Crafted Meat

The new meat culture: craft and recipes

gestalten

Content

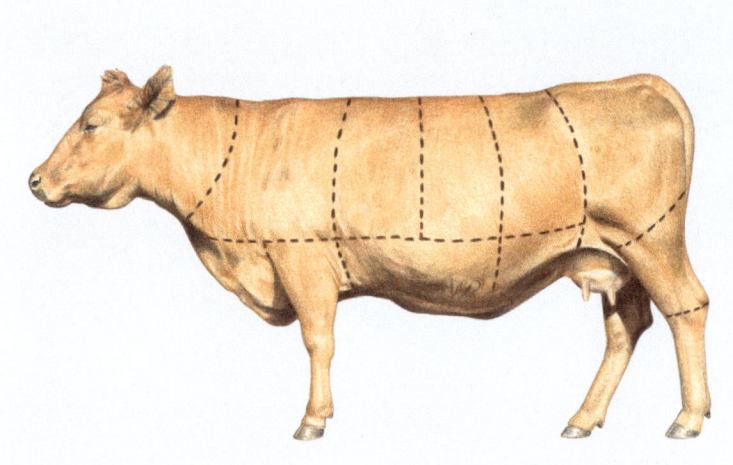

40 The cuts
42 Fresh or dry-aged
46 Beef cuts
50 Pork cuts
54 Lamb and mutton cuts
56 Poultry cuts

4 Preface –
in grandma's garden

8 The animal –
the taste of the meadows
10 Pig
20 Cattle
30 Lamb and Sheep
34 Fowl
38 Game

58 Charcuterie –
the art of butchery
60 Craft and relish
64 Raw sausage
76 Ham
85 Cured meat
86 Pâtés
87 Pies
88 BBQ

90 Know your meat
92 Storing and tasting

**96 Portraits –
heroes of the movement**
98 The new meat culture
100 Portraits

210 Recipes
212 Saussage matters
214 Recipes
244 How to make: Liverwurst
248 How to make: Salsiccia

254 Index

256 Imprint

In grandma's garden

Preface by Hendrik Haase

To this day I can still recall the special flavor of the handmade sausage my grandmother gave me every time I went to visit, cut into thick slices and layered on buttered bread. There was the hearty taste of ripened meat, paired with garlic, and the fine notes of pepper and piquant mold that had accompanied the sausage during the half year it spent ripening in the barn. Even now I can distinguish this unique taste from every plastic-wrapped supermarket sausage.

However, the times when grandma used to keep her own pigs, sheep, and chickens have passed, along with the days when the whole village gathered on the farm to celebrate the slaughter of an animal, salting ham together and cooking liverwurst in the cauldron.

Just a few decades later and I am living in the metropolis of Berlin, surprised at how little of that world remains and how hard it has become to discover the origins of the food I eat on a daily basis.

Meat and sausage have now become an everyday food on our plates—as well as a fiercely contested social theme. Books and documentaries continually uncover scandals, and for many people, wobbly YouTube clips are now the only source of information on livestock farming and the source of our sausages. Far too many animals live a life without ever having seen the sun, with troughs full of feed that makes them ill. Antibiotics and performance enhancing hormones are a further chapter in the horror story from the cramped conditions of the huge sheds. On top of this comes the fact that we are becoming increasingly conscious of the effects of cheap mass production. Industrial livestock farming consumes enormous resources and has long ceased to operate according to a healthy balance between animal, man, and nature.

Suffering in all of this is variety and taste. The consequences of this unheeding industry are uniform, tasteless meat products that are now available at discount supermarkets for less than the price of dog food. Many regional specialties, such as my grandmother's Ahle Wurscht, have almost disappeared as numerous artisan butchers have been forced to close due to price pressure. Many meat lovers have now lost their appetite, and the ascetic renunciation of everything meaty now appears to be the only solution. However, is this the whole story?

Preface

The meat rebellion
The good news is, there is another world of meat out there, a world of hope in which the origin, enjoyment, and, above all, the taste of meat have returned to center stage.

Worldwide, a movement committed to restoring dignity to meat and the butcher's craft is emerging. On farms, in butcher shops, restaurants, and street kitchens, the protagonists of this new movement are bringing about a renaissance in the enjoyment of meat. Their actions are shaped by dedication, appreciation, and passion. They are reconnecting to time-honored traditions, exploring new tastes, and gathering around them increasing numbers of followers and happy customers in search of a pleasurable alternative.

This book introduces the protagonists of this new meat movement, exploring their world, providing background information, and enabling everyone to find their own path beyond the dull monotony of industrially produced meat.

"Less meat, but better meat" is the movement's motto. But what does "better" really mean? And where can I find these tasty alternatives? Who today is still committed to honest artisanry and humane animal husbandry? And where has the taste gone that for many people is now just a memory?

This book gives answers to precisely these questions, inspiring readers, in an informative and enjoyable fashion, to set out themselves and explore this new meat culture.

Every sausage started out small
Every good steak, every sausage, and every ham begins with an animal and a livestock farmer. In order to explore this new world it is essential to know the foundations on which it is built. What we are witnessing on the farms and pastures of the meat movement is a genuine renaissance of the older breeds, which goes hand in hand with a rethink concerning the rearing and fattening of the animals.

Many of these unique creatures would have vanished if it weren't for the passionate breeders and livestock farmers who set about preserving them, believing in their unique qualities. It is thanks to these people that butchers, chefs, and meat lovers can once again draw on their rich treasure trove. Exploring the world's great variety of animal breeds is just as exciting as exploring the different grape varietals behind great wines. The diversity of flavors and terroir to be found on the pastures is the basis and precondition for every special refinement produced at the stove, in the sausage kitchen, or in the ripening cellar.

Exploring the new diversity
The numerous methods for refining and preserving meat and their various combinations, developed over the centuries, generate an unlimited variety that now make up the World Cultural Heritage of Crafted Meats. This enormous wealth of artisan cuisine is being rescued from obscurity by the movement's numerous committed activists—and in many places revitalized and reinterpreted. Exploring this rich variety of specialties takes us on an exciting journey into the history of our culture, which has always been shaped by mutual exchange. Along the way, time-honored traditions from Italy, France, Spain, Germany, and Eastern Europe meet influences from around the world.

But what is characteristic for the manufacture of genuine salami, and how do I recognize a good liverwurst? Chapter "Charcuterie" focuses on the manufacture, history, and unique qualities of the many specialties. After this look behind the scenes, handcrafted sausage and ham specialties no longer appear as the profane foodstuff they are often considered to be. Instead, they are elevated to the ranks of other highly esteemed, multifaceted specialties such as cheese and wine.

In order to explore this world, it is necessary to taste anew, embarking on one's own taste journey through this grandiose landscape. The valuable information contained in this book will assist readers in both educating their palate and finding their way around the rich array of products at the meat counter. It includes useful tips on organizing a successful tasting (page 95) and the correct way to store your booty (pages 92–93).

"Let me do it and I will understand"
Everything that one has touched, sensed, and cooked for oneself tastes different and results in a greater understanding and deeper insight than text or images could ever convey. For this reason this book sets out to inspire its readers to take the reins in their hand and explore the pleasures

of meat themselves—from nose-to-tail. And how good is it when one's own knowledge improvement is accompanied by a delicious meal? With a little application, the results obtained in the meat movement's numerous open workshops can now be repeated at home. Young chefs and butchers have developed exclusive recipes for this book, selecting favorites from their collections ideal for hobby cooks and sausage makers (from page 210). In the process it soon becomes clear that an animal consists of more than just filet. Chapter "The cuts" provides information on the important parts of the animal, beyond the familiar cuts, which are currently being rediscovered by the movement.

These practical insights into the work of butchers and cooks provide assistance when searching for the next delicacy. From now on, conversations with the butcher will take place at a higher level. This chapter also contains a list of important questions to ask the butcher when looking for good meat. (from page 40)

In pursuit of better meat we need to listen to those responsible for supplying us with this newfound pleasure. Today, farmers, butchers, and cooks committed to the new meat culture are far more than simple service providers. At their best they are trusted persons, inspirational personalities, and advisors on all meat matters. Approaching them with this awareness and the appropriate respect can result in wonderful encounters that frequently end in culinary pleasures of the highest order.

There is hope

In search of good meat and good sausage, I donned my rubber boots again to trudge through sheds and lush pastures with farmers, rose at four in the morning to join butchers at the slaughter, and ate one of the best sausages of my life. Even my grandmother would have been proud of my first self-made Ahle Wurscht. What I experienced has enabled me to understand the connections between a healthy pasture, honest handicraft, and the special taste of meat. The more I explore farming, slaughtering, and the butcher's craft, the more respect I have for this work. With every experience and every encounter I understand more about these important parts of our culture.

Back in Berlin I now have the pleasure of attending communal events again. Schlachtfesten (page 134) is a festival that honors the slaughtered animal and its meat, together with cooks, butchers, farmers, and guests from around the world. Together we celebrate this new world, which feels and tastes incredible—while my pantry fills with wonderful handcrafted works of art of unparalleled beauty and flavor.

I recommend everyone to embark on this journey of exploration, savoring its delights. This book provides sufficient inducement and inspiration. It is worth it! Here is to wishing you much enjoyment in reading this book and exploring the new meat culture!

The animal – the taste of the meadows

Pig

Pork is the most popular meat in the world and forms the basis of the majority of sausage and cold cut products that we know today. Furthermore, hearty pork fat is essential for the successful production of numerous other beef, game, and lamb specialties.

The mild European climate is especially suited to the breeding and farming of pigs. Originally reared for hardiness and a high proportion of fat, the animals were frequently kept on open pasture or shaded woods where they fed on grass, roots, acorns, beechnut, and small animals and insects. The European wild boar and Asian pigs thus developed into a wide variety of domestic breeds, each adapted to their own environment. With the old world settlers, the first European domestic pig breeds also reached America in the seventeenth century.

China, the origin of many breeds, is home to the majority of domestic pigs farmed worldwide today, followed by Europe and the USA.

In the mid-twentieth century the numerous pig breeds, with their thick layer of fat protecting them from extreme weather, were almost completely displaced by quick-growing, lean breeds. The large quantities of fat and the dark skin color of older pig breeds became unpopular. Instead of extensive farming on open pasture, the turbo-fattening of low-fat white pigs in huge sheds became the norm.

The hybrid pigs of industrial livestock farming are derived from crosses between less intensively bred pigs, which as a consequence cannot themselves be used for breeding purposes. Unable to breed new stock, pig farmers quickly became dependent on sperm banks and an involved economic system. Farmers are subject to enormous pressures with the industry demanding standardized pigs in ever shorter periods of time. In the process, diversity, quality, and taste are sacrificed. Nine out of ten pigs reared in the USA live in cramped animal factories that have nothing in common with a traditional farm. Unfortunately, things are not much different in Europe.

The pig revolution

However, for a number of years resistance has been building to this industrial monotony, with both butchers and connoisseurs increasingly turning to the meat of old breeds that have been given more space and fattened slowly on better food.

One can imagine what it would be like in the wine world if there was only one variety of grape. This is similar to the situation with today's pig farming where the great variety of breeds have been reduced to a handful. However, for artisan butchers the different characteristics of old pig breeds form an indispensable basis for their specialties.

As funny as it may sound, in order to bring about change in livestock farming and enjoy this incomparable meat, these animals have to be eaten. Butchers orient themselves to their customers, and in turn farmers to the butchers who purchase their animals. Thus the Slow Food society's motto—an organization that campaigns for the preservation of old domestic breeds—"saving through eating" is meant in all seriousness.

A question of breeding

Pigs by their nature are extremely inquisitive, using their large snouts to good effect, rummaging in the ground and continually foraging for roots and mushrooms as well as worms, snails, and other small creatures. The animals can get quite excited about these tasty carnivorous morsels. Pigs are macrosmatic animals, i.e., they have a highly developed sense of smell with more sensory cells in their snouts than dogs. Thanks to this refined faculty they are often employed as truffle pigs to search out the rare and expensive tubers hidden in the ground.

Reared on open pasture, pigs are often used as natural plows, digging and loosening the soil with their foraging while fertilizing it with their excrement—as soon as a field has been turned over, they move on to the next tract of land.

Lacking sweat glands to protect them from heat, pigs love nothing better than to wallow in mud as a way of cooling off. The dried mud is also an important protective shield against parasites and other pests.

Pigs denied the opportunity to forage outside in the soil should at least be kept on a bed of straw in which they can rummage and satisfy their curiosity. However, sufficient space is also a precondition of humane husbandry.

Hybrid pigs reared in sheds are generally granted less than one square meter of space. In contrast, Ibérico pigs reared in the woods of Spain live in a completely different world with 10,000 square meters of space per animal.

The animal

Unlike their industrial colleagues, pigs reared on open pasture get to see the sun, follow their natural behavior, and hang their snouts in fresh air.

Old pig breeds generally don't have a snow-white coat, but rather dark stripes, spots, or a completely black coat, like the English Berkshire pigs. Just like us humans, too much sun on pink skin can quickly lead to sunburn. Intensively bred pigs reared in huge sheds no longer require any protection from the sun, which is why pink is now the color we commonly associate with these animals. These pigs only see the sun or the sky briefly on their way to the slaughterhouse.

Good meat comes from good fodder

In addition to the breed, it is also the fodder and length of fattening time that has the most effect on the quality of meat. On the pasture, pigs have a varied and natural diet, frequently supplemented by grain and other diverse plants.

Old breeds, reared humanely, are never fed antibiotics (apart from in exceptional cases) and have a natural resistance to many illnesses. Good pork from slowly fattened pigs therefore needs a longer time to grow. This is the only way in which the large amounts of intramuscular fat and the meat texture required by butchers for the manufacture of good sausage and ham products can develop.

In order to survive the winter, well nourished pigs naturally accumulate a thick layer of fat during the fall months by eating protein-rich food such as acorns.

Meat from slowly growing pigs with corresponding marbling can also be dry-ripened in a fashion similar to the dry-aged meat of cattle, producing an especially tender delicacy.

The end of the pig is the beginning of the sausage

A short and quick, in other words, unexpected death, is the precondition for the processing of a pig to produce flavorsome meat of excellent quality. Careful butchers therefore slaughter pigs individually, following a long period of rest without having driven them thousands of kilometers across country in cramped lorries.

Pork can suffer a considerable loss in quality when the animals die under stress. Unfortunately, this is all too often the case on the conveyor belts of the huge slaughterhouses. Stress results in the production of lactic acid in the animals' muscles, which has the effect of denaturing the meat protein. The result is pale, soft meat that loses too much water during cooking. A long ripening, for example as required by good salami, is not possible with this meat. In order to avoid stress due to unfamiliar surroundings, rooms in good abattoirs where the pigs are slaughtered are lined with wood. Compared to their intensively bred colleagues, old pig breeds have a greater resistance to stress. Nevertheless, slaughterers are extremely careful to avoid any unnecessary or hectic noise during the slaughter.

Good fodder, humane rearing, enough time for slow growth, and stress-free slaughter result in especially juicy pork, melt-in-your-mouth surface fat, and a grandiose flavor.

Piglet

Young pigs are popularly known as piglets, and those still suckling their mothers are known as sucking or suckling pigs. After weaning they are called shoat. In Germany, suckling pigs are also known as Spanferkel, and the German name for the young of the wild boar is Frischling. The typical striped coat of young wild boars can still be seen in the piglets of certain older domestic breeds, showing how closely they are related.

Boar

Due to sexual hormones, the meat of uncastrated male pigs can have a strong taste which many meat eaters respond to with irritation or outright rejection. However, through very careful husbandry, feeding, and slaughter at the correct time, this flaw can be avoided. Nevertheless, the meat of the boar has its admirers in England and Portugal, in distinction to the rest of Europe. Unfortunately, the intensive pig farming industry has not progressed beyond the very painful method of castrating male piglets without anesthetic.

Sow

The meat of female pigs has a more intense color and a stronger meaty taste. Sow meat can absorb more salt and, thanks to this characteristic, is highly prized by butchers for the production of sausage and ham. The meat and fat of old sows is thus ideal for specialties which require a long ripening process, such as raw sausage and cured ham. In the past it was customary to slaughter the animals at the age of one or older.

The animal

SADDLEBACK

Saddleback

A typical feature of Saddleback pigs are their large, hanging, floppy ears and the eponymous saddle composed of a light stripe dividing the black skin at the level of the front legs. The breed originates from south England, which, in addition to the British Saddleback, is also the home of the Wessex and Sussex Saddleback. In Germany variants of the animal exist under the names Angler Sattelschwein and Schwäbisch Hällisches Landschwein.

The robust animals can be kept outside all year round, only requiring small huts that they can retreat to as needed.

Like many old pig breeds, Saddlebacks, with their large quantities of tasty fat, were almost wiped out during the lean meat craze of the last century. By the 1980s only a few specimens remained for breeding purposes. However, in recent times, the Saddleback has become extremely popular again and forms the starting point for new breeding programs. Nevertheless, many Saddlebacks still remain on the list of endangered livestock breeds.

The meat of the Saddleback pig is known for its copious marbling and is correspondingly juicy and especially flavorsome. The meat of the slow growing animals is also suitable for the manufacture of unique sausage and ham products thanks to the fat's fantastic qualities.

Landrace

Typical for all Landraces is their pink coloring. Further characteristics include large floppy ears and their sizes—larger than many other breeds. Landraces are reared in numerous European countries. Originally kept for subsistence farming they have now been rebred into high-performance animals.
These intensively bred Landraces are often used as breeding sows for the hybrid pigs employed in industrial farming. Over recent decades the resulting over-bred strains have displaced virtually all the old pig breeds from livestock farms. In Europe during the mid-1950s, as fat became unpopular, new strains were bred from the old Landraces to produce leaner meat after the slaughter. To this end the animals were often crossed with the Pietrain breed, known for its very lean meat. The pigs were even given an extra rib to produce a higher yield of pork chops by crossing them with Danish breeds. However, this "optimization" resulted in the animals becoming highly susceptible to stress and lacking the breed's original robustness. Today, the pig farming industry's "modern" hybrids are no longer suited for rearing on open pasture.

The meat of the "state of the art" Landraces is extremely lean with little intramuscular fat, which affects its juiciness, often leading to a rather bland flavor.

Porc Noir de Bigorre

This black pig is at home in the high-lying meadows and forests of the French Pyrenean. However, this ancient breed only just survived the changing times, and it now grazes on French open pasture where it is kept half wild.

Today's hybrid pigs are fattened for slaughter within the space of a few months. In contrast, the Noir de Bigorre needs around three times as long, and as a result produces especially high quality meat with fine marbling. This is due to the varied, natural fodder that also includes acorns and chestnuts. The meat captivates with its rich, bright red color and its special, light nutty flavor.

The meat of the Noir de Bigorre is traditionally used to make the dry-cured ham Jambon Noir de Bigorre, which is ripened for up to 24 months. Served as thin strips, it melts in your mouth. The meat of the black pig tastes best when roasted until medium rare to medium.

The animal

MANGALITSA

Gloucestershire Old Spots
The robust pig from southwest England can be recognized by its black spots on an otherwise white coat. It is popularly known as the "Orchard pig," as it is frequently found in fruit orchards where it lives all year round, foraging for whatever it can find.
The large, frugal pig is perfectly suited for rearing on open pasture throughout the year. As the slow growing animals are not suited to industrial livestock farming, they are now on the list of endangered pig breeds. However, more and more connoisseurs have come to prize their high quality meat, which, unlike the dry meat of factory farmed animals, does not shrink in the pan.

The royal family now campaigns for the preservation of the spotted pigs that are also reared on Prince Charles's farm. English butchers prize the pig, known colloquially as "Old Sports," especially for its belly that produces fantastic bacon.

Mangalitsa Wooly Pig
A wooly coat and thick layer of fat protect this pig from extreme cold in winter, making the Mangalitsa one of the world's most robust breeds. The curly red, brown, or swallow-bellied pigs are therefore also known as Wooly Pigs. Originally at home in Hungary and the Balkans, Europe's oldest pig breed has become extremely popular again amongst breeders over recent years. The close relationship between Mangalitsas and the original wild boar can be seen in the piglets, which, like young wild boar, are born with striped coats.

Mangalitsa pigs cannot be farmed intensively and in close confines, thus making them unsuitable for industrial livestock farming. Only a few pure-bred specimens remained in the 1980s following their displacement by "modern," considerably leaner pig breeds.
The wonderful creamy fat of the woolly pigs, with its low melting point, is a great delicacy and ideal for producing a fantastic lardo.

Mangalitsa meat is used to produce unique ham and sausage specialties, which in Hungary are traditionally seasoned with large quantities of paprika. The especially juicy meat with its light nutty flavor is excellent for grilling thanks to the intramuscular fat that prevents it from drying out.

Mulefoot
This breed, native to the USA, has no cloven hoof as is customary with pig's feet. This feature, similar to the hooves of the mule, has given this breed its name, Mulefoot.
Presumably descended from the Spanish pigs of the first settlers, this pig is now the most endangered breed in the USA and is preserved from extinction by breeding associations. Even characteristics such as an enormous tolerance to heat or its natural resistance to many diseases failed to stop the breed's decline.
In the twentieth century, its meat, with large quantities of intramuscular fat, was replaced by standardized, uniform, lean pork from the factory farms.

Amongst butchers Mulefoots are considered to be the perfect "ham hogs", producing wonderful ham. Today the juicy, high quality meat is popular again amongst gastronomes.

Swabian-Hall Swine
The modern history of the Swabian-Hall swine begins with its demise. As the breeder Rudolf Bühler set about saving the old breed, the robust animals were officially considered extinct. By the mid-1980s only seven specimens of the once popular species remained. Today the breed is reared by several thousand farmers in the state Baden Württemberg, Germany. This sad chapter in the animal's history has been transformed into a prime example of the rejuvenation of an old breed successfully resisting the folly of industrial farming.

The animal

WILD BOAR

Like all old saddle breeds, the Swabian-Hall originates from a cross of native Landraces with the Chinese Meishan pig. A typical feature of the animal is the white stripe across the belly and back of the coat. The finely marbled meat from the pigs reared on open pasture is of high quality and ideally suited for the manufacture of especially tasty sausage specialties.

Wild Boar

Nearly all of today's domestic pigs are descended from the Eurasian wild boar. Archaeological finds confirm that these wild pigs were domesticated and bred in the Middle East around 9,000 years ago.

The Eurasian wild boar has a black-brown, bristly coat and is therefore also known in Germany as Schwarzwild (schwarz is German for black). Following birth the piglets have a striped coat which can also be found as a relict on the young of a number of domestic pig breeds such as the Mangalitsa.

In the forest, wild boars eat acorns, mushrooms, and roots, as well as worms, snails, and even carrion if they should happen to find it. In addition to natural feed found in nature, wild boar have also developed a taste for the increasingly common cultivated corn, ransacking fields much to the annoyance of farmers. In a similar fashion, cultivated grain and potatoes can also form part of their diet. As a result, the wild boar population has increased dramatically in recent years and now has to be kept down by controlled culling.

Bagged by hunters, the meat of the wild boar forms the basis for many rustic game sausage and ham specialties. However, only the meat of sows and piglets is eaten and processed, as meat from sexually mature male boars has a strong smell and is considered unpalatable. Wild boar meat is extremely lean and has a savory pork flavor with a variety of game notes.

Ossabaw Island Hog

Following a stopover in the Canary Islands, Spanish conquistadors landed on the east coast of America, bringing with them the forefathers of today's Ossabaw Island hogs. A number of pigs subsequently escaped to Ossabaw Island off the coast of Georgia, where they returned to a natural state and still live in the underbrush to this day. In contrast to Europe, there were no wild boars on the island to mix with. As a consequence, the Ossabaw Island hog is one of the USA's most important genetic resources with the breed retaining all of its original characteristics. Unfortunately it is now an endangered breed in the USA.

The Ossabaw Island hog, closely related to the Iberian pig, is perfectly adapted to living in the wild and copes well with both heat and water. In the winter months the black or black and white spotted pigs accumulate a thick layer of fat that protects them from the cold. However, compared to their Spanish relatives, the pigs are somewhat smaller.

These robust characteristics make Ossabaw Island hogs highly suited for sustainable pig farming on open pasture. The quality of their dark meat is comparable to that of the finest Ibérico pigs. Ossabaw Island hogs are excellent for the preparation of sausage and ham specialties as well as for grilling—preferably as a whole animal over an open fire.

Bentheim Black Pied Pig

This striking, black spotted pig originates from the northern half of Germany. In the county of Bentheim in Lower Saxony, close to the Dutch border, the undemanding robust animals with their easy disposition were once extremely popular.

Bentheim pigs are renowned for their tasty back fat that can easily reach a thickness of over 10 centimeters. However, their high percentage of fat almost led to their extinction. After its decline at the

The animal

TRUPOLJE

end of the twentieth century only one breeder remained with sufficient animals to continue the breed. It still remains an endangered breed with associations campaigning for its preservation. It is part of the Slow Food society's Ark of Taste. The breed's outstanding meat is increasingly popular amongst connoisseurs in the home kitchen and gastronomy.

The meat of the Bentheim Black Pied pig has a fine marbling and as a result is incredibly juicy. Through ripening, an unusual process for pork, the tenderness of the old breed's meat can be further increased. Butchers prize the meat's special qualities whose fat has an incomparable smoothness. The meat of Bentheim Black Pied pigs is thus excellent for the preparation of distinctive sausage and ham products.

Large Black and Devon Pig

At its peak the Large Black pig was one of the most popular breeds in England and was reared in 30 other countries. Due to its origins in the south of England, the pig is also known as the Cornwall or Devon Black. Its black skin color makes the robust animals immune to sunburn, enabling them to graze freely in pastures of fresh grass and clover.
However, during the twentieth century, pigs with dark skin coloring fell out of favor, and characteristics such as a robust constitution and flavorsome meat were of little value in an age of lean pigs reared in pens.

As a result, the Large Black, whose origins date back to the sixteenth and seventeenth centuries, was almost extinct by the 1960s. Since the demand for meat from the slow growing old breeds has risen, the Large Black is becoming an increasingly common sight in the British Isles. The meat, while quite dark for pork, is extremely tender and juicy.

Pietrain

These heavily muscled pigs, renowned for producing hams of an impressive size, originate from the Belgian village of Pietrain. Beginning in the 1950s, the boars where used for the intensive breeding of hybrid pigs. As fat became unpopular, the ability of the Pietrain to produce large quantities of extremely lean meat was used as the basis for breeding lean pigs, whose meat, packaged in plastic, now fills the supermarket shelves.

The Pietrain is popular amongst breeders of old pigs for crossing purposes, lending the often very fatty meat a leaner touch. However, these white pigs with pale black spots are highly susceptible to stress and readily pass on this characteristic. During slaughter this can result in pale, soft, watery meat: So-called PSE meat (pale—soft—exudative). This meat is unsuitable for the manufacture of specialties that require a long ripening period, and butchers intending to process this meat are forced to resort to additives.

Cinta Senese

The characteristic white belt (cinta is Italian for belt) extending across the pig's neck and front legs has lent this old Italian breed its name. The Cinta Senese is considered the most important pig breed in Tuscany, and is prized by the region's fine butchers to this day. The breed originates from the hills around Siena and was probably known to the Romans. Evidence of its domestication in central Italy can be traced back to the Middle Ages.
Similar to Iberian pigs, Cinta Senese pigs are kept half wild in the forests, and thanks to their special diet produce meat with a fine, nutty flavor. However, beginning in the 1950s, this robust but slow growing pig was displaced by leaner breeds, reducing its population to just 150 animals. In recent years the Cinta Senese has enjoyed a renaissance, and is again being used in Tuscany to manufacture increasing quantities of especially tasty traditional ham and salami.

The animal

TAMWORTH

Tamworth

Originally from Ireland, the red pig was subsequently optimized through breeding in the English town of Tamworth around 1800. In the nineteenth century the robust breed spread from the United Kingdom to North America. In Canada, where it was known as "Ginger Pig," it proved especially popular for many years and was reared on numerous farms. However, unsuited to industrial pig farming, its numbers fell rapidly and the Tamworth is now considered an endangered domestic breed. Fortunately, breeding associations have been re-established and increasing numbers of chefs now prize its meat. Reared on open pasture the pig is compatible with cattle and even chickens, and copes very well with heat and bad weather.

The meat of the Tamworth pig is especially juicy, has nutty notes, and a remarkable wealth of flavors. The breed's long, fatty belly is prized by butchers for the manufacture of especially tasty bacon.

Trupolje

The wetlands of the river Sava, close to the Croatian capital of Zagreb, are home to this black spotted breed of pig, where they have been traditionally reared on the floodplain meadows and forests. Consequently, Trupolje pigs like nothing better than to bathe and wallow in small pools, and have even been observed diving for mussels to supplement their diet.

The pig's thick wooly coat is reminiscent of a Dalmatian dog's and protects the animals from cold and sun. Trupolje, like many old breeds, declined in popularity during the middle of the last century due to their fat-rich meat, and following the devastation of the Balkan war, were brought to the verge of extinction.

It is thanks to the efforts of Austrian and German zoos that the breed has survived to this day and is now being reared again. The fatty meat of these slow growing pigs is excellent for the manufacture of savory bacon and long-ripening raw sausage.

Iberian Pig (Ibérico)

For millennia the now famous black-footed, half-wild pigs have grazed between the old oak trees in the forests of Portugal and Spain. The black hooves of the pigs with their black or sometimes red coat have earned them the name Pata Negra (Spanish for black foot). In the forests of the Extramadura they can be found foraging for protein-rich acorns both night and day, a diet that lends their meat a delicate, nutty flavor.

In the past, this acorn fattening was commonly employed for other pig breeds throughout Europe. Today it is rare outside the Iberian peninsular. The famous Jamón Ibérico is only permitted to carry the suffix Bellota (Spanish for acorns), if produced from pigs reared on this special acorn fodder. This lends the meat an incomparable smoothness and wonderful flavor.

However, not every pig advertised as an Ibérico has a pedigree including a life in the forest. Due to high demand large numbers of pigs are now kept in pens. Here, acorns serve merely as supplementary fodder.

Slow growth and natural diet produce a unique wealth of flavors and intensive marbling, resulting in incredibly tender and juicy meat. The name "olive on four legs" is a title the Iberian pig has justly earned: the quality of the fat, with its valuable ingredients, comes incredibly close to that of olive oil.

Berkshire

The United Kingdom's oldest pig breed dates back around 300 years to the county of Berkshire where it was bred for the king, for whom only the best was good enough. The meat of the black animals is still considered one of the best tasting in the world and regularly beats the competition in comparative tasting. Thanks to the copious marbling, the meat has a great depth of flavors and is juicy and tender. This similarity to Kobe beef has also made the Berkshire

The animal

IBERIAN PIG

pig the most popular breed in Japan where it is known as Kurobuta (black pig).
In Europe the animals are now reared by a scattering of farmers.
In the USA, although sadly a rarity, the breed with the black coat, white feet, and spotted face is also gaining in popularity.

The Berkshire pig has entered world literature through the pages of George Orwell's novel, *Animal Farm*. The leader of the animal uprising, Napoleon, is a Berkshire boar.

Duroc
The red pigs of the Duroc breed have hanging ears and originate from the so-called Corn Belt in the American Midwest. In the past it was also known by the name Jersey-Duroc, as red pigs from the region close to New York had a large influence on the development of the breed.
Together with settlers, the pig migrated further west where it continued to develop. Its size, rapid growth, and high meat yield has made it a popular breed amongst livestock farmers. In the USA the Duroc remains one of the most commonly reared pig breeds. Worldwide it is used for cross breeding purposes to optimize meat quality and increase the yield of other breeds. What the Duroc lacks in fat it makes up for in musculature, passing on this characteristic to other breeds through crossing.

The meat of the animals is finely marbled, and with good husbandry and natural fodder, it is a tender, juicy delicacy.

Large White and German Edelschwein
Alongside the Landraces, breeding sows from England's Large White and the resulting white German Edelschwein, are the most popular animals in the industrial livestock industry for producing high performance crossbreeds. In this case the father is nearly always a Pietrain boar. Compared to other pigs, these two breeds grow extremely quickly, are relatively large, and extremely fertile. The forefathers of these high-performance animals were reared in the English county of Yorkshire where they were kept on open pasture. However, today the large animals are primarily used for intensive livestock farming in huge sheds. Characteristics such as a robust constitution and dark skin pigmentation that once provided protection against the sun are no longer required.

These breeds are of special economic interest thanks to their ability to produce a maximum increase in weight from any given amount of feed. Here livestock farmers speak of an excellent fattening performance. Shortly before this relationship reverses, with growth slowing and the amount of feed rising, the animals land in the slaughterhouse.

However, their quick growth and early slaughter at the age of a few months tends to result in a uniform, pale, lean meat lacking the wealth of flavors of meat from slow growing breeds.
Despite all this, the breeds are highly popular with the meat industry, dominating the global pig market.

Cattle

Meadow herbs, flowers, and a wide variety of grasses are the natural fodder of cattle. The great range of plants found in species-rich meadows lends herby notes to fine beef, producing a full, sustained flavor. With the assistance of their four stomachs the animals are capable of turning this diet, indigestible for humans and many other animals, into a source of nutrition. Consequently, cattle spend the majority of their day on the pasture grazing and leisurely chewing the cud.

The animal

Since time immemorial the lush pasturelands of Central and Western Europe have been an ideal ground for the breeding and farming of cattle. Today, many of the world's most popular cattle breeds originate from this cultural landscape, and the British Isles in particular, with its opulent pastures fed with generous quantities of rain, is home to many breeds. Furthermore, the Industrial Revolution in England, which gathered pace in the second half of the eighteenth century, led to some of the earliest efforts at breeding cattle for meat production, while in other parts of Europe at this time the focus was still on producing dairy cows and working animals. Old breeds are incredibly robust and perfectly adapted to their respective natural environment. The extremely hardy Highland and Galloway cattle can even find food under thick layers of snow at a time when other breeds have long been dependent on hay.

The general accusation that cattle are accelerating climate change through methane emissions is false. Cattle are capable of processing fodder which is unpalatable for us humans, and their feeding habits ensure a high variety of plant life, thus preventing the erosion of the fertile layer of humus, and binding climate-damaging gases in the soil. Their by-products include one of the best natural fertilizers there is. Cattle are thus an important part of the ecological recycling economy, especially on organic farms where no pesticides or artificial fertilizers are used.

In the wild, cattle live in herds with a clear hierarchy. Lead animals decide when it is time for the herd to move, eat, or lie in the sun ruminating. Slowly chewing, cattle herds can cover several kilometers each day.

Disputes over rank generally occur when there is competition for food, water, or lying area. In cramped sheds where the animals cannot avoid each other this can quickly lead to stress and restlessness. During skirmishes the animals naturally employ their horns, which is why cattle reared exclusively in sheds frequently have their horns removed to prevent injuries. Cattle proudly displaying their horns on open pasture are therefore a good indicator of a more humane form of husbandry.

Immediately following birth, a strong bond is formed between cow and calf that persists for several months. In husbandry systems where the calves are reared on the mother, the progeny spend a long period on the pasture with their mothers, thus enjoying conditions appropriate to their species. Calves in particular have a great need for movement, requiring lots of space to exercise their curiosity amongst members of their species.

However, this form of cattle farming is no longer the norm. The meat from cattle reared on open pasture grazing exclusively on grass has become a rarity on our plates. On intensive livestock farms, which now predominate, animals are kept in huge sheds where there are only a few square meters of space for each animal. Virtually unable to move, the animals are fed energy-rich corn and other concentrated feed instead of grass. As a result the cows' stomachs, designed for grass, frequently respond with severe digestion problems. In the USA, hormones, which are banned in Europe due to their effect on humans, are employed to further increase growth. The goal of this fattening is an extreme increase in weight in ever shorter for their age. It is no wonder that such intensively fattened and artificially

The animal

doped cattle are unable to produce high quality meat. For many cattle today the end is a long and very crowded lorry journey to the slaughterhouse. One can imagine how stressful this must be for animals that have spent their whole lives on open pasture.

Stress before or during slaughter can destroy all the efforts of years of careful rearing and feeding, even in the case of old and distinguished breeds. The meat from stressed animals that have been slaughtered incorrectly is an extremely tough affair and is unsuited for long ripening. Good slaughterers and livestock farmers thus insist on a short journey and stress-free slaughter that avoids agitating or hounding the animals. Ideally, the animals should be transported to the abattoir the day prior to being slaughtered so they can recuperate from the journey on straw bedding for a few hours.

The least stressful form of slaughter is conducted directly on the pasture using a precisely aimed bullet. The animals fall down, are slaughtered on site, and then transported. However, this form of slaughter, which is the least stressful for the animals, is not very widespread and naturally can only be employed on open pasture.

Cattle fattened on pasture with natural fodder grow more slowly and generally do not reach the same weight as their intensively farmed colleagues. The slow growth combined with plenty of exercise results in meat with fine marbling, laced with delicate veins of fat. However, in a similar fashion to pork, beef infused with fat became less popular after the Second World War as pure red meat came into demand. The resulting loss in flavor is painfully felt to this day.

Flavorsome beef has its origin in unnecessary fat and its distribution throughout the muscle. The color of the meat indicative of the greatest delicacy is therefore a red-white as opposed to a pure red. During preparation the melting fat ensures the meat stays juicy and is the precondition for the unfolding of the aromas.

Unrivaled beef can be produced on the lush pastures of Europe, America, Australia, and other parts of the world—as long as respect is paid to the origin of cattle by grazing them unnecessary using the methods of humane husbandry.

Over recent years both cattle farmers and beef connoisseurs have rediscovered the qualities of slowly fattened, older pedigree cattle breeds that produce meat with an undreamed of wealth of flavors.

Calf

Before reaching sexual maturity, generally one year after birth, young cattle are called calves. The tastiest and most humanely produced veal is obtained from animals reared on pasture together with the mother cows and fellow members of their species. The meat is light red to pink in color. Although white veal was long considered to be of the highest quality, this meat is actually obtained from calves that have been anemically reared and deprived of their natural fodder. Classics such as Wiener Schnitzel or Saltimbocca are traditionally cut from the tender topside of calf.

Bull

Sexually mature male cattle are known as bulls. Left uncastrated, they can become wild and difficult to control. Selected specimens are used for breeding purposes, while unsuited animals are fattened. Experienced breeders are experts in taming wild bulls, allowing them to mature to produce high quality beef if provided with sufficient space and open pasture. However, the readily available meat from quickly fattened young bulls is not to be compared with the quality of that from older animals, despite its pretty bright red color.

Steer

Steer are castrated male cattle, which as a result gain weight at a slower rate and are considerably more manageable than bulls. Their fattening takes considerably longer and is therefore more cost-intensive for livestock farmers. However, as a result of their slow fattening, steer can produce excellent quality meat with wonderful marbling. Time and labor-intensive steer fattening, despite its benefits, has unfortunately become very rare in this age of fast, industrial fattening. Meat from steer older than 3 years and subject to a long ripening process is some of the best meat you can put in a pan or on the grill.

The animal

Heifer

The name heifer refers to female cattle that have not yet calved. Only after the first calf does the heifer become a cow. Similar to steer, heifer grow considerably slower, thus accumulating a greater amount of intramuscular fat which results in excellent meat quality and marbling. Older specimens in particular produce the best quality beef in the world, which, after a long, dry ripening, is a great delicacy. For many people the world's best steak comes from an old heifer.

The animal

BISON

Limousin

Limousin cattle have a light to dark red coat and originate from the southwest of France. Originally popular in the region as draft animals for agriculture, farmers later utilized the breed as a supplier of especially flavorsome meat. Reared in the valleys of the low mountain ranges, Limousin cattle mixed little with other breeds over the centuries, enabling them to preserve their special qualities. However, the origins of the breed date back even further. The images of cattle in the caves near Lascaux dating back millennia show a striking resemblance to today's Limousin cattle.

The popularity of this cow as a meat breed is not just confined to France but extends around the world with the farming of Limousin in Europe, North America and Australia. Together with Charolais cattle, they are one of the most popular breeds for meat production in Germany. The animals are hardy and can be kept out to pasture all year round.

Limousin are not the largest or heaviest cattle in the world, however, they are prized for other qualities. Their meat is considered of the highest quality and is extremely popular amongst both chefs and connoisseurs. The delicate meat of Limousin cattle, when reared appropriately, is finely marbled and prized for its strong beef flavor.

Limpurger

The home of the Limpurger is southwest Germany. In the past, the oldest of Baden-Württemberg's breeds was kept by farmers of the Hohenlohe region as tri-purpose cattle. The cattle were not only deployed as working animals but also provided milk and could be fattened for slaughter. During the eighteenth century, word of the quality of the meat traveled as far as Paris where it was known as "Boef de Hohenlohe".

As this old breed could not compete with high performance cattle in terms of meat and milk production, they faced extinction by the end of the twentieth century. Today the animals are now kept as beef cattle again and are deployed as landscape conservationists. The Limpurger can even graze on the region's steep hillsides where no mowing machine could ever operate.

The meat, especially that of the pasture-reared steer, is of a special quality. Once ripened accordingly it has a strong beef flavor with light herb notes and a consistency as soft as butter.

Dexter

Dexter cattle were originally bred in the south of Ireland as small but productive "one-family cows" kept by the poorer sections of the population. The black, red-brown, or gray-brown animals were undemanding and provided enough milk for an average-sized farmer's family. In addition, the animals produced tasty meat. However, the smallest of the European cattle breeds was unable to compete in the race to produce larger and higher-yield cattle. As a result the Dexter breed was virtually extinct by the 1960s. However, the situation is entirely different when it comes to the competition of producing milk and meat of the highest quality. Here the breed leads the field.
The high fat milk is especially suited for the manufacture of special butter and ice cream specialties. Although the animals provide very tasty milk they are now primarily kept as beef cattle. Today Dexter cattle can now be found in England, North America, Australia, and New Zealand.

Shorthorn

Shorthorn cattle were one of the first optimized breeds to land in North America with the European colonists in the seventeenth century. Prized by settlers for their milk and meat, the good natured animals could also be harnessed to a plough.

The Shorthorn is considered one of the world's oldest domesticated breeds, appearing in the earliest herd books in England and Germany. This tri-purpose, small-horned breed, originally from the northeast

The animal

GALLOWAY

coast of England, has resulted in a variety of strains that specialize in milk and meat production. The "Beef Shorthorn" is a popular animal for cross breeding purposes since it serves to optimize other cattle breeds. The animals have a red, white or red-gray coat. To this day they are prized by cattle farmers for their frugal, undemanding character. The meat of the shorthorn, when reared appropriately, is of a high quality.

Water Buffalo

The formerly wild Water Buffalo was domesticated in Asia in an early period and to this day is an important working animal in the rice fields. At home in the earth's hot and wet climates, the Water Buffalo loves to wallow in pools and mud holes, cooling and protecting itself from parasites with the assistance of mud.

With their black coats and imposing horns, today these animals can also be found in Europe and North America. Their milk has a high fat content and is of a special quality. Genuine rich and creamy mozzarella is traditionally made from Buffalo milk—and not from cow milk as is customary with the industrially manufactured variety.

Water buffalo meat has a highly individual flavor, somewhere between beef and game. With less intramuscular fat than other types of beef, it is extremely lean. In order to produce flavorful and juicy sausage specialties from buffalo meat, pork fat is often added during manufacture.

Braunvieh

Alongside Simmental, Braunvieh is one of the most well known Swiss cattle breeds. The brown to gray-brown animals, with or without horns, can be found in large numbers both in the Swiss Alps, the Allägau region of Germany, and Austria's Tyrol. The animals are also renowned for their mountain climbing qualities on very steep hillsides. Alongside coat color, typical features of the breed include its black muzzle with white border, which is similar to that of a deer.

The Braunvieh is mainly found in the alpine region of Austria, Switzerland and the Allgäu region of Germany. In America the breed is known under the name, "Brown Swiss." The fertile animals are known for their longevity and are kept as dual-purpose cattle. Braunvieh produce large quantities of good milk as well as tasty meat.
Although Braunvieh are predominately used for milk and cheese production, its meat is equally as good as that of other cattle breeds.

Piedmontese

Piedmontese cattle originate from the north Italian region of Piedmont where they have kept their characteristics over many years, grazing at the foot of the Alps and in the region's small valleys. The cattle breed is related to the Zebu that migrated from Pakistan many thousands of years ago.
Characteristic features include the light, white-gray coat and the somewhat darker pigmentation around the eyes, snout and horns. In the past the mountain farmers and land owners of the alpine upland used the powerful cattle as draft animals and dairy cows. Today Piedmontese are primarily reared for their meat. The animals' good musculature can easily be seen in their gait when roaming the pasture.

With their elongated torso, these medium-sized cattle are highly prized for the good yield of meat they provide after their slaughter, which is especially tender and of a delicate flavor. These qualities have made Piedmontese into one of Italy's most popular meat breeds.

Simmental Fleckvieh

This cattle breed has its origins in Simmental in the Bernese Oberland region of Switzerland where they were kept as house cows for generations. A white head and red-spotted coat are characteristic of these animals.
The cattle are prized as a dual-purpose breed, yielding large quantities of both meat and milk. In the middle of the nineteenth century

The animal

HECK CATTLE

a Bavarian breeder began using these Swiss cattle as the basis for his breeding. The Simmental Fleckvieh, or "Fleckvieh" for short, can now be found around the world in its millions.

The breed is especially important for global meat production and is very popular in industrial livestock farming due to the high yield of prime cuts. However, under intensive fattening it reaches its slaughter weight too quickly. Simmental cattle only produce good, juicy, and tender meat through extensive husbandry, allowing the animals sufficient time to grow, combined with a lengthy ripening process.

Galloway

As far back as the time of the Romans, this black breed could be seen grazing in the lowlands of southwest Scotland, where the Galloway has a long history. These robust animals are known for their long, curly coat, which feels like the lining of a warm jacket. Galloways are known as black cattle, however, there are also red, white and multi-colored variants. A special strain is the Belted Galloway, which has a white strip of coat in the middle of its body that runs over back and belly.

A thick coat keeps the animals warm with its good insulation. Furthermore, their coat is also water resistant, making the Galloway one of the hardiest breeds worldwide. Like all robust cattle breeds the animals require virtually no medication and can survive hard winters without having to take refuge in a cow shed.

Galloways are good feed converters, coping well with poor and barren soil on which other cattle breeds would be hard pressed to find any useful fodder. These qualities make the Galloway one of the most popular landscape conservers for nature reserves.

Thanks to the variety of grasses and herbs on the pasture where they are reared, the meat of the Galloway has a special taste with a light game note. As a result of their slow growth, the dark meat has a fine marbling, thus keeping it tender and juicy.

Devon

The Devon is one of the world's oldest breeds of domesticated cattle. As early as 50 BC the Romans were struck by the red cattle on the green hills in the southwest of England. Today there are two strains: North Devon and South Devon. South Devon cattle are also known in England under the name Orange Elephants.

During the course of the seventeenth century the first specimens of Devon cattle arrived in North America with the English settlers. Today the North Devon variant is still very popular in the meat industry as a crossing breed that passes on good characteristics to other cattle. Devon cattle are known as highly efficient processors of green fodder, making them very popular as an effective meat breed on open pasture. The North Devon variant, bred for its excellent meat quality, can be found in large numbers on the vast grazing lands in Brazil, Australia, and New Zealand. Following a long, dry ripening, the meat of animals fed exclusively on grass is a special delicacy.

Highland Cattle

The wonderful Scottish Highland Cattle have a long, red-brown, shaggy coat. Despite their impressive curved horns, the animals are actually very good-natured and are considered uncomplicated by livestock farmers. The stormy, cold, and wet climate of the Scottish highlands and islands have made this cattle breed extremely hardy. Their thick, water resistant coats also protect them from extreme weather conditions. These animals are as in little need of a cow shed as they are of special food. The shaggy giants are accustomed to barren soil and moorland, which makes them extremely undemanding when it comes to food. As a consequence, Highland Cattle are very popular as natural landscape conservationists and spend the whole year in the open. Over recent decades the breed has spread well beyond the borders of Scotland and is increasingly reared in Europe and America.

Their good nature makes them especially resistant to stress, which reduces the danger the meat being compromised by anxiety during

BLACK ANGUS

the slaughter. Their slow growth and varied, natural diet consists of a variety of herbs found on pasture, which results in a very high quality, albeit lean meat, with a great wealth of aromas. This beef is often accompanied by light game notes.

Heck Cattle

The appearance of the forefathers of today's domestic cattle, the aurochs, which became extinct in the seventeenth century, can only be reconstructed from skeletal remains and cave paintings. At the beginning of the twentieth century the Heck brothers from Munich succeeded in breeding a look-alike of these primordial cattle.
Heck cattle are not a perfect replica of the impressive archetypal form with its dark, chestnut-brown to black coat, however they come extremely close to the appearance of this ancestral bovine. The animals are reminiscent of the fighting bulls in Spanish arenas, which have a similar lineage.
The original Heck cattle are extremely robust and are very popular in nature reserves and on wild pasture.
The firm meat, resulting from their varied, natural fodder, is extremely aromatic and flavorsome. The meat of these primordial cattle can be used to make unique beef salamis and cold cut products.

Charolais

The muscular Charolais cattle originate from France, although they are now reared worldwide as a meat breed. Their name is derived from the former county of Charolais in Burgundy. Characteristic features of the breed include the elongated form of the torso and the cream-white coat. While Charolais are by nature horned, strains have also been bred without horns.
The breed has a reputation for being robust and copes well with both hot and cold climates. As a result the animals can be kept out to pasture all year round.
Charolais cattle gain weight quickly, have a high slaughter weight, and a good meat yield, making them popular with both cattle farmers and butchers. Charolais cattle are popular for crossbreeding purposes.
With good husbandry and slow fattening the meat is finely marbled, and after ripening and careful preparation, has a melt-in-the-mouth, juicy texture.

Blonde d'Aquitaine

The white coated Blonde d'Aquitaine originate from the southwest of France, close to the Pyrenean, where they were originally kept as tri-purpose animals. Today they can also be found in the Loire Valley, northwest France, as well as on livestock farms in other parts of Europe. Thanks to their short summer coat the breed has no problem with heat, although they avoid cold and wet weather conditions. Generous producers of milk and meat, the animals were important in the past for farm work where they were employed as draft animals. Today the light-yellow to cream-white animals continue to be bred in an effort to refine their qualities as a supplier of especially tender meat. Whether as calf, young bull or mature steer, they are prized by livestock farmers for the high slaughter prices they command regardless of age.

With good husbandry and slow fattening, they are known for their delicately marbled and fine-fibred meat. However, as the meat can be extremely lean it is sometimes criticized for lacking flavor.

American Bison

During the last ice age wild bison migrated across the ice from Asia to North America. For generations the extremely powerful animals were an important part of the diet of native Americans who hunted them with bow and arrow. However, when white settlers reached the continent in the sixteenth century an unprecedented wave of annihilation began, reducing a population of 60 million bison, primarily located in the vast expanse of the American west, to just a few hundred specimens by the end of the nineteenth century. The impressive

The animal

TEXAS LONGHORN

animals were hunted indiscriminately—not for their meat, but in order to provide leather for equipping soldiers in Europe. American bison, whose European relative is the wisent, are now reared in increasing numbers in the USA. With the "Buffalo Commons" the idea of restoring the USA's former beauty and releasing animals into the wild has also gained support, resulting in large areas of the prairie now being reclaimed by wild cattle.

Bison have a high quality, extremely lean meat, which with careful preparation is tender as opposed to dry. Thanks to the variety of herbs on the prairie where they graze, the meat acquires a delicate, distinctly spicy flavor. The practice of drying the meat in the open air is derived from native American tradition, and Jerky Beef, which remains popular to this day, is customarily made from bison meat.

Texas Longhorn

The sight of the imposing animals on the pasture, with their horns up to two meters in length, awakens memories of classic cowboy films. The Texas Longhorn descends from the first cattle that trod North American soil some 500 years ago, and is one of the few North American breeds that has adapted perfectly to its new environment.

As the buffalo disappeared from the great plains they were replaced by the Longhorns who also coped well with the barren soil. To this day the animals are known for their special hardiness, resistance to diseases and longevity—characteristics that many intensively bred cattle now lack. The Texas Longhorn is therefore known by breeders as a "genetic goldmine."

Nevertheless, the breed, whose characteristic skull has become an icon of the American south, was almost extinct by the beginning of the twentieth century. Slow-growing cattle breeds that specialized in wild fodder were no longer desirable in an era of barbed wire fenced, industrial livestock farming. However, the Longhorn is now extremely popular again amongst meat lovers. Although the meat is extremely lean, with good ripening it can be very tender.

The Texas longhorn is not to be confused with the English Longhorn, also known as a meat breed, which originates from the British Isles and whose long horns curve downwards.

Hereford

This breed originates from the English county of Herefordshire, where they were bred at the start of the industrial revolution in the middle of the eighteenth century. The hornless animals were easy to transport by train and were designed to service the increased demand for meat in the big cities.

From England they spread to North and South America where to this day they remain one of the most popular cattle breeds. Hereford cattle are robust and can be left out to pasture all year round. They cope well with cold, heat, and rain, and are thus suited to the Australian climate where they can be found in large numbers. The brown cattle are easy to recognize by their pale white heads.

Hereford cattle have become one of the most popular beef breeds worldwide. It is also popular in industrial livestock farming, although it has a tendency to put on fat under such conditions. With good husbandry, ripening, and fodder, the meat is of excellent quality, finely marbled with a full flavor.

Chianina

These large and extremely powerful cattle served as models for animal sculptures as far back as Roman times. Steer of the Chianina breed can have a shoulder height of over two meters. For centuries the world's largest breed of cattle served as a reliable partner for the farmers of central Italy. The natural power of the porcelain-white draft animal became obsolete in the twentieth century with the mechanization of agriculture. Today the breed, which originate from the eponymous Chiana Valley in Tuscany, is prized above all for its extremely flavorsome meat. However, as the breed is not suitable for intensive and quick fattening,

The animal

CHIANINA

fewer and fewer farmers are rearing the noble animal.
The famous Bistecca alla Fiorentina, a one and a half kilo T-bone steak, is traditionally cut from the short loin of steer from the Chianina breed. In the Tuscan village of Sestino the "Sagra della Bistecca Chianina" is celebrated each summer, a large festival held in honor of the cattle.

Angus

The hills of the counties of Aberdeen and Angus in the northeast of Scotland are the birthplace of the famous Angus cattle. With their black, sometimes red coat, they are a short-legged, hornless breed. Of medium size compared to other cattle, Angus can quickly put on weight and fat, developing an impressive musculature. As a result it has become one of the world's most popular meat breeds and is reared in large numbers both in Europe and the USA. In the USA Angus are amongst the most frequently used animals for meat production. As the cows cause few problems during calving, the breed is also used for crossing in order to pass this characteristic onto other cattle.
As Angus cattle tend to accumulate a lot of fat the breed fell into disgrace for a period. Today, as a long ripening process requires a good fat layer, and marbled meat is favoured and its popularity is on the rise again.

Aubrac

In the seventeenth century Benedictine monks bred this breed of cattle in the monasteries of the Massif Central in southwest France. The influence of the Swiss Braunvieh on the wheat-gray Aubrac is clearly evident in the white ring around the muzzle. On the pastures of the volcanic plateaus the cattle developed into a highly robust and frugal breed with good musculature. The sparsely populated region, in which the famous Laguiole knife is also forged, is unsuitable for the cultivation of grain, however it offers large pastures with a great variety of grasses and herbs which make ideal cattle fodder. The meat of cattle grazed on such pasture is of a special quality. Following the mechanization of farming after the Second World War and the decline of the region's artisanal food producers, Aubrac cattle also disappeared from the pastures. However, since the 1980s the breed has enjoyed a renaissance and is amongst the best that France has to offer.

Kobe Cattle and Wagyū

The meat from Kobe cattle has gained an international reputation and is often described as the best and most expensive meat in the world. The breed behind the high-priced meat specialty is the black Japanese Tajima, known in the rest of the world as Wagyū ("Wa" = Japanese, "Gyū" = cattle).

The name Kobe is reserved for cattle that were born, reared, fattened, and slaughtered close to Kobe in the south Japanese prefecture of Hyogo. An exclusive specialty is the fattening of heifers in the region of Matsusaka, whose meat, according to connoisseurs, is of an even higher quality than that of the Kobe bulls.

Over recent years the Wagyū breed has also been taken up by cattle farmers in Europe, the USA, and Australia. In contrast to Japan, where the animals are mainly kept in cow sheds and fed concentrated feed, Wagyūs throughout the rest of the world are generally kept on pasture.

The legend that animals in Japan are massaged with Sake and played music only applies in rare cases, however, the majority of animals are granted many months of slow growth.

In Japan Wagyū beef is traditionally part of the meat fondue known as Shabu-shabu. Cut into very thin, fine slices it quickly cooks in the broth. As a prime example of perfect marbling, the meat has an especially tender, extremely juicy, and melt-in-the-mouth texture.

Lamb and sheep

Tender lamb and mutton are used to make the famous sausage specialty, merguez, and even the popular pastrami originates from a ripened mutton specialty from Romania. In addition to their soft wool and tasty milk that is used to produce fantastic cheeses, sheep are mainly prized for their delicious meat.

The animal

Today's domestic sheep are descended from the wild sheep known as Mouflon, which can still be found living wild in Europe's forests. In contrast to pigs and cattle, sheep cannot be kept all year round en masse in cramped sheds. As a result, the majority of sheep have access to plenty of green fodder in open pastures and spacious pens. In many regions sheep have become important landscape conservationists, employed as natural lawn mowers that keep the turf short and dense.

In regions where pork is not eaten for religious reasons, the meat of sheep, lamb, and ram has always played an important role. Over the course of time, in addition to breeds reared for large quantities of wool, meat breeds with greater muscling and a higher slaughter weight than pure wool breeds also emerged.
The names of popular meat breeds such as Oxford, Shropshire, and Dorset point to the long tradition of sheep breeding in England. However, meat sheep such as the Texel, Ile de France, and the Rhönschaf were also bred in Holland, Germany, and France.

Dual-purpose breeds, such as the widespread Merino sheep from Spain, can be used for both wool and meat production. However, during the previous century the focus on just one characteristic, exploited for maximum profitability, has resulted in the displacement of many old breeds by more productive strains. Sheep breeds typical of a particular region, such as the German White Polled Heath or Moorschnucke—species that are well adapted to their native moorland where they serve as indispensable landscape managers—have thus become endangered domestic breeds. Grazed on an undisturbed landscape, the meat of these animals is an incomparable delicacy with a great wealth of flavors.

Today the majority of sheep are reared in Asia, Australia, New Zealand, and the British Isles. Strong exporting countries such as New Zealand and Australia now supply their lamb throughout the world. Refrigerated, it ripens in the containers on-board ships during transit. However, it is worthwhile to take a closer look at where the lamb on offer comes from. Today it is not uncommon to rear lambs on food such as genetically modified soybean and grain in order to improve their performance. Even antibiotics can be employed as a performance enhancer for conventional fattening. However, the robust sheep with their four stomachs are completely adapted to green fodder and cope well on open pasture.

In order to produce tender lamb, it must be hung long enough, preferably dry-hung in the air and not kept for long periods in shrink-wrap plastic. Connoisseurs prefer the ripened meat of young sheep, as opposed to that from lambs just a few months old. In order to ripen, lamb, like the meat of cattle, requires a layer of fat that protects the meat from drying. Lambs that have been slaughtered too young often lack this characteristic.

Lamb can be air dried, smoked, and processed into ripened sausage specialties. Like the meat of goats, lamb is often very lean, which presents butchers with additional problems, especially with specialties that require a long ripening process where the results can be somewhat dry.
Fresh lamb is primarily used for braising and pan-frying. Thanks to the meat's pronounced, intense flavor, it lends itself readily to stronger and more adventurous seasoning.

The animal

SWISS WHITE ALPINE SHEEP

Lamb
All sheep up to one year old are known as lambs. So-called milk lambs, which can be a maximum of six months old, have especially pale meat. Unfortunately, this meat is frequently lacking in flavor. Lambs for fattening can be up to 12 months old.

Hogget
Lambs that are slaughtered in their second year of life are called hoggets. Following dry ripening, their meat is a special delicacy and is often underrated.

Sheep
Sheep is a general term referring to all female animals older than one year. Compared to pale lamb's meat, it is dark red in color with fine marbling and stronger taste.

Wether
Wether refers to castrated male animals. The meat of these animals is considerably stronger in flavor than that of sheep.

Ram
Rams are uncastrated male animals older than one year. Due to its strong flavor, ram meat is not particularly popular.

Fowl

Today, no other meat lands so frequently on our plates than that of fowl. Numerous patés, confits, and terrines are traditionally manufactured from fowl—usually from these birds' delicate, aromatic innards.

In the past, chickens were primarily seen as egg suppliers. Today their meat has also become extremely important. On small-scale farms, freely roaming chickens were a natural part of the fauna, and the rooster crowing on the dung heap in the early morning became a typical symbol of farm life.

Domestic geese, in addition to providing a festive roast, also served as guard animals, sounding the alarm with their loud honking at the sight of any intruder.

The turkeys of North and South America were domesticated by the indigenous populations long before the arrival of the first settlers. In Europe the breeding of turkeys subsequently replaced the rearing of peacocks that had been widespread up until that time.

From the middle of the last century onwards, poultry farming underwent a grave development. Huge chicken coops, devoid of sunlight, sprung up primarily for the rearing of quickly growing hybrid breeds raised for their extreme performance and record fattening time. Hybrid breeds are derived from inbred lines designed to reproduce one specific characteristic on a large scale. The hens of laying breeds reared in this manner lay enormous numbers of eggs, while, in contrast, the roosters hardly accumulate any meat and are unsuited to fattening. For this reason millions of male chicks are killed every year immediately upon hatching.

Intensive poultry farming has become one of the saddest chapters in the history of industrial animal husbandry. Many of the birds fattened within the space of a few weeks suffer pain, and are regularly administered antibiotics during their short lives as a preventative measure. However, the greatest problem with intensive poultry farming is the lack of space in the coops, with the birds often lacking sufficient room to even stretch their wings.

Consequently, good poultry comes from animals that spend the majority of their life in the open. Here the animals have enough space to follow their natural behavior. Increasing numbers of poultry farmers who pursue quality over quantity are now taking this route, employing the methods of humane husbandry. The meat of these animals possesses a more pronounced and varied flavor, which is also reflected in the processed meat specialties.

Chickens spend more than half of the day in the open, pecking and searching for food. Along with ducks and turkeys, chickens are omnivores and happily supplement their plant-rich diet with snails or worms. Geese eat grass and herbs but also grain, which is why the wild Graylag goose, which congregates in large flocks, is feared by many farmers.

To care for their plumage, chickens bathe in sand to rid their feathers of dirt and parasites. Waterfowl, geese, and ducks require access to bodies of water for bathing, cleaning their plumage, and diving for food.

In order to protect themselves from birds of prey, fowl like to hide in hedges, trees, and bushes. If such brushwood is unavailable, open aviaries can also serve as a source of protection. With the aid of small, mobile chicken coops, poultry farmers can also provide such shelter on treeless open ground. By nature, chickens spend the night in trees. Today these are replaced by suitably raised bars.

The animal

SWEDISH FLOWER ROOSTER

As in the case of cattle and pigs, ambitious poultry farmers are increasingly drawing on a virtually forgotten diversity of breeds for the rearing of free range fowl. In contrast to the intensively bred hybrid fowl, there are many especially tasty old breeds which are both more robust, easier to rear, and perfectly suited to being kept outdoors all year round.

Rediscovered dual-purpose breeds such as Les Bleues, Sundheimer, and Sulmtaler lay large numbers of eggs as well as accumulating sufficient meat, meaning both hens and roosters can be usefully reared. The blue-footed Les Bleues originates from the well-known Bresse chickens, which in France are also reared free range. Kept outdoors and fed a natural diet, the animals require considerably longer to reach an appropriate slaughter weight however they are less frequently ill and, thanks to slow growth and natural food, produce meat of a far higher quality.
A specialty is roosters raised as capons. The young, castrated roosters grow more slowly and are heavier than normal roosters—they even accumulate intramuscular fat that makes their meat especially juicy and flavorsome. In France and Italy capons are traditionally served as a festive roast at Christmas. However, as they are often castrated without anesthetic, the rearing of capons, although free range, remains subject to criticism.

In contrast another frequently criticized fowl specialty, the goose liver delicacy known as foie gras, can be produced completely naturally from free range geese without the rightly rejected force feeding. If geese are given a natural environment and appropriate food they naturally develop a fatty liver, which they normally accumulate as a reserve for their long migrations southwards. The incomparable taste of this pain-free alternative is now gaining ground on its force fed counterpart.

Processing
The countless cheap poultry products on supermarket shelves have virtually no traditional roots, and are primarily understood to be a reaction of the food industry to the lean meat craze of recent decades. They are often relatively tasteless products and the cause of a sad end to the life of the animals.

The animal

WILD DUCK   CANADA GOOSE

Chickens, ducks, geese, and turkeys consist of more than just breast meat, and when correctly roasted, cooked, or made into pâtés, rilletes, and confits, they make a special delicacy.

In the past, an effort was made to utilize every part of the fowl. This included, in addition to the breast fillets, the supposedly inedible cuts, innards, and fat. This approach gave rise to the numerous traditional, artisanal fowl specialties that we know today.

As a rule chicken meat is extremely lean, and in contrast to pork and beef, is little suited to the manufacture of sausage specialties requiring a long ripening. As a result, poultry meat is often mixed with that of other animals for the purpose of processing and ripening. Thanks to their higher fat content, ducks and geese are better suited to the manufacture of air-dried specialties, and are a delicacy when lightly smoked. Duck meat can also be used to make excellent fresh sausages—a special delight.

Game

The diversity of wild game roaming the forests, mountains, and meadows is every bit as colorful as the plant world. Fallow deer, red deer, roe deer, and wild boar are the most frequently hunted animals. Wild geese, ducks, pheasants, and partridges are known as game birds.

The animal

Hunting is strictly regulated and restricted by closed seasons. Even the quantities of game that can be killed in the wild are regimented and not up to the whims of the hunter. Hunting as a simple adventure sport is increasingly under fire. As a result, types of hunting common in the past are now prohibited. Nevertheless, hunting still plays an important role in nature preservation.

Wild boar, especially on the European continent, are becoming a menace with the large scale cultivation of corn. An explosion in their numbers is resulting in severe damage the agricultural industry. Inquisitive wild boars are also making an appearance in cities as they search for food. The Benelux countries are plagued by hundreds of thousands of wild geese descending on the countryside. In light of these developments, butchers are now faced with the challenge of producing tasty specialties from these animals. Meat lovers should seize the opportunity and view game as a flavorsome alternative and explore the existing diversity.

DEER

Enclosures
A number of game species—above all red deer, fallow deer, and wild boar—can also be kept in enclosures. This was a practice familiar to the kings of past centuries who, as early as the Middle Ages, established deer parks. Kept in enclosures and fed a special diet, these animals could be reared to produce more fat, and thanks to the easily accessible food, were somewhat heavier than fellow members of their species living in the wild.

In captivity a number of domestic breeds can be crossed with their wild forefathers. Known as backcrossing, this method can be used to produce half wild, slow growing breeds with their own specific qualities. New Zealand is home to the largest game industry by far, with the animals, primarily deer, kept in huge enclosures. Reared to produce venison, this industry has advanced to become one of the country's most important economic sectors.

The flavor of the forest
Game meat is darker than that of domesticated breeds and has a stronger, sometimes pungent flavor. The animals' diverse natural diet, foraged from the woodlands, can thus be experienced directly on the tongue. With the correct fodder, these typical game flavors can also be found in the meat of bison and a number of old cattle breeds. To this day, the fattening of half wild pigs on acorns in the forests of Spain and Portugal is a popular method for lending meat this special flavor.

In the past, game meat, following a long and sometimes imperfect ripening, often displayed a flavor known as haut gout. This pungent note of decay divides opinion, however, due to improved refrigeration, it is now rarely encountered. Like beef, game also needs to be hung and dry-ripened for a number of days. The length of the ripening depends on the type of animal and its size. Following ripening, game is softer and has a more intense aroma, with the meat from young animals generally more tender than that of older animals.

Game animals, thanks to plenty of exercise and the absence of breeding influences, produce extremely lean meat, which, if prepared carelessly, can quickly become dry. As a consequence, it is often larded with pork bacon. Extra fat, generally from domestic pigs, is also added to improve game sausage. Game is also used to manufacture a variety of different sausage specialties, cold cuts, and pâtés. Even jerky, such as the dried meat from wild springboks, known in South Africa as Biltong, can be made from game.

The cuts

Fresh or dry-aged

When following these tips, storing fresh or dry-aged meat at home is not a problem. There is no fixed or general rule as to how long meat can be stored.

The cuts

How do I store good meat at home? In a refrigerator, freezer, or in a suitable pantry?

In principle, meat—regardless of whether fresh or dry-aged—can also be stored at home. Generally it is advisable to use fresh meat from the butcher, stored in the fridge, as quickly as possible. If it is to be kept for longer then it should be frozen. For fresh meat in airtight vacuum packs, a refrigerator with a temperature of 32–36°F / 0–2°C provides optimal conditions. For shock-frozen meat a deep freezer is best, and dry-aged meat should ideally be stored in a special meat-maturing fridge as used in butcher shops and restaurants, or shock-frozen. Dry-ripened sausages and hams can be stored in a pantry, but only at a suitable room temperature that does not cause the fat to melt. More sausage know-how is provided in the chapter "Know your meat" (see pp. 90–95). Anyone who likes to experiment can also ripen good meat in special dry-aging bags in a normal fridge. There is no fixed or general rule as to how long meat can be stored. After all, the initial products differ in terms of the activity of the microorganisms, the percentage of fat, and quality. However, consumers should adhere to the use-by-date specified by producers.

As a general rule, all food should be subjected to a sense test before eating—in particular by smelling—in order to check whether it is still fresh.

How does a butcher recognize good meat?

Both PSE and DFD meat is the result of faulty practice in abattoirs, which not only results in poor quality meat but also exposes the animals to extreme stress in the last moments of their lives. PSE is a designation only applied to pork, whereas DFD applies to beef and in rare cases, pork.

If an animal is exposed to stress shortly before being slaughtered, its adrenalin level rises, energy reserves are rapidly used up, and the pH value sinks too quickly. This results in pale, soft, and watery meat—negative qualities that lend the meat its title: PSE (pale, soft, and exudative). In addition to these obvious deficiencies, the meat acquires a mealy to dry consistency, regardless of how it is prepared.

While PSE meat is much too pale, in the case of DFD meat exactly the opposite occurs. It is not without reason that the acronym DFD stands for dark, firm and dry—and the meat is too dark, firm, and dry for a specific reason.

As in the case of PSE, the stress which the animal is exposed to shortly before being slaughtered has an immediate, negative effect on the quality of the meat due to the organism's increased consumption of glycogen. If, following a slaughter, insufficient glycogen is available to produce the lactic acid required for the ripening of the meat, then the valuable commodity deteriorates, resulting in inferior DFD meat.

Meat color

The color of meat is an important quality indicator for the butcher. Thus good beef is characterized by deep red muscle tissue and white fat, while pale red meat is indicative of an animal that has been slaughtered very young and is of a lower quality and inferior flavor. If one is looking for first class veal, it should be dark to light pink in color. High quality pork should be deep red in color, not too pale (see PSE meat). The most intensive red is to be found in the muscle tissue of lambs. Variations in the color of the meat from breed to breed is shown very clearly in the case of beef: with its contrasting, bright white veins of fat, Japanese Wagyu displays a deep red color. US beef, thanks to the addition of corn to the feed, is lighter red, while the meat from German Angus cattle is a dark red due to the exclusive use of grass fodder. As a general rule, if the meat appears unusually dark or darker than one is used to, this is a sign that the animal, in accordance with its nature, has had a lot of exercise—a clear indication of humane animal husbandry.

The cuts

Marbling

Intramuscular fat—commonly known as marbling—is a visible quality feature of good meat and is largely dependent on three factors: breed, exercise, and diet. Of all the animal breeds, only cattle, pigs, and sheep are naturally disposed to the accumulation of intramuscular fat. Lots of exercise and a natural diet are ideal preconditions for the formation of the fine, fat veins, which can be considerably enhanced by feeding the animals additional concentrated feed such as corn or wheat in the final weeks prior to slaughter. However, the intensity of marbling varies considerably from breed to breed. While the bison of the North American prairies are renowned for lean meat with little fat infiltration, the meat of original Japanese Kobe cattle has the highest level of marbling of any beef in the world. The fat stored in connective tissue is largely responsible for the meat's tenderness and flavor, which, thanks to the fine, fat veins, retains its juiciness even when grilled or fried.

Pioneer work

Although it has not played a great role in Germany up until now, using marbling as official criteria for the classification of meat has long been practiced in countries such as the USA and Japan. The assessment and quality grading of meat is conducted according to the BMS—the Beef Marbling Score. Meat with a score of 5 on the BMS scale can have an excellent degree of marbling between 8 and 12. In addition to marbling, the BMS scale also takes into account the texture and color of the fat and the meat.

What should I ask the butcher?

Behind all good meat there is a breeder who is both knowledgeable and passionate about his trade. He has consciously chosen breeds with a good genetic disposition, allowing his animals and their meat sufficient time to fully develop. He practices humane animal husbandry and fattening, and only slaughters the animals when the meat is at its height with respect to both flavor and development.

With simple questions asked over the counter, every meat lover can check whether their butcher of choice really does know about his meat and meat products. If the answers are unsatisfactory or evasive then it is probably better to look for an alternative supplier.

Questions about the animal:

- Where do the animals used for the specialties come from?
- How were the animals kept and what fodder did they receive?
- How old were they and how were they slaughtered?

Questions about the manufacture:

- Which cuts did he butcher himself and which specialties did he make?
- How was the meat ripened and for how long?
- Which methods were used to refine and preserve the specialties (see pp. 60–63)
- What seasoning or seasoning mixtures were used?
- What other ingredients were used in the manufacture of the specialties?

Beef cuts

What was perfectly normal for our grandparents is now being rediscovered by today's butchers and cooks: the art of using every part of the animal. The resulting conscious use of unfamiliar cuts such as spider steak, tri-tip, flank, or tomahawk is now part and parcel of the nose-to-tail movement and increasingly common amongst quality-conscious butchers and meat suppliers.

The renaissance of the forgotten cuts

This is not exactly a surprise for experienced meat experts. After all, these virtually forgotten cuts are often the most exciting parts of the animal and have considerable culinary value. In order to obtain these cuts, methodical work and fine artisanry are required. Here the butcher's rule of thumb applies: "Let the knife do the work, not the muscles!" However, the danger of landing in the wrong filet or damaging cuts when butchering cattle remains. With a sharp knife, the carcass is first divided into two halves and then into a forequarter and a hindquarter. If the butcher only intends to ripen the prime cuts, they first butcher the side of the animal, and then ripen the cuts. If they intend to ripen the whole side in one piece, then they butcher it after ripening. There are many ways of cutting the loin located in the hindquarter. Traditionally the belly—consisting of the flank, skirt, and top butt flap—is cut out. Other butchers cut the carcass into Pistola and forequarter with plate section.

While in the Middle Ages the fatty parts were considered the classic prime cuts, today the pan-fried cuts such as sirloin, tenderloin, entrecote, T-bone, and porterhouse have acquired this status. Nevertheless, secondary cuts, which in the past were considered inferior, such as flat iron, Onglet, flank, spider, Teres Major, tri-tip, and skirt, are also ideal for frying—however, this is only the case when the meat used is of excellent quality and originates from animals who have enjoyed additional fattening with an energy-rich fodder such as corn or barley. The innards, which are removed directly after the slaughter and are not ripened, are also enjoying increased popularity. On the other hand, pan-fried cuts such as tenderloin, sirloin, and entrecote, originate from those muscles least used by the animal, while braising cuts such as cheeks originate from the muscles that receive a lot of exercise. Although today more than ever, efforts are made to allocate every individual muscle its own, independent culinary status, the cutting and trimming of pan-fried and braising cuts still produces enough meat, fat, and trimmings for the butcher to make delicious sausages by employing traditional artisanal techniques.

Other countries. Other cuts

The pole position is occupied by the Americans, who produce many more cuts from an animal than the Germans or the French. However, there are also exceptions, such as the spider steak cut from the leg, which is highly regarded by meat lovers in Germany and England, but is virtually unknown in the USA. A further difference is to be found in the manner in which the loin is subdivided during butchering, i.e., where the cut is made between the entrecote and porterhouse.

In order to obtain a perfect piece of meat, a further essential processing step is required: the ripening of the meat, which is closely connected to its sensory evaluation, i.e., a piece of meat that scores well with consumers in terms of tenderness, juiciness, taste, and aroma. While beef immediately after slaughter is tough and lacking in flavor, meat ripened for 30 days—during which time the enzymes in the meat begin to break down the protein structures after 14 days—delights the senses with its flavor and incredible tenderness. Furthermore, anyone who wants to produce meat with the ultimate flavor will opt for the supreme discipline of dry-aging, which is celebrating a comeback amongst butchers, cooks, and meat lovers.

Whether an unfamiliar spider steak, a handmade sausage, or a laboriously dry-ripened porterhouse from humanely reared cattle, the respectful utilization of the whole animal not only results in new, sustainable taste experiences, but also ensures that the meat lover can enjoy them with a good conscience.

Ripening

When is a steak a good steak? When it is tender and has a good flavor is how the majority of meat lovers would answer. In order for these two characteristics to develop to the fullest, meat needs to ripen. The animal's muscle protein, which has hardened after the slaughter, initially results in tough, unpalatable meat. After around 14 days the curse is lifted thanks to the enzymes in the meat that then begin to break down the hard muscle fibers to produce soft, tender meat. The question that remains is what method is to be used for the optimal ripening of the precious meat.

Aqua Aging

In the ripening method developed by the master butcher Dirk Ludwig (pages 122-123), the meat is immersed in mineral water and ripens in a special plastic container for four weeks. The mineral water creates a barrier, protecting the meat from oxygen and bacteria, allowing it to ripen without decaying. In distinction to the wet ripening methods in common use, meat subjected to aqua aging ripens without acquiring any musty notes. An essential feature of

The cuts

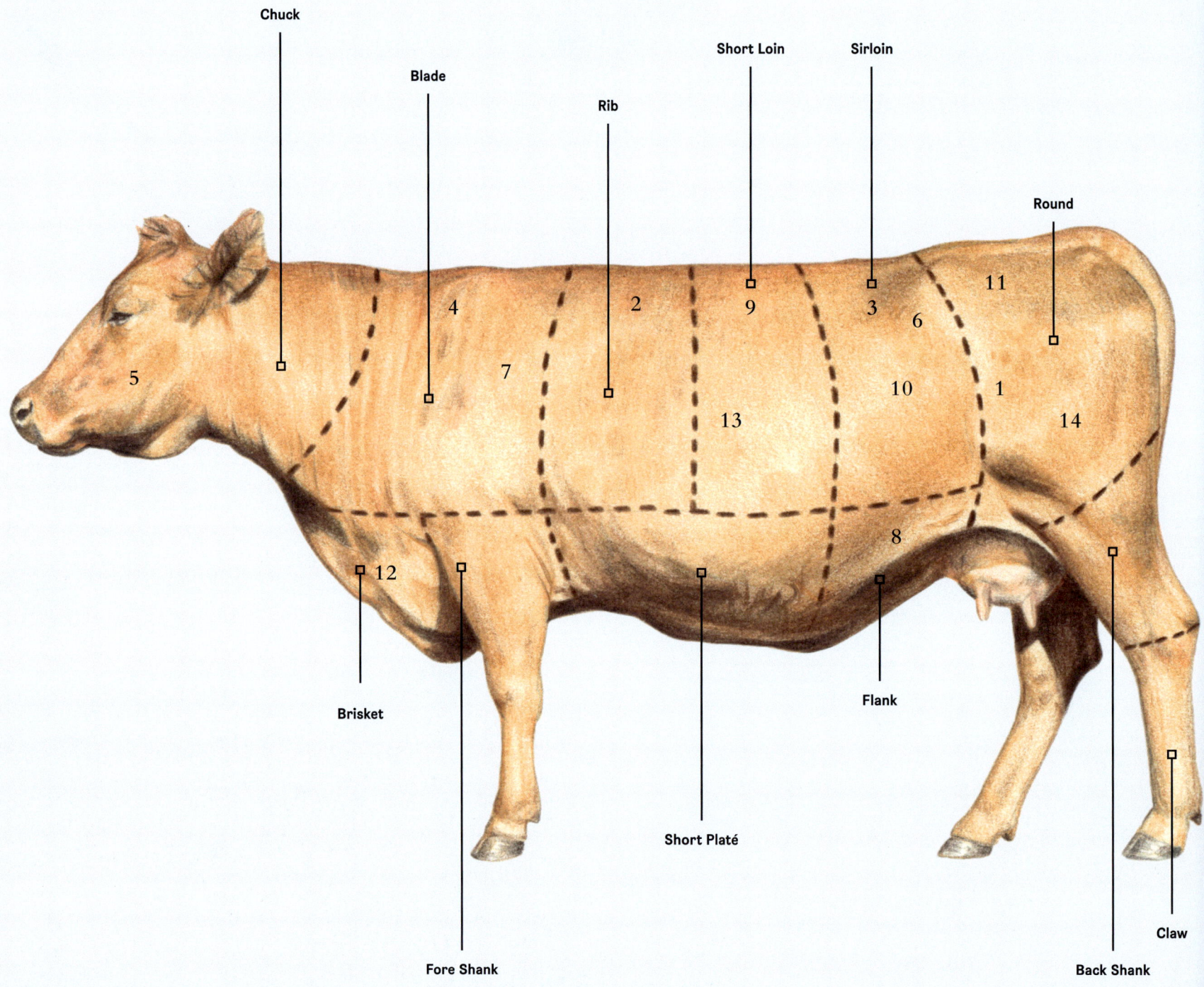

this method is using correct proportions of water, minerals, carbon dioxide, and meat—a secret closely guarded by the meat expert Dirk Ludwig.

Wet/foil aging and Wet-aged

Of all the available types of ripened beef, it is clear that the most commonly sold variety is wet-aged. With this method, the cuts, removed from the bone directly after slaughter, are sealed in vacuum packed bags when they ripen, where they are left to soak in their own juice for at least 30 days. The advantage of this ripening method is that the cuts of meat lose very little weight and are considerably more tender. However, wet-aged meat is not as rich in flavor and often acquires a metallic and slightly sour taste due to the bacteria that find ideal conditions for the production of lactic acid in this wet environment. Renowned meat suppliers use this ripening method in order to preserve the original flavor of high quality meat.

Dry-ripening

The method favored by the new meat movement is dry-ripening, a method generally reserved for high quality loin cuts. However, this ripening method, which has enjoyed cult status in America for decades, is actually an old hat: around 40 years ago master butchers dry-ripened meat on the bone in order to increase its shelf life. While the method was employed in the past for all manner of cuts, today it is mainly rib-eye, striploin, T-bone, and porterhouse cuts that are hung in the impressive ripening chambers in order to refine their flavor. As a rule the meat ripens at a controlled humidity of 85% and a room temperature of 45°F/7°C for 21 days, during which time it loses an impressive 30–50% of its weight. Tenderloin should be removed from the bone after around seven days of ripening, otherwise it can acquire the taste and consistency of ham. After the ripening has been completed the cuts are trimmed, the dried outer layer carefully removed, and the meat prepared like a conventional steak. This sophisticated and laboriously ripened meat is prized by gourmets for its tenderness and incomparably intense, primal flavor—a special delicacy that has its price, and not just because of the exquisite cuts of meat. The time investment, storage expense, and weight loss of up to 50% all contribute to the high price.

Butchering diagram

1. **Hanging Tender:** A steak known as Nierenzapfen in Germany and Onglet in France. Intense meat flavor.

2. **Tomahawk:** Rib-eye with an extra-long bone. Ideal for frying.

3. **Sirloin:** The hip of the cow. As steak, it is perfect for frying.

4. **Beef Rib and Côte de Boef:** From the rear loin. Cut into slices, it is also popular as cutlets and is an especially juicy cut.

5. **Cheeks:** Typical cut for braising and very popular in gourmet cuisine.

6. **Porterhouse:** Steak with bones in a characteristic T shape from the rear of the loin. Larger filet component than a T-bone.

7. **Ribeye and Entrecote:** From the front of the loin and ideal for frying. With the rib eye center, one of four strands of muscle.

8. **Bavette Flanchet:** From the flank. Lean meat but nevertheless with intense flavor. One of the most popular steaks in the USA.

9. **T-Bone Steak and Bistecca alla Fiorentina:** Cut from the rear of the loin with a classic T-shaped bone.

10. **Filet Mignon and Tenderloin:** The most tender and highly prized cut from the loin. Generally known as filet.

11. **Strip Loin and Rump Steak:** From the rear of the loin with the typical fatty edge.

12. **Brisket:** Classic cut for the smoker and very popular in the USA. From the front of the breast.

13. **Back Ribs and Spare Ribs:** Cut together with muscle from the rib cage. Ideal for the smoker.

14. **Tri-tip:** Short-fibred meat from the niche between the sirloin and the thick flank. Perfect for the grill and in the past was reserved for dignitaries.

Tip
Pieces of meat suitable for sausages and cold cuts: muscle, trimmings, and fat from the whole animal. Finely or coarsely chopped in the cutter and packed into natural intestines.

Pork cuts

The contrast couldn't be greater: while pork is the most popular meat amongst German consumers, apart from filet cuts, it has rarely found its way into gourmet cuisine. However, thanks to the rediscovery of unfamiliar secondary cuts, the breeding of old pig breeds, and the great enthusiasm for hand made sausage specialties, this has now changed.

Roots of the pig enthusiasm

The increased interest in special or secondary cuts such as the German Kachelfleisch, Spanish Pluma, and Papada is naturally reflected in butchering which demands special skill and know-how. In addition to the special cuts, removing the cutlets is one of the most difficult moments during butchering—even for experienced master butchers. Solid mastery of the craft is also required for making sausages, where cuts such as the pig's head are also highly prized. After the head has been boiled in the pot, the remaining section composed of rind, muscle, fat, and connective tissue, known as the mask, is removed from the skull and processed to make cooked sausages. For the manufacture of traditional blanched sausages, belly, shoulder, backfat, and the pig's dewlap are utilized.

Warm meat processing

Warm meat is perfectly suited to the manufacture of cooked and blanched sausages such as liverwurst, blood sausage, ham sausage, Wiener and Frankfurter sausages, and aspic. However, the practice of butchering immediately after slaughter is now very rare as maintaining a slaughtering facility is no longer economical for small butchers. However, for the sake of the traditional handicraft and on the grounds of taste, there is much reason to recommend warm meat processing, which must be carried out within 40 minutes after the slaughter of the animal when the warm meat has a natural pH value of up to seven. Thanks to this high pH value, which is a result of the meat's natural phosphate, the salinity is reduced. This means that more salt can be added to the sausage mass, which improves the taste, as well as enhancing the flavor of any added herbs and spices. Furthermore, an additional binding agent such as phosphate is no longer necessary. Thus the butcher obtains a sausage with good binding qualities by purely natural means. In contrast, phosphate is often added to pork that has been butchered when cold in order to obtain the required binding quality. This meat has a pH of 5.6.

Ripening

In contrast to beef, pork requires considerably less ripening time. After 48 hours, pork from shed-reared pigs has the ideal degree of ripeness and is ready for sale or further processing. In the case of pork from free range pigs, longer ripening periods are advisable in order to obtain the desired tenderness. A number of courageous butchers such as Heiko Brath and LiVar pig breeder, Frans de Rond have even attempted to ripen pork, which is only possible with old breeds and meat of an appropriate quality.

Culinary playground

Pork can be prepared in a variety of ways. Some cuts are best suited to braising, others to frying, and more still are only suitable for sausage making. Over the course of time three versatile classics have emerged: cutlets, the neck of pork, and the haunches. The latter can be used for both air-dried and cooked ham specialties, as well as for fresh meat cuts for roasting. The topside is perfect for making ham, while the silverside—including the rind, scored in a diamond pattern—is ideal for oven roasted pork with crackling. In addition to the favorites, there are other cuts such as pork belly and the extremely tender cheeks, which have only recently grown in popularity. The pork belly is also the source of bacon, which has achieved cult status amongst some meat eaters and is now an integral part of the burger culture. In contrast, the backfat of the peaceful quadruped is primarily used to lard larger roasts, while Kachelfleisch, Secreto, and Presa are typical side cuts that are still to be discovered by many meat lovers.

The cuts

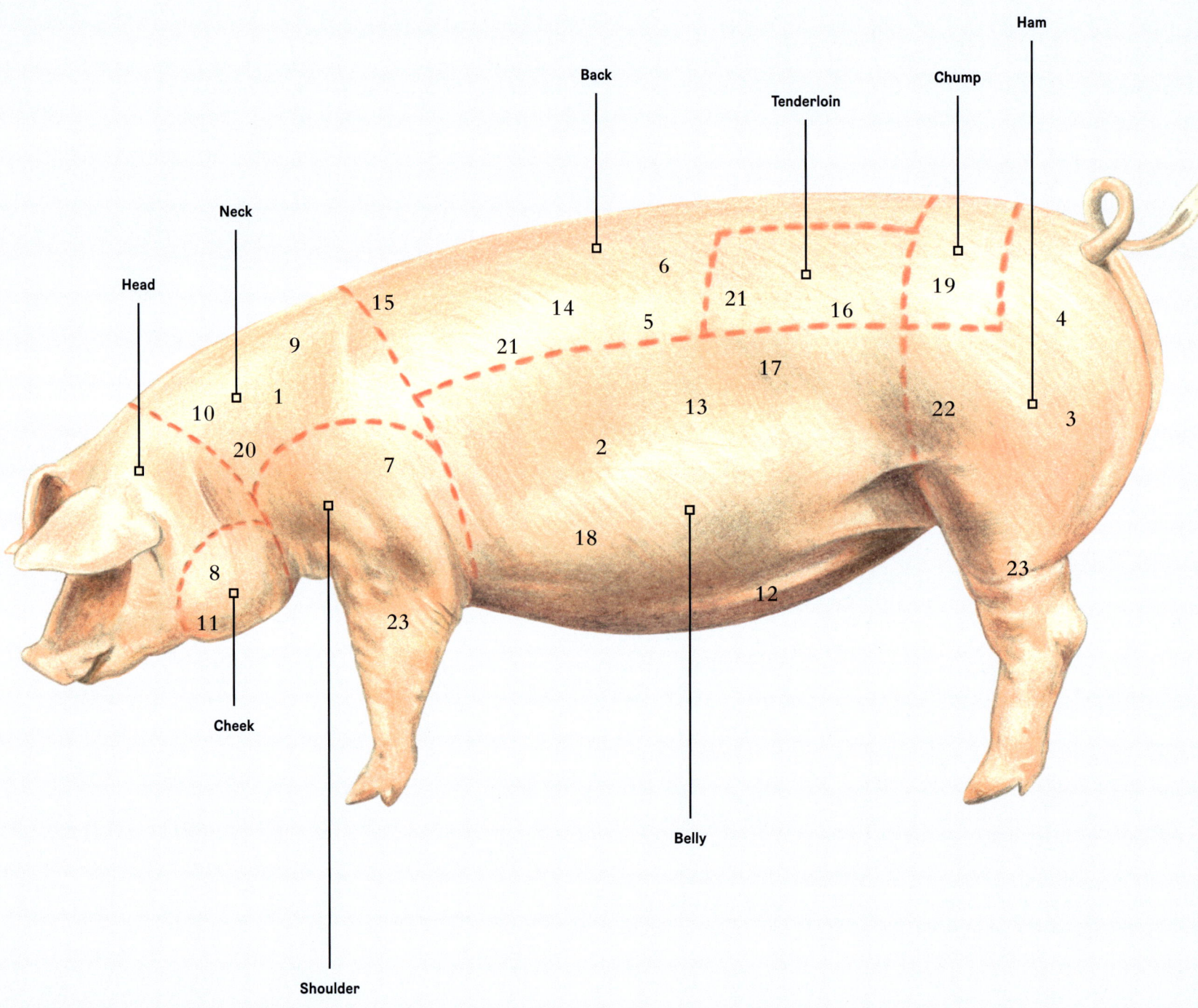

52

Butchering diagram

1. **Boston Butt:** Cut from the neck, consisting of muscle, fat, sinews, connective tissue, and bones. Classic American BBQ dish. Smoked, it is plucked apart to make the dish, pulled pork.

2. **Ribs:** From the rack, with a relatively high percentage of fat and a melt-in-your-mouth texture. Known in Spain as Costillas, they are an essential part of a genuine American BBQ.

3. **Jamon:** Spanish for ham. Composed of the topside, silverside, sirloin, and rear ham hock.

4. **Kachelfleisch:** Term for a German cut, also known as Fledermaus (bat). Located on the hip bone of the ham, it is traditionally used for making sausages. Also ideal for frying.

5. **Loin ribs:** From the upper part of the pork loin. Smaller, curved, and with less meat than spare ribs. Also known in the USA as baby back ribs.

6. **Pork loin:** Known in Spain as Lomo. A very fine cut which contains the tenderloin, loin roast, and cutlets. Very juicy and lean.

7. **Paleta:** Spanish for shoulder of ham and the counterpart to Jamon. Composed of shoulder and front ham hock.

8. **Papada:** Spanish for pork dewlap and a special cut from the cheek area. In the Spanish cut, Papada is part of the cheek muscles.

9. **Pluma:** Spanish for feather. Triangular, flat cut from the front of the loin. Good marbling, remains juicy when grilled.

10. **Presa:** Spanish name for a shoulder steak. Rich marbling and intense red meat. Perfect for grilling and smoking.

11. **Pork cheeks:** Known is Spain as Carillera. A cut from the muscles of the lower jaw, very lean and ideal for stewing.

12. **Pork belly:** High percentage of fat and fat infiltration. Dry cured and cold smoked to make the highly popular bacon.

13. **Spare ribs:** Ribs from the upper belly, also known as St. Louis Cut. Less meat than back ribs.

14. **Rack of pork:** Large, compact part of the back musculature with a high percentage of connective tissue and extremely juicy. Can be cut into numerous cutlets, perfect for frying.

15. **Secreto:** Translated, it means secret pork filet. Coarse-fibred, fan-shaped cut hidden between the loin and backfat. Richly marbled.

16. **Pork tenderloin:** Known in Spain under the tuneful name Solomillo. Located beneath the rack on both sides of the spine. Fine-fibered with little fat.

17. **Spare ribs:** Cut from the upper, meatier part of the rib cage and the lower, less meaty belly ribs.

18. **Pork membrane:** Fine, net-like fatty tissue from the diaphragm. Perfect for holding together dishes such as roulade. Almost completely dissolves during cooking.

19. **Pork schnitzel:** Usually cut from the loin or leg, it is generally beaten flat with a meat tenderizer to break the muscle fibers.

20. **Neck of pork:** A popular cut, richly marbled and very juicy. The section of neck with bones is generally cut into cutlets.

21. **Chop:** From the loin and with bone. Includes the central loin chops and the especially lean rib chops.

22. **Thick flank:** From the leg and part of the ham. Very fine-fibered, it is lean and juicy meat. Ideal for roasting, cooking in fine slices, or for ragout and goulash.

23. **Ham hock:** A cut from the leg with a high proportion of connective tissue and lean meat.

The cuts

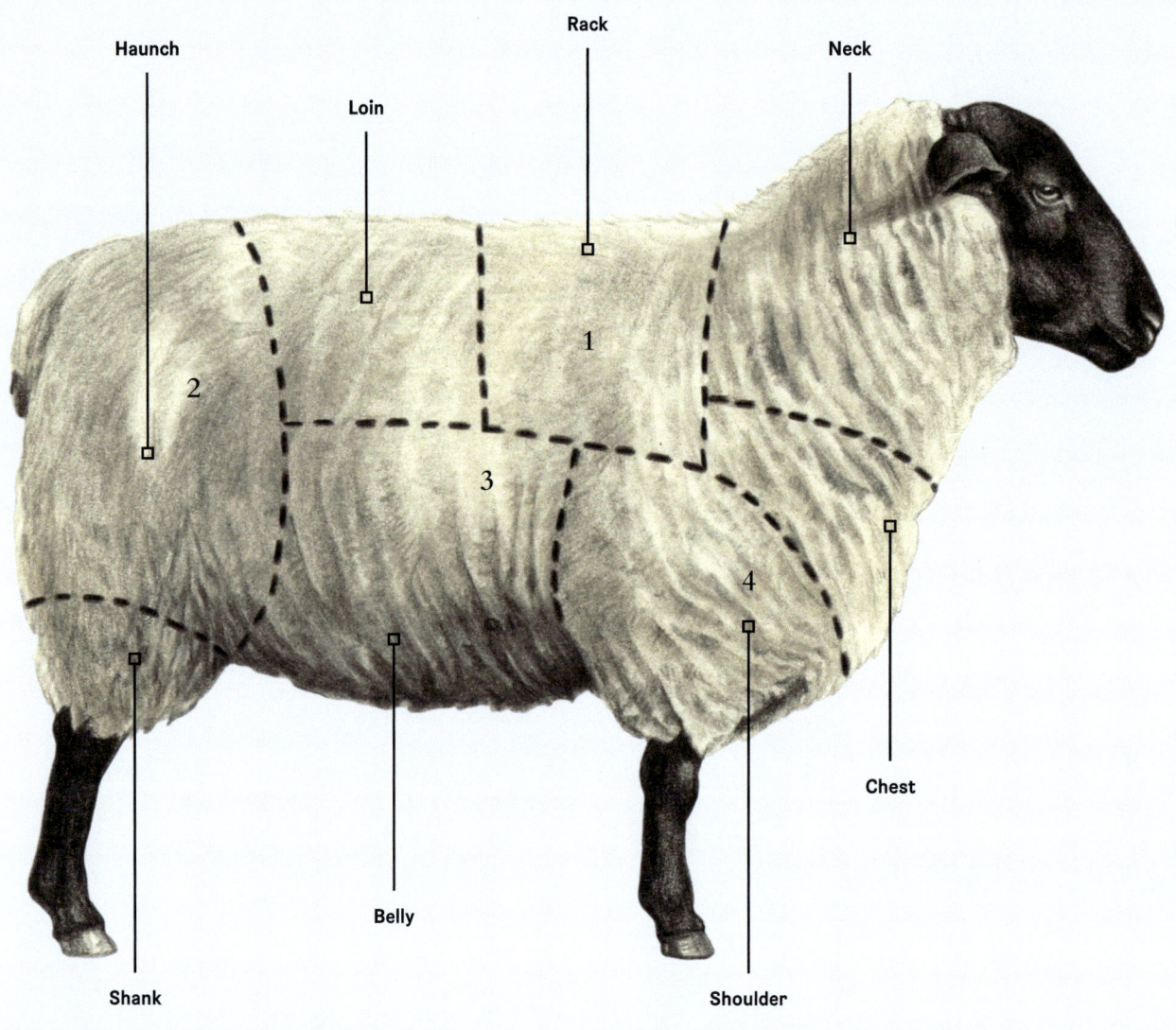

Lamb and mutton cuts

They are thought to be the first animals domesticated by man, are extremely adaptable, and in addition to wool, milk, and tallow, also supply delicious, nutritious meat. Sheep.

The cuts

Piquant delicacy beneath lambskin

Lambs, which provide the best meat, often have names that provide an indication of their origin, such as Limousine, salt meadow, or Pauillac lamb. And that for a very good reason: the origin of the animals provides information on both their natural food and the aroma of the meat. In the case of lamb, the animals' diet—for example whether they have grazed on Mediterranean herbs or grass from fields close to the coast—has a decisive influence on the taste of the meat. Lamb from animals reared in coastal regions, often called Pré-Salé or salt meadow lamb, is characterized by a slightly salty taste, while lamb from mountainous regions such as the Pyrenees or the volcanic Vogelsberg region in Germany, grazing on wild herbs and grasses, has an additional piquant note. In addition to origin and fodder, age and the proportion of fat are the most important quality criteria for lamb.

The butchering of a lamb is conducted in a similar fashion to the butchering of cattle—albeit on a much smaller scale. After the severing of the head, which is especially prized as a delicacy in the Arab world, the legs are cut off, the loin is sawn out together with the cutlets, and finally the breast and shoulder are removed. The lamb's relatively small muscles dictate the limited number of cuts, which traditionally consist of the neck, the loin or saddle, legs, skirt, breast, shoulder, and hocks. The most versatile cut is the loin, also known as saddle of lamb, which consists of the double cutlets, loin roast, loin cutlets with noisettes, and tenderloin, and which can also be roasted whole. In addition to lamb filets, the lamb cutlets—known in England as chops—are especially popular amongst passionate grillers. While the leg of lamb is predestined for braising, the shoulder of lamb is used in Ireland to make the traditional Irish stew. In addition to its range of uses and culinary possibilities, lamb is especially prized amongst gourmets for its delicacy and intense flavor.

Butchering diagram

1. **Loin or saddle of lamb:** Cut from the back with a relatively high percentage of connective tissue. Ideal sliced into cutlets and fried in the pan or roasted whole.

2. **Leg of lamb:** The most popular cut for roasting, it is tender and full of flavor. Leg of lamb is perfect for steaks and skewers, and lamb hocks for braised dishes and stews.

3. **Lamb ribs:** Composed of seven or eight ribs from the breast. Best marinated and then braised or grilled.

4. **Shoulder of lamb:** Cut from the forequarter. Smaller than a leg, with a lot of fat and connective tissue, it can be used in a variety of ways.

The cuts

Poultry cuts

The ideal chicken breast—which consumers tend to grab out of habit when buying poultry—should be tender, low in fat, and with a delicate flavor. However the chicken has so much more to offer.

The cuts

Poultry and its characteristics

Anyone looking for good meat who buys a humanely reared chicken will be surprised to see that the breast is a good deal smaller than that from shed-reared chickens, which are almost exclusively bred for their breast meat. This meat will also be firmer as the muscles from free range animals quite simply get more exercise. These special meat characteristics are also found amongst non-domesticated game birds such as partridge, wild duck, or grouse. In addition to rearing conditions tailored to the animals' needs, the species of bird, breed, gender, age, and food influence the eating pleasure. The conscious selection of a free range meat breed that was also given a final fattening with concentrated, natural feed such as corn, buckwheat, or cream, is the best way to ensure one has both a happy and a high quality chicken on one's hands. The delicate, lean meat for which chicken is renowned is primarily obtained from young animals, while the meat of older animals and boiling hens tends to have a tougher texture. Chicken should always be well done, and, in the case of good quality meat, will retain its juicy consistency despite the heat of the cooking process.

Chicken is traditionally butchered to obtain the breast, legs, and wings, although the feathered part of the wing is generally cut off. However, the chicken also holds a number of special cuts in store, such as the Sot-l'y-laisse, supreme cut, and drumsticks. Freely translated, Sot-l'y-laisse means "the fool leaves it there," which leaves no doubt as to the exquisite character of this very delicate, filet-like piece of poultry, which lies almost undetected towards the rear of the chicken above the legs. The cut known in Europe as supreme cut, and in the USA as broiler airline breast, is primarily a matter of aesthetics, with the upper wing bone left attached to the breast filet for the sake of appearances. The part of the chicken known as the drumstick refers to the lower leg, and in the case of the butterfly cut, prepared using a special technique in which the breast filet is cut with a sharp knife parallel to the chopping board and opened up to produce a butterfly shape—appearance is again the primary concern.

Butchering diagram

1. **Breast:** The most tender part of poultry—very low in fat and extremely popular. Best cooked together with the skin. Without skin: poached, steamed, or cut into slices.

2. **Wing:** Best known as chicken wings—darker meat than the breast and needs to be cooked longer. Perfect coated in breadcrumbs, deep-fried, or grilled.

3. **Leg and thigh:** Dark, firmer meat thanks to good blood supply—the top part of the leg is commonly known as a drumstick.

4. **Sot-L'y-Laisse:** Very delicate, small, filet-like pieces of meat that are tender, with juicy consistency and intense flavor.

Charcuterie – the art of butchery

Craft and relish

The fruity-smoky note of a fine German mettwurst, the sweetness of an air ripened ham, the piquant and lightly sour taste of salami: many of these exquisite flavors have their origin in centuries-old techniques which remain part of the charcutier's craft to this day, serving to both preserve the meat and provide incomparable pleasure.

The origin of the charcutier's craft

The practice of traditional home slaughtering is the birthplace of the majority of the artisanal sausage and ham specialties that we know today. As it was not possible to eat all of an animal immediately after slaughter, methods had to be found to preserve the meat.
Before the invention of refrigeration there were few means to keep meat cool, so methods such as heating, salting, smoking, and fermentation have been used as a means of preservation for centuries.

In addition to preservation, the chopping of tough and fatty cuts of meat enabled all parts of the animal to be used and made palatable. Even animal products such as blood, which fresh and pure doesn't taste good, makes a tasty addition to sausage. Thanks to the artisanal skills of the butcher, even these parts of the animal can be turned into a tender and aromatic delicacy.

Due to the use of cuts of meat and animal products commonly considered ignoble, the sausage has gained a reputation as a product made from scraps. However, for butchers and meat connoisseurs, there are no ignoble parts of an animal—wonderful flavors can be enticed from every piece. It all comes down to preparation and artistry.

Pig is synonymous with sausage

In the past, the processing of the animal began immediately after its slaughter. Butchers refer to the meat from freshly slaughtered animals as warm meat. Although it is harder to cut, the resulting specialties have a better flavor. In addition, it is better at binding with water than cooled meat, which is decisive for the consistency of a sausage and its texture. The qualities of warm meat are especially important for the manufacture of cooked and blanched sausages such as liverwurst and Lyoner. However, it also lends raw sausages such as the German ahle wurscht their characteristic flavor.

Today few butchers slaughter on their premises, which is the precondition for processing warm meat. In the majority of cases, the journey from the abattoir to the butcher is too long to make use of the characteristics of warm meat. Today the processing of cold meat is the norm. Pork is considered cold meat when it is processed more than 3 hours after slaughter. In the case of beef this period is around twice as long. In many cases this meat needs to be mixed with additives in order to produce a satisfactory sausage.

After the rough butchering, the cuts are prepared by the butcher for further processing. Parts such as the haunches, belly, and neck—used to make hams, bacon, and Coppa—are cut and trimmed, i.e., sinews and excess fat are removed.

The pieces of meat and fat for the sausages are generally coarsely cut and then mixed with the remaining offcuts left over from the larger joints of meat.

After the butchering comes the chopping—the meat grinder and the cutter

All sausage specialties are made of chopped meat. Before the invention of faster automatic machines, the chopping of the meat into fine pieces was laborious manual labor that employed the large butcher knife. Today butchers have a range of machines at their disposal for this processing step. Ultimately, the size of the pieces of meat and the mixture of fine meat dough and coarser chunks determines the sausage's mouthfeel and texture, and thus the taste.

For salami the meat is generally coarsely chopped. Today butchers use a meat grinder for this purpose. Inside the machine the meat is conveyed via a spiral shaft to a knife rotating in front of a perforated disc. By using discs with different sized holes the butcher can select how fine or coarse the resulting mass will be.

For a much finer mass, such as that that needed to make Frankfurter sausages or leberkäse, a so-called cutter is used. Here the meat is placed in a revolving tub equipped with a series of knives rotating at high speed. In similar fashion to a kitchen blender, the meat is cut into very small pieces to produce a very fine sausage mass. However, the high-speed knives can easily cause the protein in the meat to coagulate, which is why ice is generally added to cool the mass. The ice also promotes binding, resulting in a firm and juicy sausage.

Time to fill: Sausage mass and intestines

In contrast to mincemeat, the goal with sausage mass is for it to bind. This is achieved by mixing the mass by hand in a trough, or mechanically in a sausage mixer. The additional ingredients, which are sometimes mixed into the mass during chopping in the grinder or cutter, include spices, salt, and further ingredients depending on the recipe. The resulting sausage mass has the texture of a slightly stiff dough. In order to test whether the sausage has the right consistency, butchers place a piece of the mass in their outstretched palm and turn their hand over. If it remains adhered to the hand, the mass has the right binding quality and can be used.

In the final step, the seasoned and mixed mass is filled into casings. Today, in addition to cleaned natural cow, pig, and sheep intestines, artificial gut made from cellophane, collagen, and plastic is also used. In the case of some specialties, the animal's bladder or stomach serves as a casing.

During filling the challenge is to stuff the gut without creating any cavities. Any resulting air pockets will quickly lead to bacterial growth, and the sausage will go bad during the ripening process.

Preservation methods and their little helpers

Fresh or raw sausages such as frying sausages or salsicca do not keep very long and need to be quickly cooked and eaten. All other types of sausage are preserved in a further series of steps—some for a few days, others for many months.

1. Heating

The simplest method of preserving raw meat is to heat it. Sausages such as mortadella, German fleischwurst, and Frankfurter sausages are carefully blanched at 70–80°C/158–176°F. With the application of heat the sausage mass coagulates and a range of microorganisms are killed. The resulting sausage has a firm consistency, and when refrigerated it keeps for some time, although not for long periods.

2. Salting

Raw meat is composed of 80% water. Water is the breeding ground for many microorganisms that have the potential to make meat inedible. Through the addition of salt during sausage manufacturing, and the generous salting of large pieces of meat such as hams, an initial quantity of water is extracted from the meat. Once absorbed, the salt also creates a climate inhospitable to many microorganisms. In addition to these qualities, salt also improves the sausage mass's binding qualities and enhances the taste of the various specialties. Many of the names for sausage such as saussage, or saucisson, refer to the importance of salt during manufacture as the root salus is derived from the Latin word for salt.

3. Curing

The use of so-called curing salts containing nitrate or nitrite is another preservation method that has been practiced for thousands of years. However, this was often used unwittingly as many salts naturally contain nitrate.

It is only in the last 120 years that the precise action of curing salt has been known and employed in its pure form. Nitrite can combat microorganisms that remain unaffected by pure salt, thus enhancing the preserving properties of sausage and ham.

In addition, curing salt generates a fine cured flavor and a bright red color thanks to the way the nitrite combines with the coloring agent in the muscle, lending it stability. Left uncured, such sausage and ham products would tend to be gray in color. Butchers call this process reddening. Heating the sausage accelerates the process.

For long-ripened products a mixture of cooking salt and saltpeter is commonly used. The saltpeter must first be broken down into nitrite within the sausage, so that the process takes somewhat longer, resulting in an improved flavor.

4. Smoking

In the past, meat was smoked directly over the fire or close to the hearth. Today food artisans have smoking chambers at their disposal that enable both the quantity of smoke and its temperature to be precisely regulated. Hot-smoked specialties are smoked at a temperature between 50 and 100°C. At these temperatures the meat not only acquires a smoky flavor but also cooks.

During cold smoking the temperatures are considerably lower, between 15–30°C/59–86°F. The cold-smoking process can take hours, sometimes even days, and is generally employed to produce specialties with an especially long shelf life.
The substances contained in the smoke not only combat unwanted mold, yeasts, and microorganisms—they also provide a special aroma, with each type of wood adding its

own unique characteristics. Consequently, charcutiers pay special attention to the combination of woods, selecting them to enhance each individual specialty.

5. Ripening, fermentation and drying

The salty environment inside salami or ham not only repels microorganisms, but also attracts those that like salt. A number of these organisms have earned a place as important helpers in the ripening of artisanal manufactured meat products. The goal in the ripening of sausages and hams is to allow these beneficent helpers to gain the upper hand, and, thanks to a special climate, displace the unwanted microorganisms. The process is similar to that employed for other specialties such as sauerkraut, where fermentation also plays an important role. The food source of these little helpers is sugar, which they convert into lactic acid, which is why it is common to add a little wine or sugar to the sausage mass. Today, in order to give the good microorganisms a helping hand, so-called starter cultures are frequently used, giving the little helpers a head start.

The mold that forms on the skin of sausage and ham specialties during the long ripening process also provides additional protection from external factors, preventing other harmful molds from gaining a foothold. In addition, the mold breathes oxygen, preventing the sausage from going rancid.

The endless variety of combinations

These different elements of the charcutier's craft have always been employed in various combinations. Frankfurter sausages are blanched, cured, and smoked. Black Forest ham is salted, smoked, and then air-ripened. According to region and climate, meat products have been preserved using unique combinations of these techniques. Over the centuries this has resulted in the rich palette of artisanal specialties, with their endless variety of flavors, that we enjoy to this day.

On the following pages you will find a selection of the most important specialties that exemeplify the various styles of this artisanal meat culture. Each one of them represents thousands of regional varieties worldwide.

Raw Sausage

Salami

For many people salami is the epitome of good sausage. Finely cut on crusty white bread, or thick, pure slices on a wooden platter, everyone has their own memories of the intense flavors of this specialty that often undergoes a long ripening. Tender and soft, or a robust texture; strongly seasoned, or a fine play of flavors. Above all it is Italy, where the climate is especially suited to ripening, that this type of sausage has been brought to perfection. Today, salami is popular throughout the world.

In its country of origin this sausage specialty is available in hundreds of different varieties. At first glance the variety appears endless. Salame Milano, Salame Felino, Salame Fabriano—nearly every region in Italy is proud of its very own variety of salami. The origin of the word salame, the singular for salami, goes back to the Latin word for salt, and means something like salt meat or salt sausage.

At a time when sausage was primarily a food of the poor population, salami was made from donkey, mule, or even horse meat. However, today the majority of salami is made from pork.

The manufacturing principle is the same for all salami-like sausages. Meat, cut into pieces, is preserved with the help of curing salt, natural fermentation, a protective layer of mold, and air-drying. Salami is called a fermented sausage, because, like sauerkraut, cheese, or wine and beer, fermentation is an important part of the natural ripening of the salami. Natural airborne lactobacilli, or microorganisms added as a starter culture, transform the sugar in the meat into lactic acid, thus generating an environment in the sausage that is inhospitable to other microorganisms. The addition of wine and sugar accelerates the fermentation process in the sausage. As soon as the good microorganisms have won and other bacteria no longer have a chance to multiply, the sausage will keep for a long time. The mild sour taste of salami is an indicator of this manufacturing process that employs acidification.

In order to avoid cavities in which unwanted bacteria could multiply during ripening, thick sausages, after filling in intestine casings, are bound with twine or a net that is knotted every few centimeters.

After a short while, mold develops on the skin of the sausage in the ripening rooms, forming a protective film against unwanted external influences, keeping out harmful natural types of mold. Today, butchers also have the option of spraying on these good molds before ripening in order to help this process along. Ripening with the assistance of mold also adds an additional depth of flavor to the sausage.

The individual character of the regional specialties is to be found in their very own microclimates. Every ripening cellar and every butcher's shop has its own distinct fermentation aids and mold varieties that have developed over centuries, which have been preserved up to this day. In a similar fashion to wine, these highly specific milieus constitute the sausage's terroir. In today's highly modern, stainless steel production facilities—rigorously disinfected following each shift—this traditional flavor can only be simulated and is rarely matched.

Following fermentation and reddening with curing salt, the sausage loses moisture during the long dry-ripening. The mold and balanced climate of the ripening room, along with the appropriate humidity and temperature, ensures that this process takes place slowly and evenly.

During ripening, salami can lose up to 50% of its weight, resulting in a concentration of the flavors. During air-drying the relationship between acidity, piquancy, and salt content are harmonized.

The quickly and hastily produced salami of large sausage factories often lacks sufficient time to ripen. Using phosphates and ripening additives, manufacturers attempt to reduce water loss and bind as much liquid in the sausage as possible, which, it goes without saying, has a dire effect on the taste. In Italy, smoking is not traditionally employed, which is why the majority of salami are air-dried specialties.

Good salami has a balanced relationship between acidity, salt, meat, and piquancy. The art is to generate as much flavor as possible during ripening without upsetting the rich balance of flavors.

Sliced salami is a standard ingredient in Italian appetizer culture and, in addition to olives, cheese, and grilled vegetables, can be found on many antipasti plates. The slices of savory sausage can also be found in Italy's version of the sandwich, the panino, and naturally, softly melted on pizza.

Charcuterie

Salame Milano

Salame Milano is the most popular variety in the world, and for many people it is the mother of all salami. It is traditionally manufactured in the metropolitan region of Milan, where in 1909 Italy's first modern sausage factory opened business. To this day, Milan-style salami is copied en masse by the sausage industry, and has unfortunately become a relatively mundane product.

Salame Milano is traditionally manufactured from pork, fat, and beef. The sausage meat is ground more finely than that used for other salami, and it is said that the pieces of fat in the sliced salami should be about the size of grains of rice. Salt, pepper, saltpeter, crushed garlic, and a shot of wine are added to the meat. After drying, the salami ripens for several months, losing up to 30% of its weight. However, industrial variants are not granted this much time, and are usually ripened in plastic casings as opposed to natural intestines.

Salame Finocchina

Fennel is the herb that gives this dry-ripened Tuscan specialty its characteristic flavor. Before pepper imported from distant climes became affordable, fennel was a popular seasoning, which, especially in its wild form, lends the sausage a certain sharpness and full-bodied flavor.

Salame Finocchiona, traditionally manufactured from heavy pigs of the Cinta Senese breed, ripens in two to three months and, in addition to the fennel, has a fine garlic flavor.

Due to its soft crumbly texture, it has a tendency to break when cut into slices, but this is a typical feature of the salami, not a flaw. As a shot of wine is also used in the manufacture of the specialty, Chianti—also typical for the region of Tuscany—makes an excellent accompaniment to Finocchiona.

Salame Felino

This salami specialty originates from the valleys of the Apennine Mountains close to Parma. The village of Felino is the birthplace of this sausage specialty, which can have a length of up to two meters—although its diameter seldom exceeds five centimetres. It is manufactured from coarsely ground pork seasoned with whole peppercorns and garlic marinated in wine. The Felino ripens for a minimum of two months in the part of the intestine known as the rectum, which, due to its thickness, is especially suited for ripening.

In order to avoid cavities, which could have a negative effect on the sausage, the Felino is bound with twine and knotted every few centimeters.

Diagonally and oval cut Felino, with its melt-in-your-mouth texture, is a classic appetizer and tastes fantastic with a lively Lambrusco—also typical for the Emilia-Romagna region.

Soppressata

Soppressata is pressed during the ripening process, lending it a somewhat flat shape like a round salami that had been trodden on by someone. The expulsion of the air during storage under pressure is very important for the ripening of the sausage, preventing the formation of cavities. This is especially important for sausages filled into large intestines such as that of cattle and which then undergo a long ripening.

The Italian pressed sausage is manufactured in a similar fashion to that of salami, employing coarsely cut pork from the shoulder and rump. Originally from southern Italy, it can now be found in central Italy, and above all in the northern city of Venice. The specialty "Soppressata di Gioi" can be recognized by its cross section—a pale white core of pork fat. Thanks to Italian immigrants, sopressata is now also popular in the USA, where, as elsewhere, it tastes delicious as an appetizer with olives and Italian bread. Soppressata is now also popular as a pizza topping.

Saucisson sec and Saucisse sèche

The French words sec and sèche, which effectively mean dry, already point to the air-drying process typical of salami.

French style salami supposedly goes back to Italian merchants who brought salami with them from their home country, inspiring butchers in the trading city of Lyon to manufacture this type of sausage. Lyon is also home to the well known French salami, saucisson rosette. Somewhat larger than usual, the sausage is named after the end of the rectum, the rosette, in which the meat is filled for ripening. The sausage's strong flavor is the result of a long ripening process that lasts for up to 12 months.

The typical saucisson sec is somewhat smaller than the rosette and is mostly made of pork meat and fat that is roughly cut and ground. In France, in addition to salt, pepper, and curing salt, different fruits, nuts, and cheese such as Roquefort or Beaufort, depending on the variety, are added to the meat. It is also common to add a shot of vermouth or wine to the sausage meat.

Once filled, the sausages are fermented and air-cured. This can take from between a few weeks to many months—traditionally with the assistance of mold, which provides extra flavor.

Another popular saucisson, a soft variety from Lyon, is the "Saucisson de Lyon" containing pistachio nuts, which, following a four to seven week ripening, are added to casseroles or baked in brioche pastry.

N'duja

The fire red and equally sharp 'nduja is a salami from southern Italy. A prized feature of the specialty, originally from Calabria, is that is reminiscent of soft German mettwurst, making it ideal for spreading on bread. As its innards were originally used for the spreading, it received the name 'nduja in reference to the French andouille. In the past all the leftover parts of meat were used for the sausage, which included a lot of fat, the meat from the pig's head, and its innards. The sausage meat was then mixed with large amounts of Calabrian chili, which gives the 'nduja its fiery sharpness. After the meat has been filled into the pig's large appendix, it is cold smoked for a week and then left to ripen for several months.

The specialty sobrassada, found on Mallorca, is similar to 'nduja but is not smoked. A special delicacy is the "Sobrasada de Mallorca de Credo Negro," which is manufactured from the black pigs of the Balearic Islands.

'Nduja and sobrassada are especially tasty on lightly toasted white bread and form the basis for sauces or pizza toppings. Ripened 'nduja can now also be bought packaged in jars.

Hungarian Salami

Old pig breeds reared in Hungary such as the Mangalitsa pig, and old English breeds like the black Berkshire and Cornwall pigs, supply the special taste of this traditional Hungarian salami.

On the great Hungarian lowlands, the country's breadbasket, more than enough grain was produced to fatten hordes of pigs. In Budapest and Szeged the fattened animals were used to produce the two most famous, and now protected, varieties of Hungarian salami, known under the names Szegedi szalámi and Budapesti téliszalámi.

Hungarian salami is seasoned with salt, pepper, caraway seeds, and Hungarian paprika powder. After filling, they are smoked for several weeks over beech wood at a maximum temperature of 12°C/54°F, and subsequently dry-hung for at least three months for fermentation and ripening. Traditionally, this salami is fermented without the addition of starter cultures that would accelerate the process. Due to the very warm summer months, the manufacture of the raw sausage was limited to the colder season, which is why it is also known as Hungarian winter salami. Thanks to the Tisza and Danube rivers, the two cities have humid climates, ideal for the formation of mold needed for the ripening of the sausages in the cellars.

Cut into slices, Hungarian szalámi is delicious as an appetizer or served on gray bread. A fresh white wine or a classic blond beer makes an excellent accompaniment.

Charcuterie

CHORIZO

After dry curing, the majority of sausages have a typical horseshoe shape. However, the Spanish specialty is also produced in long strings of individual sausages. The variety of chorizo filled in the pig's large intestine is known as morcón. It is thicker, ripened longer, and, due to the intestine, is somewhat misshapen. In addition to the cured varieties, chorizo is also available as a fresh sausage that can be grilled or fried. Chorizo can also be found in Spanish-speaking America where it is also made from game, beef, or poultry. In Mexico there is a green variety with fresh herbs, seasoned exclusively with green paprika. Chorizo tastes excellent when added to Mediterranean stews, but also fried or grilled. Together with scrambled egg, the sausage is a traditional feature of Spanish appetizers (tapas).

Cabanossi

Cabanossi are generally long, smoked, raw sausages made from robust, coarse sausage meat. Heavily seasoned with garlic and paprika, these thin sausages of pork or beef are especially popular in eastern European countries.

Due to their appearance, long varieties of cabanossi are often sold as sausage whips. The rugged texture, thanks to the coarsely ground fat, is characteristic for cabanossi, as is the strong smoky note that results from hot smoking.

Cabanossi are traditionally eaten whole from the hand without any trimmings. However, the spicy specialty is also delicious in hearty soups and stews. In the USA they are a popular topping for pizzas. Unrefrigerated, cabanossi keep for a long time.

CABANOSSI

Chorizo and Chouriço

When Spanish conquistadors, returning from the American continent, brought red peppers back to Europe in the sixteenth century, an air-cured raw sausage specialty was developed on the Iberian Peninsula that is now available in many varieties. What they all have in common is the bold seasoning with hot paprika. The spicy capsaicin that it contains functions like a natural preservative, which was also used in the past for the preservation of pork.

Red peppers were soon dried over an open fire to make a paprika powder, which to this day is known as Pimenton de la vera and is used to season chorizo. Due to the smoke passing over the drying paprika, the powder acquires a mild, smoky note.

The fine, marbled meat of the black Ibérico pigs is traditionally employed for the manufacture of chorizo. However, modern white pig breeds are now also used in its manufacture.

Along with the paprika powder, wine, garlic, and Mediterranean herbs are also added to the coarse sausage meat. In a number of Iberian regions, nuts, pig blood, and pumpkins are also added.

The sausage meat is subsequently left to marinate for several days before being filled into intestine casings, smoked, and hung out to cure. Depending on the region and the butcher, chorizo can be seasoned to produce sausages with varying degrees of spiciness. As a fermented raw sausage, the chorizo, following several weeks of ripening, has a mildly sour taste.

Kiełbasa

Many of Poland's sausage specialties originate from the rural practice of home slaughtering. Kielbasa, the Polish word for sausage, is traditionally available in many varieties and recipes. Characteristic for many of the sausages is the creased surface that results from the hot smoking, sometimes over an open fire. In the former royal seat of Krakow, a number of unique sausage specialties were developed over the centuries, providing only the best for the king's table. The Krakow-style kielbasa (Kielbasa Krakowska) are made from both beef and pork.

During manufacture a small portion of the meat is finely ground, while the rest is divided into coarsely cut pieces. After seasoning with fresh garlic, mustard seeds, salt, pepper, and other spices, the sausage is hot smoked and then blanched; this is followed by a second, cold smoking. Due to the coarsely cut meat, the sausage has a highly distinctive flavor and robust texture. In addition, traditionally smoked kielbasa have a wonderfully rustic, smoky aroma.

Kielbasa tastes best in hearty soups and stews, but also fried or grilled, cut into slices, and served on a fresh slice of sourdough bread.

Sucuk

Sucuk is the Turkish sausage specialty, although it can also be found in the Arab region, Central Asia and the Balkans.

The heavily seasoned raw sausage is traditionally made from beef and lamb, and liberally seasoned with garlic, cumin, pimento, and cayenne pepper. The sausage is filled into the round section of intestine known as the jejunum, or in long sections tied off in pairs—the form of the sausage depends on the intestine used.

The recipe varies from butcher to butcher and includes some fiery varieties. The typical taste of sucuk is due to the dry-curing, which results in a loss in weight and an intensification of flavor. Caution should be exercised with the readily available industrial copies that almost always contain monosodium glutamate (MSG).

The sausage is traditionally cut into medium-thick slices and briefly fried in the pan until lightly crisp on the outside. It is also added to the Turkish egg dish menemen, where, alongside scrambled eggs, it is briefly fried in the pan together with tomatoes, bell peppers, and fresh herbs. Prepared in this fashion, sucuk makes a tasty addition to a hearty breakfast.

FINE METTWURST

Teewurst and Fine Mettwurst

Teewurst is a smooth form of the German specialty mettwurst, made from pork and pork fat. This spreading sausage has its origins in Poland where it is served in the traditional English fashion, in sandwiches accompanying afternoon tea. The sausage obtains its characteristic texture from the addition of large quantities of pork fat and finely diced meat, which is produced by the high-speed knife of a cutter machine.

Teewurst is subsequently hot smoked and undergoes lactic acid fermentation for a number of days, which lends the sausage its fine sour note. Unfortunately, this type of sausage has gained a bad reputation due to its industrial counterparts. However, there are fantastic-tasting varieties of teewurst with incomparable creaminess and flavor.

Teewurst tastes excellent when thickly spread on moist sourdough bread. Alternatively, fine varieties can be enjoyed pure as an appetizer in the fashion of a pâté.

BOCKWURST

Knacker and Bockwurst

As its name suggests, a well-made knacker should produce a juicy "knack" sound when bitten into (knackig: German for crisp/firm). The meat for this raw sausage specialty is ground until medium-coarse, strongly seasoned with pepper, curing salt and mustard seeds, and, in a number of cases, further seasoned with caraway seeds and a pinch of mace. Recipes vary, depending on the butcher and the type of meat used for the sausage. After cold smoking, knackers are air dried to produce the desired texture—the longer the drying, the harder the sausage.

Knacker can be eaten cold, although they taste best when briefly heated in water. They are also excellent when served with hearty stews, sauerkraut, or dishes such as the north German grünkohl (kale)—topped off with a dash of mustard and a cold beer.

Landjäger and Kaminwurzen

In the past, these small, raw pork and beef sausages tied in pairs, served as a handy snack for agricultural workers, and to this day can be found in the rucksacks of many hikers.

Charcuterie

Landjäger are made from relatively coarse sausage meat and, after a short ripening phase, are air cured and finally dry smoked for up to one day. Very popular in Austria, Switzerland, and southern Germany, these sausages are traditionally angular in shape due to pressured strorage spaces. Similar to the landjäger are the kaminwurzen, which in the past were hung in the chimney above the domestic fireplace (kamin: German for chimney). In contrast to the landjäger, the kaminwurzen are not pressed and therefore have a round form.
Landjäger can be stored without refrigeration, drying over time. It is recommended to try out sausages with different degrees of hardness. They are excellent with rustic, buttered bread, pickles, and a cold, blond beer.

LANDJÄGER

Ahle Wurscht

Ahle wurscht, which basically means old sausage, is a raw sausage specialty from central Germany that undergoes a long ripening. It originates from the long home-slaughtering tradition of the region of North Hessia, and is manufactured from heavy sausage pigs, which can be up to one and a half years old. The pigs are processed by the butchers while they are still slaughter-warm, meaning shortly after slaughtering. No chemical additives are used since the natural enzymes still active in the meat can be used for ripening.
The sausage mass is seasoned with pepper, salt, saltpeter, and garlic pickled in brandy. A number of butchers also add mustard seeds or a pinch of caraway seeds. The coarsely ground and seasoned sausage mass is subsequently filled into intestines of varying diameters, before ripening in special curing chambers for up to 12 months depending on the caliber of the sausage. A number of butchers also smoke the sausage briefly before ripening.
Ahle wurscht is available in different forms: as the circular dürre runde, the long stracke, or in a club-shaped variety. Characteristic of this type of air-dried raw sausage is its soft texture, which is reminiscent of marzipan.
Ahle wurscht tastes great in thick slices on dark sourdough bread, or enjoyed pure, simply for the taste. In order to enjoy them at their best, it is recommended to cut the slices relatively thick so that the sausage retains its typical texture.

Cervelat and Schlackwurst

Sausages known under the name cervelat or zervelat can be found in both Switzerland and Germany, however, the manufacturing processes employed are fundamentally different. The Swiss cervelat is a small, thick, smoked, blanched sausage, which is very popular grilled over a campfire. In contrast, the German zervelat is a short-ripened raw sausage—in other words, very young salami.
The name cervelat is derived from the Latin word for brain, cerebellum. In the past, pig brains were much more common as an ingredient in sausage mass than they are today, although it no longer plays a role in the manufacture of many of these specialties.
Today the German cervelat is usually made from a mix of pork and beef. The finely ground sausage mass is seasoned with salt, pepper, curing salt, and sometimes a shot of brandy. The cervalet is then traditionally filled into the pig's schlacke, or rectum. For this reason the specialty is also known in a number of regions as schlackwurst.
Cold smoked for several hours, the sausage is ready to eat after a short ripening period of one to two weeks, or even after a few days. Due to the short ripening, zervelat sausage is relatively firm and has a fine sour note, however, it is quite soft compared to salami ripened for a longer period. In Germany it is primarily eaten as a classic filling for sandwiches.

Lap Cheong

Lap cheong, the Asian version of the raw sausage, is characterized by its sweetish taste. The sausage mass is prepared from poultry meat, pork fat, and liver, and coarsely diced and seasoned with soy sauce, rose water, and rice wine. Filled in small, compact formats, lap cheong is available in fresh, soft, or long-ripened and smoked varieties. The air-cured varieties can be very hard indeed. Unfortunately, it is now common to enhance the sausage's appearance and shelf life with the addition of food coloring and preservatives. Traditionally, good sausages naturally contain no such additives.
Cut into thin slices, lap cheong is a common ingredient for stir-fried dishes prepared in the traditional wok, and is sometimes used as a filling for the Chinese dumplings known as Dim Sum.

Blanched sausage

Wiener and Frankfurter

The naming of these now world famous, slim sausages can be somewhat confusing. Frankfurt is the original home of a lpure pork, long-blanched sausage that today is known as frankfurter sausage. A butcher who moved from Frankfurt to Vienna subsequently manufactured this type of blanched sausage in Austria using pork and beef. This version of the sausage is now known as wiener sausage. Together with European immigrants, the sausage traveled to America where it is now an indispensable part of the hot dog.
The method used to manufacture both wieners and frankfurters is very similar. The meat, with the assistance of crushed ice, is ground very finely in a cutter to form the sausage mass. It is then seasoned with white pepper, mace, and curing salt, which is responsible for the pink color. The sausage mass is then filled into thin sheep intestine, known in Germany as saitling, which is why, to this day it is also known in southern Germany as the saitenwürstchen. The

Charcuterie

sausage is then smoked until it obtains its characteristic color and, as the final step in the production process, it is blanched. The sausage should then have a nice crisp snap, with a soft, juicy interior.
Closely related to the Frankfurter sausage is the bockwurst, which, while somewhat thicker, is made in a very similar fashion. Popular in Berlin as an accompaniment to bockbier, a strong seasonal beer, it has subsequently become known under the name bockwurst.
The cervelat, popular in Switzerland, is also a blanched sausage manufactured in a similar fashion. The small, thick sausage is traditionally cut crosswise at the ends, skewered and roasted over an open fire on long sticks. Similar sausages in Slovenia and the Czech Republic are known under the name Špekáčky. The Swiss name cervelas is derived from the Latin for brain, which in the past was used in the manufacture of the sausage. The Bavarian town of Regensburg also boasts a somewhat thicker version of this sausage, where it is traditionally cut open, grilled, and served in a bread roll with pickled gherkins, horseradish, and sweet mustard.

WEISSWURST

Weißwurst and Boudin blanc

Weißwurst is an indispensable part of a hearty Munich breakfast. The well known adage that weißwurst shouldn't be eaten after 12 o'clock midday originates from the time when the sausage was still sold raw and fridges were a rarity. However, weißwurst are now usually sold pre-blanched, have a longer shelf life, and only need to be carefully heated in lightly salted water before eating. As in the case of all blanched sausages, caution needs to be exercised here as the weißwurst can burst if boiled.
The Bavarian weißwurst is made from veal, pork rind and the meat from the head of the calf, with the total quantity of veal making up a minimum of 51%. The ingredients are chopped into a fine sausage mass in a cutter with the addition of crushed ice, and then seasoned with freshly chopped parsley, grated lemon rinds, pepper, mace, and ginger. The mass is then filled into pig intestines and tied into small sausages. As a preservative measure, the weißwurst is then blanched for 20 minutes at 70°C/158°F, and tastes best when freshly cooked. As weißwurst does not contain any curing salt, which normally lends a sausage its red color, it is white to light-gray after blanching.
The Bavarian weißwurst is typically eaten without the casing, and dipped in sweet Bavarian mustard. It is also delicious with a fresh pretzel straight from the oven and a freshly poured wheat beer.
The French boudin blanc is a close relative of the Bavarian weißwurst, and is traditionally manufactured with the addition of eggs, milk, and dried, grated white bread. In contrast to the Munich weißwurst, the boudin blanc also lands in the frying pan or on the grill.

Leberkäs

Despite what one may think, not every leberkäse contains liver (leber is German for liver). To this day, original Bavarian leberkäse does not contain any liver whatsoever. It is assumed that the name was originally derived from the vernacular for the form of the leberkäse loaf, which resembles a loaf of bread, and not the organ.
The fine meat dough is made from a mixture of beef and fatty pork, sometimes liver and onions, finely chopped in a cutter and seasoned. In the case of coarser versions, roughly cut meat is added to the fine sausage mass. The meat dough is then filled into rectangular molds and baked in the oven until it obtains its characteristic brown crust. The white variety of leberkäse, often known as kalbskäse, is made without curing salt and lack the pink coloring as a result.
Cut into thick slices it is traditionally served in semmel—as bread rolls are known in Bavaria—together with sweet mustard. It is also delicious as a fine cold cut.

Mortadella

Mortadella is one of the most popular Italian specialties and originates from the region around Bologna. As a consequence, Mortadella Bologna is also a protected geographical indication (IGP). The name of the specialty is derived from myrtle berries, which, prior to the arrival of pepper, were used to season the sausage.
The specialty can be recognized by its distinct velvety-pink color, pure white pieces of fat, and the yellow-green sprinklings of pistachios that are revealed within each slice.
The pork used for mortadella is first passed through the cutter to produce a very fine sausage mass, followed by the addition of coarsely diced fat—traditionally the firm fat from the neck of the pig—and pistachios. The mixture is then seasoned with salt and pepper. In some regions a little garlic is also added. The mass is then filled into intestines. In its region of origin, mortadellas can be up to 100 kg / 220 lbs. in weight. The filled raw sausage is then cooked in a convection oven at a maximum of 90°C/194°F, which, depending on the size of the sausage, can take up to one day. Industrial copies lack the flavor of the artisanal original, which is reminiscent of a very fine meat loaf. Bologna, popular in the USA, German fleischwurst, and the French

Charcuterie

saucisse de Lyon, are all descended from this specialty. A good mortadella has no smoky notes, and neither does it have the typical taste associated with a blanched sausage.

Mortadella is often cut into thin slices, and tastes delicious with white ciabbata bread. However, the special combination of hearty fat and the Mortadella's fine sausage mass is best enjoyed thickly diced, as traditionally served in Italy. It is also good in combination with fresh pasta and is an excellent filling for tortellini and ravioli.

Fine blanched sausages of a larger diameter, available today as a range of cold cuts, are prepared in a manner similar to that of wiener or frankfurter sausages. The main difference is the diameter and the meat filling, which is sometimes composed of coarsely cut meat. As in the case of wieners, the meat is fed into a cutter along with ice where it is processed to produce a fine sausage mass with the aid of the quickly rotating knife. Filled into large diameter intestines, the sausages are then blanched for one to two hours at around 70° C / 158° F. The length of the blanching phase is dependent on the thickness of the sausage. This is generally followed by a short smoking, which provides additional flavor and an outer protective layer.

STADTWURST

GELBWURST

Lyoner, Fleischwurst, Stadtwurst, Jagdwurst, Extrawurst, and Gelbwurst

The main difference between specialties such as fleischwurst, stadtwurst, and jagdwurst are the proportions of pork and beef used and the mixture of fine and coarse sausage meat. Other varieties from this family of sausage include the Austrian extrawurst and the specialty known in Germany as lyoner.

Lyon has a long tradition of coloring sausages—which at the time were generally white to gray—through the addition of seasoning. Before the discovery of curing salt at the end of the nineteenth century, which gives sausages a pink hue, use was made of the dying properties of spices such as saffron to produce an appetizing color. To this day, fine blanched sausages made without the addition of curing salt are known in southern Germany as gelbwurst (yellow sausage). However, the reference to Lyon is primarily historical in character as the sausage mass of a traditional cervelas de Lyon is not as finely cut as fleischwurst, has a much coarser cross section, and has little in common with a fine blanched sausage. Furthermore, it is prepared in the oven and added to stews, as opposed to being eaten cold in slices.

Stuffed Pig's Stomach

Stretching the sausage meat with the addition of potatoes has a long history. Kartoffelwürste (potato sausages) are common in many regions of Germany and Switzerland.

The Palitinate region of Germany is home to a special type of sausage made from a mixture of meat with potatoes and other vegetables, which is traditionally stuffed into a pig's stomach. In its region of origin, the so-called Saumagen is not just a butcher's specialty. It is also a popular dish prepared at home in the domestic kitchen, with every family having their own special recipe.

Stuffed pig's stomach is known in the USA as Seimaage or Hog Maw. Another relative of the German specialty is Haggis, traditionally filled in a sheep's stomach.

The first step in making a Saumagen is tproducing the sausage mass from pork and fat, which is mixed with diced potatoes, carrots, leeks, onions, and other vegetables. In order to produce a varied consistency, coarser ground meat or whole chunks are added to the finely ground forcemeat. The mass is then seasoned with fresh herbs such as marjoram, thyme, and spices such as nutmeg, garlic, salt, and pepper—together with a dash of regional white wine. The mixed and seasoned mass is then stuffed into a cleaned pig's stomach, which is tied at both ends with twine. Butchers take care that the stomach is not filled too tight, as otherwise there is a danger of it bursting during cooking. Thus tied, the Palitinate Saumagen is cooked at a low simmer for several hours, after which the stomach is tightly filled and ready to serve. Freshly cooked and cut into thick slices, Palitinate Saumagen is traditionally served with sauerkraut and mashed potatoes. However, the specialty also tastes fantastic briefly fried in the pan, ideally accompanied by savoy cabbage in cream sauce and dark gravy.

STUFFED PIG'S STOMACH

Frying sausage

Bratwurst, Fränkische, Nürnberger, Merguez, and Boerewors

Whether it is fresh herbs, exotic spices, or ingredients such as wine, milk, or eggs, there is virtually no limit to the seasoning of a frying sausage. Over centuries, numerous regional varieties were developed worldwide that are as diverse as the butchers that produce them.
In the case of the German bratwurst, theory has it that the syllable brat is not necessarily derived from the German word braten (German for roast or fry), but has its origins in the word brät, the German term for sausage mass. Internationally, frying sausages are also known as saucisse, saussage, or salcicca—words that all have their origin in the Latin word for salt.
The main distinction between the various types of frying sausages is whether they are sold fresh, i.e., raw, or whether they have been quickly blanched after filling in order to improve their shelf life. In contrast to fresh, red frying sausages, blanched frying sausages are a velvety white. Blanched frying sausages, manufactured without casing, are known in Germany as wollwurst. This sausage ohne Darm (without intestine), fried and served with a hot sauce, is a popular snack in Berlin known as currywurst.
In Germany the state of Thuringia and the region of Franconia are renowned for their frying sausage specialties. The classic Franconian frying sausage is made of coarsely ground meat and traditionally has a pronounced marjoram note. The sausage mass used for the fränkische sausage known as bratwurstgehäck, is stuffed in the bändel, a special part of the pig's small intestine. Genuine fränkische sausages can thus be identified by the thin white strip of fat down the side of the intestine. As a rule, Franconian sausages are sold unblanched, i.e., raw.
The nürnberger, also from Franconia, is stuffed in thin sheep intestines that are tied to form small, short sausages, and are traditionally grilled and served with sauerkraut. Cooked in a broth containing vinegar and onions, they are served as saure Zipfel.
Compared to the Franconian sausages, those from Thuringia, which are also sold fresh, are made of a somewhat finer sausage mass. As early as the Middle Ages, they could be found roasting over the glowing charcoal embers on the region's grills.
In Italy, coarse, fresh frying sausages are known under the name salsiccia, and every region has its characteristic varieties with their very own seasoning. Salsiccia is eaten raw, fried or pressed out of its casing and added to soups.
In South Africa coarse frying sausages are known as boerewors, which, in addition to beef and pork, can also contain game such as Antelope or Springbok. The farmer's sausage is traditionally rolled into a spiral and fried or grilled.
The deep red, North African merguez sausage has also gained international popularity. The spicy sausage is sold raw and originates from the region's Muslim-influenced cuisine, which means it does not contain any pork but is instead made from lamb, mutton, and beef.

Cooked sausage

Leberwurst

The manufacture of leberwurst originates from the long tradition of home slaughtering that aspired to preserve all parts of an animal. Therefore the best leberwurst is made slaughter-warm, i.e., shortly after the animal has been slaughtered. In Germany it is Thuringia and Palitinate that are best known as the rustic versions of this specialty.
The sausage mass, composed of pre-blanched pork rind and fresh liver, is ground and then seasoned primarily with marjoram, pepper, and salt. Further ingredients, depending on the recipe, include steamed onions and additional seasoning such as mace or garlic. The sausage mass is then stuffed into gut casings or jars and boiled. In a number of regions the sausages are filled in intestine casings and subsequently smoked.
The different varieties of leberwurst primarily differ in terms of texture, with traditional types tending to be rather coarse, although very fine varieties can be produced with the aid of the modern cutter. Without the addition of curing salt, leberwurst is gray. This is actually its original color and not an indication of inferior quality.
Especially fine leberwurst is made from veal and calf's liver. The livers of grown cows are not suitable due to their slightly bitter taste.

Hearty leberwurst tastes best thickly spread on a slice of full-flavored sourdough bread, accompanied by pickled gherkins and some freshly sliced apple. The tradition of eating leberwurst warm, fresh from the pot, is a practice dating back to its origins in the age of home slaughtering. Ideal with potatoes boiled in their skins, some freshly ground caraway seeds, butter, and salt.

Charcuterie

LEBERWURST

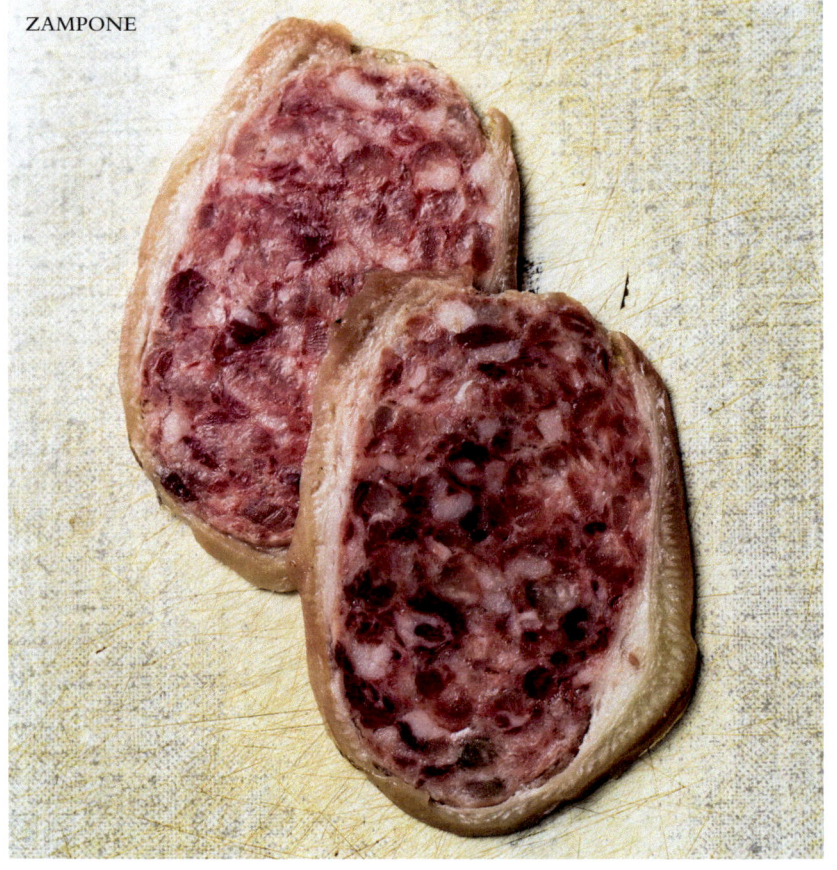
ZAMPONE

Zampone and Cotechino Modena

Zampone, the "big foot," is a popular festive dish in Italy at Christmas and New Year. It is said that the filled and cooked pig's trotter brings good luck. However, this rustic specialty also has its place in the country's high-end gastronomy.

The legend states that the art of stuffing sausage meat into de-boned pigs' trotters originates from a time when intestines were in short supply. Without their much needed casings, resourceful butchers developed the practice of carefully cleaning and de-boning the trotters until only the outside remained.

Zampone is part of a culinary tradition that prides itself on using all parts of the animal. In the past, the filling primarily consisted of hard to use scraps of fatty meat, or even rind and head meat. This specialty originates from the region of Emilia-Romagna, renowned for its rich sausage culture.

The filling for Zampone is composed of coarsely ground meat from the neck, head, and shoulder of the pig together with back fat and fatty rind, with the rind in particular contributing to the specialty's melt-in-the-mouth texture. The sausage mass is seasoned with fresh garlic and spices such as cinnamon, cloves, pepper, and salt and then injected into the de-boned trotter with a sausage filler.

There are also versions where the mass is filled into normal pig intestines. Cotechino Modena has a similar taste to Zampone but looks like a normal sausage. Before the Zampone can be served, it needs to be cooked for several hours. During this long period of gentle cooking even the tough rind develops a soft, tender consistency. However, anyone who wants to spare themselves the long preparation time can buy Zampone pre-cooked and vacuum packed as a convenience product. Cotechino and Zampone are traditionally cut into thick slices and eaten warm—when cold, the specialties quickly lose their creaminess. Together with beef, veal, and chicken, Zampone and Cotechino are traditional ingredients in the hearty Piedmontese stew Bollito Misto. As a New Year's dish, the filled pig trotters are usually served with mashed potatoes, polenta, and lentils, which are also considered to bring good luck in Italy.

Haggis

References to filled stomach, stuffed with meat and innards, can be found as early as Homer's Odyssey. Sausage mass made from hard to use innards such as heart, liver, and lungs, stuffed in stomachs, has a long history. The national dish, haggis, traditionally stuffed in sheep's stomachs, is now known around the world thanks to the movements of Scottish migrants.

Haggis is made from lamb and innards which are chopped, boiled, and then coarsely ground to make the sausage mass. Mixed with oat groats, seasoning, and stewed onions, it is then stuffed into sheep's stomachs. After tying, the stomachs are boiled for several hours. The oats in the sausage mass absorb fat and liquids, ensuring that the end result is a tightly filled stomach. Today haggis is mainly produced using artificial gut instead of the traditional sheep's stomach.

Though this rustic specialty is met with skepticism from many people, it has a wonderful savory flavor and, when enjoyed warm with mashed potatoes and pureed rutabaga, it makes a fantastic feel-good food for cold days.

Charcuterie

Andouille and Kokoreç

This French specialty divides opinion as andouille is traditionally—and exclusively—made from innards, more precisely the small and large intestines of the pig, in a labor intensive process.

The carefully cleaned intestines are first treated to a long soak in salt water, after which they are roughly bundled, rolled together, and then stuffed into large intestines. This is followed by a long, cold smoking over beech wood for several days, after which they are boiled for several hours.

In Brittany the pig intestines are inserted into one another, one at a time, with the last layer consisting of a large cow's appendix. As a result, slices of this sausage, known as andouille de Guémené, look like tree stumps with their concentric circles.

The smallest version of andouille is the so-called andouillet, which is grilled like a sausage.

The grilling of intestines and innards wrapped around each other is also practiced in Turkey, where the specialty known as kokoreç is grilled over charcoal like a kebab on a spit. As soon as the kokoreç is crispy on the outside, it is cut into small pieces, seasoned, and served in bread.

In the USA, andouille refers to a smoked sausage specialty made from coarsely cut and ground ham. Mainly found in Lousiana, this sausage has little in common with the French original.

Presssack, Presskopf and Schwartenmagen

A somewhat more rustic version of pig head found in aspic is the German presssack, one of the many sausage specialties made from the innards, the meat of the head, and pieces left over from the slaughter. It is designed to make use of all parts of the animal. The meat and the rind are first boiled in a stock until soft, cut into small pieces, and then mixed with seasoning. Classic sausage herbs and spices such as marjoram, pepper, pimento, and onions are employed, as are cloves and nutmeg. For the mass of the red presssack, fresh pig blood is also added. White presssack is made without blood or curing salt that would turn the meat red. The casing for the mixture of broth and meat is traditionally a pig's stomach. In a number of regions in Germany this specialty is therefore called schwartenmagen, vernacular for pig stomach. After filling, the tied sausage is boiled, and in some cases cold smoked. The Presssack is traditionally pressed between two boards during manufacture in order to achieve an even distribution of the meat filling.

Dipped in a vinegar marinade and served with fresh onions, presssack is served as part of a typical Bavarian cold platter and is excellent with beer.

PRESSSACK

Headcheese, Fromage de tête, and Schweinskopfsülze

For many butchers the best part of the pig is not the filet but the cheeks at the side of the head. Contrary to expectations, the meat of the head can be a real delicacy, and when boiled it constitutes the basis for many aspic dishes.

In France, the pig-head in aspic is known under the name fromage de tête, while in the English speaking world it is known as headcheese.

Using a broth of vinegar, seasoning, and vegetables, the head is boiled until the meat is almost falling off the bones. Selected pieces of meat are then diced and poured into terrines together with the broth. A number of varieties contain additional ingredients such as onions, gherkins, and mustard seeds. Upon cooling, the broth congeals due to the high concentration of gelatin in the bones and connective tissue, producing the aspic with its firm texture. In many cases the meat is also cured prior to setting, which can be recognized by the red color of the meat in some varieties of aspic.

Cut into thick slices, aspic is delicious with potatoes boiled in their skins, together with a dollop of tartar sauce. Thinly cut and sprinkled with vinegar marinade, fine aspic makes a delicious appetizer.

Blood Sausage, Boudin Noir, Flönz, Rotwurst, and Zungenrotwurst

The manufacture of blood sausage is one of the oldest of the butcher's skills, and has many varieties worldwide. It can be served warm and fresh straight from the pot, smoked and ripened for long periods, or prepared with special ingredients such as nuts and fruits.

The basis of every blood sausage is a filling composed of fresh blood, blanched fat, and rind. The mass, depending on the recipe, is seasoned in a variety of ways before being stuffed into intestines. Further ingredients, such as the white pieces of fat characteristic of German rotwurst (red sausage) or specialties such as flönz from the Rhineland region, are subsequently added to the mass. After stuffing, the blood sausages are boiled for a period of time dependent on their thickness. During boiling, the protein in the blood coagulates, giving the red-brown sausage its firm texture. In order to improve its preservation properties, blood sausage is often cold smoked after boiling.

Allowed to ripen for longer periods, blood sausage turns black and loses weight. This specialty, known as black sausage, has a more intensive flavor after dry-ripening and is a special delicacy.

Rotwurst is often eaten as a cold cut. However, the rich flavors of many blood sausage specialties are best enjoyed when served cut into thick slices, lightly tossed in flour, and fried in the pan. Warm blood sausage, such as the soft French boudin noir, goes well with sauerkraut and potatoes, and is excellent with caramelized apples and braised onions.

Charcuterie

PANHAS

Black Pudding, Grützwurst, Morcilla, Pinkel, and Panhas

Adding coarsely milled grains like oats or pearl barley to rustic, cooked sausages is a long tradition. These ingredients ensure that the mixture of stock, blood, ground fat, and meat has a firm consistency once cooled. The grain soaks up the savory juices and lends the sausages a special texture. In some regions, stale bread is also added to the sausage mass.

In Germany, grützwürste (groat sausages) without blood are known under the names knipp or pinkel. However, liver and blood sausage mass is also mixed with grain to produce an especially creamy texture. The western German specialty panhas contains buckwheat, and in Spain rice is added to the blood sausage known as morcilla, while the English black pudding contains oat groats and flakes.

Groat sausages are eaten warm, either heated in water or fried in the pan. They are ideal as a filling accompaniment to mashed potatoes and hearty vegetables. Eaten warm directly from the pan, they have a melt-in-your-mouth texture.

Corned Beef

Curing cuts of beef unsuited for frying or roasting, such as brisket, using salt and saltpeter, and then cooking them until soft, has a long history. This method is successfully used to make tender and hearty specialties from supposedly tough cuts of meat, and has the added benefit of improving their keeping properties. It is thought that the name corned beef is derived from the coarse grained corns of salt that were used in the past for its manufacture.

In the British Isles, this method of conserving beef became popular at the time of the industrial revolution. So-called corned beef was one of the world's first industrially produced preserved meats, and was soon packaged in cans. This long-life convenience product could be easily transported and spread from the United Kingdom to the rest of the world on shipping routes. To this day, the popular German seaman's dish, labskaus, contains the cured brisket of beef now known as corned beef.

Canned corned beef usually consists of finely chopped meat in jellied aspic. However, there are also versions with more coarsely cut pieces of meat in terrine mould or artificial gut.

In America the cured beef brisket is usually left whole, cooked in marinade, and thinly cut. Sliced in this manner, it forms an essential ingredient in the popular reuben sandwich.

Ham

Boiled Ham, Prosciutto Cotto, Jambon Blanc, and Spalla Cotta

Good boiled ham is a tender, juicy delicacy. In France such specialties are known as jambon blanc, and in Italy prosciutto cotto, where the shoulder of pig is also prepared in this special fashion to produce spalla cotta.

Boiled ham is traditionally made from the haunch of the pig that is separated from the carcass and freed of bones. Rind, sinews, and excess fat are removed, and the meat cut to shape.

SCHWEINSKOPFSÜLZE AND CORNED BEEF

In order to speed up the curing of the thick pieces of meat, a solution of curing salt is injected directly into the meat and, to ensure an even curing, the injected hams are repeatedly turned and massaged to distribute the brine. A number of butchers also rub the meat with herbs such as rosemary, or spices such as juniper berries, which lend the boiled ham special aromatic notes.

The hams are then placed in molds and pressed to keep the pieces of meat together and prevent the formation of cavities. Alternatively, the hams are tied up in special nets or tightly bound using strong twine. Pressed into shape, the meat is then boiled for several hours, during which time the pieces of meat adhere to one another to form a single, solid piece.

The food industry also employs this process to produce cheap ham imitations from a variety of meat scraps, which is why boiled ham tends to have a bad reputation. However, artisanal specialties can be wonderfully aromatic.

At the end of the boiling process the ham will have assumed the shape into which it was pressed. In some cases the hams are then briefly smoked. Good boiled ham is tender and juicy, and, when cut into slices, makes an excellent appetizer together with bread and a glass of wine. It is also great with freshly made pasta.

Prague Ham, Burgundy Ham, and Honey Ham

The cold smoking of ham as a means to extend its lifetime—on top of curing and boiling—has a long tradition in the Czech Republic. In distinction to the usual boiled ham, the Prague version is left on the bone and subsequently smoked, although there are also de-boned varieties, such as the specialty known in Czech as Pražská šunka, which today is also available canned.

PRAGUE HAM

HONEY HAM

This special variety of ham is traditionally manufactured from pigs of the old Czech saddleback breed, Pøeštice, which have been fattened on whey and potatoes in order to produce the optimal proportions of fat and lean meat.

In the middle of the nineteenth century, the Prague butcher, František Zvìøina, began to refine this traditional specialty, and by the end of the century, Prague ham was being manufactured in large quantities, first spreading to Germany before becoming popular in Austria, Hungary, and later in Paris.

In the past Pražská šunka was manufactured from lightweight pigs and the hams were generally no heavier than five kg. However, today's hams can be considerably heavier. The cut pieces of meat are first salted by hand and rubbed with a mixture of curing salt, sugar, and herbs. Stacked on top of each other in barrels, they are subsequently cured for five to six weeks in brine. After curing, the meat is soaked for several hours in warm water, and then placed in the smokehouse where it is hung over beech wood for half a day. Following the smoking process, the hams are boiled and finally cooled in cold water. Good Prague ham is juicy and light pink in color, with a lustrous golden-yellow sheen on the outside. Pražská šunka is eaten as a cold cut, but also grilled whole over charcoal, cut into pieces, and served warm in bread. The juicy texture of the cured, boiled ham in combination with the light smoky aroma makes the Prague ham a special delicacy.

Charcuterie

Katenschinken, Dielenschinken, and Ammerländer Schinken

The constantly high humidity of regions north of the Alps poses difficulties for the natural ripening of air-dried specialties. Consequently, greater use has been made of smoke for preserving sausages and ham specialties in northern and central Europe.

In northern Germany, and in the region of Schleswig Holstein in particular, this resulted in a smoked ham on the bone know as Katenschinken or Dielenschinken. The Ammerländer Schinken from Lower Saxony is also produced in this fashion. The roofs of farmhouses, known as Katen, were traditionally of the thatched variety, which meant that stone chimneys were outlawed due to the danger of fire. The farmers thus hung the salted hams over the open fire, letting the smoke escape through the gable. The name Dielenschinken originates from the tradition of hanging hams for ripening in the large halls, known as Diele, of traditional ffarmhouses, which are commonly referred to as Low German houses. The valuable joints of meat hung above the heads of the house's occupants are still known as Schinkenhimmel (ham heaven). In the dense northern forests, pigs were traditionally fattened on a varied diet that included acorns. The wood of the forests was used for both heating and the smoking of hams, with the slow-burning beech wood being especially popular. As the wood smoulders for long periods, to this day it is still popular for the slow smoking of ham. The pig haunches are trimmed and cut according to the "Hamburg round cut," and repeatedly salted and cured over a period of three to eight weeks. The subsequent long, cold smoking over beech wood lasts several weeks or even months, after which the hams are ripened for a period before being cut and sold. Holsteiner Katenschinken, a smoked specialty, has a delicate smoky note and a fine nutty flavor, and is popular today served thinly cut with asparagus or on bread. However, it can also be found diced and fried in scrambled eggs and in many other north German dishes.

HAM ON THE BONE

SMOKED HAM

Black Forest Ham

The fresh air of the Black Forest is home to an especially aromatic ham specialty that has been smoked over fir wood. This ham owes its character to the dry air of the Black Forest in which, following smoking, it can be air-ripened for long periods—a process which has been employed in the region for centuries and is now protected by the EU.

Black Forest ham (Schwarzwälder Schinken) is boneless, which means the manufacturing process begins with the de-boning, i.e., cutting the bone from the pig's haunches. The pieces of meat are then rubbed with curing salt, pepper, garlic, and a special mixture of herbs. During the subsequent water loss, brine forms, within which the meat ripens for several weeks. The region's butchers then allow the ham to rest for a while, which is termed, nachbrennen—an additional phase of dry curing during where the curing salt and herbs are absorbed deeper into the meat.

The Black Forest ham is then traditionally smoked over fir wood, which is available in large quantities in the region. In the past, stonework smokehouses were used; today automated smoking chambers are the standard method. The hams hang for three to four weeks at 20°C/68°F over smoldering sawdust and fir tree branches, during which time the ham loses around a quarter of its weight. The smoking is followed by a dry-ripening phase lasting several weeks, which lends the specialty its refined flavor. Black Forest ham has a nutty, spicy flavor with a characteristic smoky note. Diced or cut into fine strips, it is used in a multitude of traditional dishes, lending them a hearty flavor. Thinly cut, the ham is delicious on black bread accompanied by an artisanal brewed beer.

Parma and San Daniele

Northern Italy is not just renowned for its sausage making, but also for air-dried ham specialties. The dry, fragrant air of the hills around Parma, and the microclimate of the small Friulian town of San Daniele, are home to a number of ham specialties that are known throughout the world and carry the EU's protective seal.

In northern Italy in particular, pigs have been reared for centuries. In the past, the animals were fattened on acorns from the forests and later from the region's rich harvests of grain. For the ham specialties Prosciutto di Parma and Prosciutto di San Daniele, only pigs from

CULATELLO DI ZIBELLO, SAN DANIELE, AND PARMA

northern and central Italy are used. There are precise specifications as to the breeds of pigs to be used and the regions from which they must originate. Only animals from the breeds Large White, Landrace, and Duroc are used during manufacture. It is also stipulated that they must be more than nine months old and heavier than 150 kg / 330 lbs., which is a very heavy pig by today's standards. The animals are fed exclusively on corn, barley, and in the case of Parma ham, the whey from the regional Parma cheese production. Unfortunately, there are no specifications concerning the rearing conditions, which remain a secret to this day. In the middle of the twentieth century, industrial production methods were introduced at the two sites, with Parma alone now selling almost 10 million units per annum.

The production of the north Italian hams begins with the trimming of the pig haunches, resulting in the typical rounded ham shape. In the case of Proscuitto San Daniele, the trotter is left on the leg, and the ham is lightly pressed during storage, producing its characteristic guitar shape. Following trimming, the hams are rubbed with sea salt and then allowed to rest for a number of weeks. Less salt is used in Parma, which lends it a milder flavor compared to its Tuscan cousin. During the salting phase, the hams are repeatedly massaged and rubbed with fresh salt, and after around two months, the salt is washed off and the hams left to dry. During the special air-drying process, the hams are hung on huge, high wooden frames. The ripening rooms have open windows on opposite sides, allowing a free flow of outside air. As a result of the continuous draft, the hams dry slowly, losing weight. In order to prevent the hams from drying too quickly, those parts of the meat not covered by rind are smeared with a mixture of lard, salt, and pepper. After seven months in the fresh air, the hams are moved to darker, less well ventilated rooms for further enzymatic ripening, and within the space of half a year they begin to acquire their special flavor. Toward the end of the ripening process, the butchers briefly insert a porous horse bone into the meat, smelling the bone to assess the progress of the ripening. This last ripening phase can last from one to three years.

According to the regulations, ham from Parma and San Daniele must be ripened for at least one year and pass a quality inspection before being sold with its characteristic branding.

Northern Italian Prosciutto has a slightly sweet flavor, which is termed dolce by the Italians. Cut into wafer thin slices, the ham has a captivating aroma. It is popular as an appetizer and as a standard ingredient in many Mediterranean dishes.

Charcuterie

JAMÓN IBÉRICO DE BELLOTA

Jamón Ibérico Bellota and Serrano

The secret of the unique taste of Iberian ham is to be found in the holm oak forests in the southwest of Spain, the so-called Dehesa. This is home to the semi-wild Ibérico pigs, whose diet, in addition to wild herbs, primarily consists of the rich supply of acorns, with the black pigs eating up to 10 kg / 22 lbs. of this rich source of protein during the course of one day.

In the past, this special acorn fattening was practiced throughout Europe, however, today it is mainly restricted to Spain, the home of Jamón Ibérico, and Portugal. In the French Pyrenean, the Bigorre breed of pigs, related to the Ibérico, are also fattened on acorns for the production of a ham delicacy, and the popular German Westphalian ham also used to be produced from pigs fattened on acorns.

The various quality classes of Jamón Ibérico are determined by the fodder: ham from free-range pigs that have accumulated at least 40% of their weight from eating acorns is termed Jamón Ibérico de Bellota and is the best this specialty has to offer; Jamón Ibérico de Recebo is the name for ham from pigs that have only been fed shredded acorns during the final fattening period; and ham sold under the name Jamón Ibérico, without a suffix, can be produced from domestic pigs crossed with the black pigs. These animals are generally kept in pens and are not fed acorns.

Thanks to the rich diet and slow growth of the older breeds, the meat of the Iberian pigs fattened on acorns has a special marbling. The unique qualities of the meat and fat are ideal for a long ripening that can last for two or sometimes even four years.

Before the haunches are hung out to ripen, they are covered in sea salt and cured for just over one week. After this period they are washed and stored at a low temperature and high humidity for two months, during which time the salt is absorbed into the meat. Only after this treatment are the hams are hung in the well ventilated ripening rooms, known as secadero, for between six and twelve months. In contrast to Italian hams, the exposed parts of Spanish hams are not smeared with lard but are allowed to ripen in the air. In the secaderos the hams sweat out there own weight in liquid.

After the months-long air-ripening, the hams are transferred to darker and cooler ripening cellars called, bodegas, where there is a slightly higher humidity and the hams begin the final phase of ripening, which can last a number of years. It is during this phase that the hams develop their special flavor.

As the black pig's trotter is traditionally left on the Jamón Ibérico, the specialty is also known under the name Pata Negra.

Ripened Iberian ham is typically stored upright on a stand placed on a table, with paper-thin slices cut from the ham with a long knife. However, it is now also available in individually packaged sections. Genuine Jamón Ibérico de Bellota is characterized by an unbelievably complex depth of flavor. It has a unique combination of meaty and nutty flavors and a melt-in-your-mouth texture.

Serrano ham, also from Spain, is manufactured in a similar fashion to the Italian air-dried specialties. However, in contrast to Jamón Ibérico, it is manufactured from white domestic breeds, not the black pigs. Etymologically, the name Serrano originates from the mountainous region where the special air is responsible for the ripening of the Spanish ham on the bone.

Country Ham, Virginia Ham, and Smithfield Ham

Early settlers from Europe imported the tradition of salting and smoking hams for the purpose of preservation to the east coast of the USA. In North and South Carolina, Tennessee, and Virginia, this led to the development of country hams, which, to this day, are popular in America as a festive dish.

Notable amongst these is the Smithfield Ham from Virginia, which was traditionally made from pigs fed on the remains of the harvest from the region's large peanut plantations. Thanks to this special fodder, the ham acquired an especially fine, sweet, nutty flavor. However, the regulations specifying that the pigs be fattened exclusively on peanuts were loosened considerably in the 1960s.

For the production of these American country hams, the pig haunches are first salted for two to three months, during which time they are regularly turned and massaged. The pieces of meat are then filled into close meshed nets and smoked over hickory and red oak wood. The subsequent dry ripening in special, temperature controlled ripening rooms lasts from several months to over one year. Country hams are sold in various age classes, on and off the bone. Long-ripened varieties have a wealth of flavors comparable to the best European hams. In America, country hams are prepared whole and traditionally served at Easter and Christmas. The ham is first soaked in water over night in order to take the edge off the highly salty taste. The remains of the herbs, salt, and mold are then brushed off and the country ham is boiled in water until it reaches a core temperature of 70° C / 158° F.

The skin is then removed from the ham and the surface fat is scored in a crisscross pattern to form diamond shapes. Rubbed with honey, brown sugar, or maple syrup, and garnished with cloves stuck into the meat, the ham is then placed in the oven for glazing. The roasted and glazed ham is cut into thin slices and eaten with gravy or as a filling for sandwiches.

Culatello

For some people, Culatello is the king of the hams, although, strictly speaking, it is somewhere between a sausage and a ham. It originates from the Parma region, or more precisely the city of Zibello, home to the traditionally manufactured and ripened Culatello di Zibello, which is now protected by both the EU and associations such as Slow Food. The original is made from pigs several years in age of rare breeds typical in Tuscany and Emilia-Romagna. Thanks to the black pigs' special fodder of chestnuts, acorns, and corn, the Culatello di Zibello acquires a fine nutty flavor.

The meat used for this specialty is taken from the rear, inner part of the pig's haunches, pared from the bone, and removed of fat and sinews. The meat is first salted and then placed in brine composed of salt, pepper, garlic, and wine, soaking into the meat over several weeks. To ensure even penetration, the pieces of meat are repeatedly massaged by hand.

The salted pieces of meat are then filled into pig bladders and bound with a strong thread to form a wide meshed net, resulting in the typical pear shape. Thus bound, it ripens for over a year in the region's ancient ripening cellars. Traditionally, Culatello is only produced during October and February when the valleys of the Po plain are shrouded in a thick, cold mist. The special ripening climate and mold cultures of the ripening rooms lend the specialty a unique depth of flavor.

However, today's mass-produced Culatellos from large processing plants outside the region, operating all year round, generally lack these qualities. Artisanally produced Culatello from the meat of old breeds is a rare product, and having it thinly sliced is a highpoint on any appetizer plate.

Coppa

In addition to the traditional pigs' haunches, especially tasty air-dried hams can also be made from pork neck and shoulder, as in the case of the Italian specialty coppa or capocollo, which can be traced back to Roman times.

The region of Emilia-Romagna is home to special varieties of coppa such as Coppa Piacentina—now a protected designation of origin—made from heavy domestic pigs. For the specialty's characteristic ripening and flavor, pork with a higher percentage of intramuscular fat is required, which is now hard to find with the dominance of today's lean meat breeds.

In France, Coppa de Corsa is produced from Corsican pigs, which are very similar to Ibérico pigs, of one year and older. The Corsican wild pigs, known as Australe, have a varied diet of chestnuts and acorns from foraging in the island's forests and meadows, which lend the Coppa de Corsa its light, nutty flavor.

Coppa is prepared by cutting the rind and sinews from the pork neck and trimming the outer fat. Cut into pieces, the meat is salted and rubbed with sugar and spices such as pepper, bay leaf, cinnamon, and cloves. Thus prepared, the pork necks ripen for a period in the curing brine, during which time the pieces of meat are repeatedly massaged in order to ensure the even absorption of flavors and curing salt. The pieces of meat are then washed, dried, and stuffed into large cow intestines or wrapped in a pig's diaphragm. The Coppa is then fastened with a hemp cord or alternatively pressed in a close meshed net. In this cylindrical form, the Coppa is air-cured for at least half a year, during which time it loses almost half of its weight.

Cut into slices, the final product is dark red and laced with white fat, which gives Coppa its soft texture and juicy consistency, complemented by a full-bodied, lightly sweet flavor.

With the right fodder, this can be augmented by nutty flavors and delicate wood and mushroom notes. Freshly sliced, Coppa is served as an appetizer or as a melt-in-your-mouth topping for pizzas.

COPPA

Bresaola

In the Alpine valleys, the tradition of preserving beef by salting and air-drying dates back to the Middle Ages. In the northern Italian Alpine region of Valtellina the climactic conditions are ideal for the ripening of dried meat. The valley's fresh breeze and humidity ensure that the specialties slowly lose moisture, resulting in an especially tender Bresaola. As a result, Bresaola della Valtellina is an EU protected designation.

For the manufacture of Bresaola, lean pieces of the cow's haunches are trimmed of outer fat, dry-salted, and rubbed with a mixture of pepper, bay leaves, garlic, cinnamon, cloves, and curing salt. The pieces of meat are then left to cure in the brine, to which some producers add a shot of wine. During this phase the pieces of meat are repeatedly massaged in order to enhance the absorption of the brine. Finally, the meat is stuffed into natural intestines and hung up to dry. During this ripening period, lasting at least two months, air-drying and fermentation processes within the meat contribute to the specialty's

Charcuterie

long shelf life. A white mold also forms on the outer skin that helps protect the meat from outside influences.

During dry-ripening the beef loses almost half of its weight. Bresaola is typically cylindrical in form, although there are brick-shaped varieties which have been pressed during ripening.

An especially tasty variety of Bresaola is produced from the meat of Piedmontese cattle. In the Asti region and around Venice, Bresaola is also manufactured from horsemeat, and there are even varieties made from venison thigh that are often refined with the addition of red wine. The somewhat smaller version of Bresaola is known as Slinzenga, which is made from the coarser section of the beef haunch and is generally more strongly seasoned.

Cut into wafer-thin slices, Bresaola is popularly served as a carpaccio with a few drops of lemon juice, oil, parmesan shavings, and arugula salad to make a delicious appetizer.

BÜNDNERFLEISCH

Bündnerfleisch

The Canton of Graubünden in the west of Switzerland is renowned beyond its borders for its air-dried and deep red beef specialty, Bündnerfleisch. After grazing on the Alpine pastures throughout the summer, mountain farmers used to slaughter those animals that couldn't be kept over the winter, using the meat to make sausage and cold cut products for their own consumption over the winter months. The best pieces were cured and preserved by drying in the Alpine air, and to this day the best Bündnerfleisch is made from the meat of old cows. The manufacture of Bündnerfleisch resembles that of its cousin, Bresaola. Meat from the cow's haunches is trimmed of fat and sinews, cured, seasoned, and then marinated in a spice brine for several weeks. Washed and stuffed into nets or stocking-like gauze, the pieces of meat air-ripen for three to six months, during which time they are pressed several times per day, which explains Bündnerfleisch's rectangular form. The pressing is designed to prevent the exterior from drying out too quickly, ensuring a juicy consistency throughout.

In order to meet the high demand for what was once a farmer's specialty, Bündnerfleisch is now manufactured from beef imported from South America. Today, the majority of the meat ages in ripening chambers that simulate the appropriate Alpine climate the whole year round—a break in production over the summer months, which was customary in the past, is no longer necessary.

Before the invention of slicing machines, Bündnerfleisch was diced and used like bacon for regional potato and flour dishes. Today, the specialty is generally cut into thin slices, and can be best enjoyed with dark bread baked from a wood-fired oven together with a glass of red wine. The fine slices can also be rolled and filled with arugula or cream cheese.

Jerky, Billtong, Ch'arki, Pemmican, and Meat Bars

Ch'arki is the name given to the protein-rich strips of meat traditionally dried over a fire and used as travel provisions by the Native American Quechua tribe from Peru. This dried meat specialty subsequently found its way to North America with Spanish immigrants where it became known as jerky.

The drying of meat in the open air or over a smoldering fire is one of the oldest preservative techniques known to man. Through the removal of water the easily perishable foodstuff keeps for long periods and is lighter and easier to transport.

The natives of North America primarily used this method to preserve the rich supply of buffalo meat. Lean meat is preferred for the production of jerky, which is why the meat of deer, moose, or other wild animals is often used. Domestic pigs are not particularly suited to this form of air-drying as their meat is generally too fatty. Today lean beef is primarily used in the manufacture of beef jerky.

Before drying, the majority of the fat is removed from the meat. Cut into thin strips, it is then salted, marinated in a spiced brine, and finally dried—in a number of varieties it is also cold smoked. The most important thing is that the meat is dried as opposed to roasted or boiled. A related variety of dried meat is the South African Biltong, which, in contrast to jerky, is cut into fine strips after drying. In Africa, Biltong is made from game such as springbok or ostrich and, in contrast to jerky, is often marinated with a little vinegar.

Another relative of jerky is the Chinese specialty Bakkwa, which is traditionally eaten during the Chinese New Year festival. Marinated in soy sauce and honey, Bakkwa has a distinctly sweet flavor.

Bars made from ground dried meat mixed with nuts and fruit were called pemmican by the natives of North America, and today modern versions, known as meat bars, are sold in the USA as a savory snack.

South Tyrolean Bacon and Alto Adige Bacon

North of the Alps, smoking is the traditional method used to preserve ham—south of the Alps it tends to be drying and ripening in the fresh air. South Tyrolean bacon is produced right in the middle of the Alps, where a symbiosis of the two techniques has traditionally been

BEEF JERKY

TYROLEAN BACON

employed to refine and preserve the meat of pig haunches. In the past, the region's mountain farmers slaughtered their pigs in the cold winter months to produce the energy-rich bacon with its good preservative properties, which served as part of their staple diet during the following year's arduous farm work. However, only a small proportion of today's South Tyrolean bacon is now made from the region's pigs, with the majority of the raw ingredients now imported. Bacon from real Tyrolean pigs is specially labeled as farmhouse bacon, and is made from older pigs with a correspondingly richer marbling. Genuine Tyrolean farmhouse bacon is thus of a higher quality but in shorter supply.

The first step in making the bacon is to remove the bones from the pig's haunches, paring the meat so as to form a heart shape when opened out. Known in this form as hammen, the hams are then rubbed with salt and—depending on the manufacturer—a seasoning mix primarily consisting of pepper, bay leaves, rosemary, and juniper berries. Salted and given a herb crust, the hams are cured for several weeks, during which time they are turned repeatedly. Today the climate of the winter months, the traditional curing season, is simulated all-year-round in special ripening rooms.

Following the curing phase, the hams are hung and lightly smoked over wood with a low resin content, which is followed by the dry-ripening phase lasting for over half a year in rooms ventilated with mountain air. During this time, a fine mold with a scent of fresh porcini mushrooms forms on the hams, lending the bacon its fine, nutty flavors.

After ripening, the Tyrolean bacon is golden-yellow on the outside, has a deep red interior, and is laced with white fat. Thanks to the sparing use of salt, South Tyrolean bacon has a very mild flavor, composed of a perfect balance of smoky and air-dried notes.

In the mountains of Tyrol, the bacon is cut into small, thick slices, and served with bread and pickled vegetables as part of the cold platter known locally as Märende. Diced, it also forms an essential ingredient in the Tyrolean pan-fried dish Gröstl, not to forget the savory Tyrolean bacon dumplings.

American and English Bacon

Bacon, cut into thin slices and fried in the pan together with fried eggs, sausages, and baked beans, is an essential part of any full English breakfast. English bacon, in contrast to American bacon, is primarily cut from the loin, although, in addition to this lean section, also includes part of the adjoining, fatty belly.

In contrast, American bacon is cut entirely from the pork belly, which is laced with plenty of juicy fat. In England these long strips are known as streaky bacon. Canadian bacon, however, is cut exclusively from the lean pork loin and has little in common with the juicy varieties from America and England.

However, what all these varieties of bacon have in common is the production method—An initial curing followed by smoking. The sections of meat are first placed in brine, or sometimes just rubbed with salt, and cured for several days. In the case of the classic streaky bacon, the skin is usually removed from the belly prior to curing. Depending on the butcher, a special seasoning mix may also be added to the curing salt and sugar.

Today, in the case of industrially manufactured bacon, the curing brine, which may also contain liquid smoke flavoring, is injected directly into the meat to save time. Clearly, such methods are incapable of producing the rich array of aromas of slowly cured and properly smoked bacon.

After curing, artisanal produced bacon is first rubbed and dried before being smoked on a hook over smoldering sawdust. Un-smoked bacon is sold as green bacon.

Bacon can be enjoyed in a variety of ways. Slices of bacon fried in the pan or roasted in the oven are known in England as rashers, and, in addition to finding their way onto the breakfast table, also make a crispy addition to burgers. Especially lean cuts of meat are often wrapped in bacon to keep the meat moist and to add flavor. So-called pig candy is produced by roasting slices of bacon in the oven with maple syrup, honey, or raw sugar to produce small crispy delicacies. Strips of bacon glazed with chocolate are also delicious, as are spreads such as bacon jam, a relish made from roasted bacon. Today's bacon-mania knows no limits.

Charcuterie

BELLY BACON

Pancetta is a popular appetizer, and when lightly fried in the pan, makes a delicious accompaniment to many dishes. The creamy pasta dish, carbonara, is traditionally prepared using diced Pancetta—or even better, Guanciale—turning this Italian staple into a special delicacy.

Lardo and Lardo di Colonnata

As early as Roman times, slaves working in the marble quarries of the Apuan Alps are reported to have received white bacon as an energy-rich food. However, long after the end of the Roman Empire, the pork backfat, called lardo, continued to provide nutrition for quarry workers during their arduous labor in the mountains. To this day, the special microclimate of the Tuscan mountains, with only moderate temperature fluctuations, is ideal for the special ripening of the white pieces of bacon fat.
The popular lardo specialty from the small Italian mountain village of Colonnata, where it is packed into large boxes made from Carrara marble and salted for several months, has become renowned worldwide.

However, salting and ripening as a means of preserving backfat is practiced in other regions. In the Aosta Valley, simple wooden boxes are used instead of marble, and in other regions and countries north of the Alps, pork backfat is also smoked.
Lardo is made from older pigs rich in fat, preferably from those breeds renowned for their especially thick layer of backfat. Hungary is also home to especially tasty white bacon produced from the abundant backfat of the Mangalitsa wooly pig, which is smoked and then blanched. This specialty, known as szalonna, is frequently seasoned with large quantities of paprika.
In the case of Lardo di Colonnata, the pieces of fat are rubbed with salt and a seasoning mix of pepper, rosemary, bay leaf, sage, cloves, cinnamon, juniper berries, and nutmeg.

Pancetta and Guanciale

The more refined versions of bacon originate from Italy where they are known as Pancetta and Guanciale. In contrast to classic bacon, these specialties are not smoked but salted and dry-ripened, which lends them an especially fine, elegant flavor. The round shape is a characteristic feature of Pancetta, distinguishing it from other ripened pork belly specialties.

To make Pancetta, the pork belly is first trimmed to form a rectangle and then salted by hand. In order to accelerate the ripening process, sugar is added to the mixture of salt and diverse Mediterranean spices, which in the case of Calabrian Pancetta, includes large quantities of native chilies. The cured pork belly is then rolled up and sewn together on the open side with twine. In order to provide additional protection from outside influences, the roll is then wrapped in a pig's bladder or diaphragm that is bound tight with twine.
Guanciale is similar to Pancetta in terms of both its manufacture and taste. However, it is made from pork cheek, not belly. A characteristic feature of Guanciale is the dark seasoning mix composed of coarsely crushed pepper and other spices that is applied to the outside. The fat and meat of pork cheek have a special quality with a somewhat stronger flavor.

In cross-section, Pancetta displays a fine spiral of red meat and pale fat, and the flavor is characterized by fine, sweet notes. Cut into thin slices,

LARDO

Charcuterie

After the marble boxes have been rubbed with fresh garlic, the pieces of fat are stacked in piles, with a mixture of salt, pepper, fresh garlic, and spices sprinkled between each layer. The mixture is then sealed with a large marble lid. The pieces of fat ripen in the resulting brine for a period of at least six months.

Lardo is white with a delicate pink tinge. Specially ripened with herbs and spices, it has an amazing depth of aroma, which is reminiscent of the finest herb butter. The white bacon tastes wonderful on bread still warm from the oven, and in Italy fine slices of Lardo are also added to pizza and fresh pasta shortly before serving.

Cured meat

Pastrami

In Romania Pastramă is the name given to a mutton specialty that is cured, smoked, and then boiled prior to eating. In the second half of the nineteenth century, Romanian Jewish emigrants brought this method of preparing and preserving meat with them to the east coast of the USA.

Today, pastrami is an important part of the local deli culture where it is popular as a filling for sandwiches composed of layers of thinly cut slices.

In Turkey and the Balkans there are similar specialties made from beef or lamb known under the names pastýrma and pastërma, although they differ greatly from their American cousins in both taste and preparation. Nevertheless, etymologically, pastrami always means the same: to preserve or conserve.
In America pastrami is primarily made from beef brisket, however it can also be cut from the shoulder or topside. Freed from any excess fat, the trimmed pieces of meat are cured in brine seasoned with garlic, pepper, coriander, and curing salt for several days, sometimes several weeks.

The pieces of meat are then dried and rubbed with a dry seasoning mix, the so-called rub, composed of coarsely ground pepper and other spices. Encased in this thick spice crust, the beef is now placed in the smoking chamber where it is cold smoked for several hours, sometimes up to one to two days. This additional smoking distinguishes pastrami from corned beef, a cured specialty also made from beef brisket.

After smoking, the pieces of meat are boiled for several hours until they are soft and tender.
Like all slow-cooked specialties, the connective tissue of the marbled meat is softened and loses its elastic properties, resulting in a juicy, crumbly texture.
The pastrami of New York delis is generally quite tangy. Together with a creamy cabbage salad called coleslaw, pastrami is an important ingredient in the popular Rachel sandwich, served with mustard and gherkin. Good pastrami is juicy, with a melt-in-the-mouth texture and a flavor composed of a harmonious balance of cured meat, spices, and delicate smoky notes.

PASTRAMI

Kassler, Geselchtes, and Rauchfleisch

Boiled, cured, and cold-smoked pork is a common ingredient in many rustic dishes, and, preserved in this fashion, is also found in numerous stews.
In Germany it is sold as Kassler, Geselchtes, or Rauchfleisch. The rustic southern German and Austrian specialty, Bauerngeselchte, also falls into this category, although it is generally smoked for longer.
The manufacturing principle is the same for all cured, smoked meat specialties. The meat is first cured in brine and then lightly smoked at a low temperature. Parts such as pork neck, ribs, cheeks, belly, and shoulder are commonly used, although in some regions the knuckle of pork is also cured and smoked prior to cooking in the oven.
For the specialty known in Germany simply as Kassler, the lean pork loin is used. A master butcher by the name of Cassel is reputed to have invented this specialty in Berlin in the nineteenth century. In Austria, pork loin preserved in this manner is known as Selchkarree, karree being the Austrian term for loin. In Switzerland it is known under the name Ripple.

Kassler loin can be served fried, roasted in the oven, or boiled. The fattier parts such as neck, cheeks, and belly can be added to stews, and cooked slowly to add a hearty flavor with light smoky notes. Care should be taken with the preparation of leaner cuts such as Kassler loin, which has a tendency to dry out if cooked for too long or at high temperatures. Kassler baked in bread dough is therefore a popular method of preparation that prevents the meat from drying out.

Charcuterie

GRIEBENSCHMALZ

Pâtés

Pâté en croûte

Recipes for fine French pâtés and terrines go back to the Middle Ages, where fine meat preparations, elaborately baked in pastry, adorned the tables of the royal houses. Today, every region in France offers its own varieties of this specialty, and many families have their own recipes for pâtés with a crispy pastry crust (en croûte is French for under the crust).

The manufacture of pâtés baked in pastry requires the combined skills of the butcher, the cook, and the patissier. Though pâté en croûte is prepared by many butchers in France, it is also a discipline that has been mastered by chefs in many fine restaurants. Pâtés that have not been elaborately baked in a pastry crust, but prepared directly in a mold are known as terrines.

The mixture used for fine pâtés and terrines, as opposed to the mass used for sausages, is generally finer and known as farce. However, the dividing line between normal forcemeat and farce is no longer so clear-cut as modern machines, such as the cutter, are now capable of producing very fine sausage mass.

As a rule, pâtés are composed of a mixture of a finely cut meat dough, coarsely cut lean pieces, innards such as liver, and other ingredients that can include fruit, mushrooms, nuts, noble truffles, and goose liver as used for the specialty foie gras. Depending on the recipe, poultry, pork, beef, or game can be used, sometimes in combination. The mixture is refined with brandy, herbs, and a variety of spices. A special delicacy is the Pâté de foie gras, which contains large quantities of the goose liver specialty and is also produced en croûte.

The next steps in the preparation are quite elaborate. First, the farce is filled into a terrine mold lined with pastry dough. This is done in layers so that the other ingredients are enveloped by the farce. When this is complete, the dough at the sides is folded over the filled mold and covered with a pastry lid. In order to allow the steam generated during baking to escape, small chimneys made from paper, clay, or folded aluminum foil are stuck into round holes cut into the pastry lid.

During baking, the filling beneath the pastry casing tends to shrink so that any resulting cavities are often filled with a stock that gelatinizes upon cooling. After baking, the pâté en croûte has a golden-yellow crust.

Pâté en croûte is best served cold cut into thick slices together with a fresh salad and vinaigrette, rounded off with a dash of sweet-sour preserve.

Pâté de campagne

Pâté de campagne, a simple French country terrine, is the rustic cousin of the noble and elaborately prepared French terrines and pâtés en croûte. Nevertheless, a well-made pâté de campagne is a far cry from a run of the mill meat loaf. This variety of country terrine has its roots in Brittany.

A pâté de campagne is generally prepared from lean and fatty pork, liver and bacon, with finely chopped onions, fresh herbs, spices, salt, and, depending on the recipe, cognac or wine added to the coarsely cut meat. This mixture is then marinated in the fridge for several hours before it is ground until medium coarse. Eggs, and in some cases coarser cut meat, are added to the resulting mass. The goal is a compact but heterogeneous pâté mass composed of a variety of fine and coarse pieces of meat.

The pâté de campagne is baked in a terrine mold that has been lined with pork membrane from the diaphragm, and sometimes with additional fatty bacon. The challenge when baking is to prevent the pâté from drying out, which results in a crumbly texture. The farce should have a solid consistency, with the fat providing the necessary juiciness. The pork membrane, folded over the top of the filled mold, ensures a compact farce and provides a smooth surface for the formation of the pâté's characteristic brown crust.
After baking, the specialty is cooled and served in thick slices. Pâté de campagne tastes wonderful with rustic country bread, accompanied by small pickled gherkins and a glass of French vin de pays.

Rillette, Confit, Schmalzfleisch, and Griebenschmalz

Gently cooking meat in rendered fat, allowing it to cool, and covering it in a layer of fat, is a preservation method with a very long history. Farmers used this method to conserve valuable stocks of meat over the winter months until the next slaughter. This specialty is traditionally made from pork, poultry, duck, and goose. However, fish, rabbit, or game can also be preserved in fat using this method.
In Germany these specialties are known as Schmalzfleisch or Potsuse. The popular Griebenschmalz (lard with greaves), with roasted apple and onions, is produced in a similar fashion.

In France, where these specialties are known as rillette and confit, this aspect of the butcher's art has been brought to perfection. As far back as the Renaissance, the poet François Rabelais raved about the brown pork jam from the city of Tours. On the banks of the Loire in northwest France, there is a proud tradition of producing rillette according to a local recipe. The city's butchers are renowned for first roasting the pieces of meat at a higher temperature, which gives the meat its golden brown color, lending the Rillettes de Tours their special roast flavors.

The secret is in the gentle, slow roasting of the meat in its own fat, a process that can last several hours, sometimes up to half a day. In contrast to frying, which requires a temperature of 180°C/356°F, rillette is cooked at a much lower temperature of around 80°C/176°F. If the meat does not fall apart on its own after cooking, it is generally pulled apart or rubbed by hand. The resulting fine, long meat fibers, the so-called rillettes, are what give the dish its name.
Larger pieces of meat that are roasted and conserved in the fat whole are known as confit. Goose and duck, especially the legs, are frequently preserved in this manner.
Rillettes are seasoned with salt, pepper, and depending on the recipe, with further herbs, and wine or spirits. The conserved meat is traditionally stored in small dishes or preserving jars.
In order to increase its shelf life, the last layer in the dish usually consists of pure fat, forming an air-tight seal protecting the meat from outside influences.
Rillettes taste delicious as an appetizer spread thickly on crusty white bread, accompanied by a few small French pickled gherkins, known as cornichons, and a cool glass of white wine from the Loire.

Pies

Shepherd's Pie and Pork Pie

Without protection, meat cooked in the extreme heat of the early wood-fired ovens, or directly over the open fire, quickly burned or dried out. In the past, instead of expensive pots and casserole dishes, it was common to use a protective casing of simple dough, which in prehistoric times and antiquity often consisted of nothing more than flour and water. Mixed with vegetables and herbs, the meat cooked slowly in these baked casings, retaining its moisture without burning. Once cooled, these meals in their pastry casings were not just easy to handle and transport, but also lasted longer thanks to the protective layer. These early types of pies were known as coffyns, in other words, small chests or coffins in which the meat was baked together with the vegetables. However, the thick, hard pastry of prehistoric times and antiquity was generally not eaten.

In the Middle Ages the term pyes appeared for the first time in English. Richly ornamented, filled pastries were extremely popular as an intermediate course at the royal court as a means of entertaining guests. They were filled with all kinds of game and poultry, however, whether birds such as the magpie were also used, or whether it was just the form of the bird's nest that provided the inspiration for the name, is unclear.

England has a long tradition of pie making. During the industrial revolution English housewives cooked their husbands whole meals in pie form. The filled specialties were taken down the pits by mineworkers and eaten while working. English settlers also took the pie tradition with them to Australia, New Zealand, and the USA, where today it is the sweet varieties filled with various fruits that dominate. However, English pies are traditionally savory, filled with meat and vegetables. Historically, sweet pies are a relatively modern development.
Popular fillings for meat pies include pork (pork pie), lamb's kidneys (kidney pie), and poultry and game (chicken pie and game pie). Today, the coarsely cut meat is generally pre-cooked together with vegetables and a dash of stock, wine, or beer, before being filled into a mold lined with pastry. The pie is then sealed with a pastry lid before being placed in the oven. After baking, the tender meat is encased in a hearty meat sauce, with the pastry—especially the gold-brown crust—providing a crispy counterpart.

Over time, in order to save pastry, ceramic baking dishes were developed and are still used to this day. The resulting pies have a pastry lid, but no pastry base or sides. The traditional shepherd's and cottage pies baked in these dishes are made from a mixture of finely chopped meat and vegetables, and covered with a layer of mashed or grated potato. The potato crust, like the pastry, protects the meat from drying out, resulting in an extremely juicy dish.
Meat pies are available today in various round shapes and as little tartlets. They are also common in a half-moon shapes, where the pastry has been folded over the filling to form an envelope with the open side closed with the pressure of a fork.
Pies can be eaten cold but are best enjoyed warm with a freshly pulled malted ale.

Charuterie

BBQ

Pulled Pork, Spare Ribs, Brisket, and Whole Hog

The word barbeque originates from the Spanish term barbacoa, which was used by Spanish immigrants to describe the method of preparing meat traditionally practiced in the Caribbean. The Taíno people named their sacred fire sites, where they roasted meat wrapped in agave leaves, barabicu. In the Caribbean region, whole animals were also slowly roasted on large frames directly over the fire. Together with the Spaniards and the slaves transported to the American plantations via the Caribbean, this method of preparing meat found its way to the southern USA, where it is now known as barbeque, or BBQ for short.
To this day fiercely fought competitions are still held in the southern states to decide who makes the best barbeque. At the numerous championships, so-called pitmasters (pit refers to the fireplace) from various regions compete for the honors.

In Texas, beef is the main meat subjected to the BBQ treatment. The popular barbequed brisket, a breast of beef that has been cooked in the smoker until the meat is almost falling of the bone, originates from this state. Memphis, Tennessee is renowned for its slowly cooked pork ribs and the tender shoulder of pork from the smoker, known as pulled pork, which is traditionally served in a sandwich with a sweet tomato sauce. Kansas City is known for its highly spiced, dry marinades that are rubbed into the meat before smoking.

However, the supreme discipline—and for many people the only genuine BBQ—is the roasting and slow cooking of whole animals. Whole hog BBQ, the roasting of a whole pig over glowing embers, is especially popular in North Carolina. The meat, removed from the bone and chopped into pieces, is traditionally served on the plate or in a roll with a vinegar sauce.
In contrast to the quick grilling of sausages, burgers, and steaks over hot embers, a genuine barbeque at lower temperatures takes considerably longer, requiring careful attendance over several hours, sometimes even days.
The secret of the BBQ is in the slow cooking of the meat by indirect heat. As a result of the hours of slow cooking, even marbled and relatively tough cuts of meat, such as brisket, can be turned into a melt-in-the-mouth delicacy.

Before the meat finds its way onto the grate of the BBQ oven, it is rubbed with a dry spice mix (dry rub) or marinated.
With the so-called smoker, the meat is not grilled directly over the embers but at a sufficient distance to ensure it cooks slowly—as well as smoking in the smoke wafting over the meat. In the classic BBQ oven, the embers are contained in an adjoining firebox from which heat and smoke are directed to the meat via a pipe. The challenge for the pit master is to prevent the meat from burning or losing too much moisture and fat during the long period in the oven. After cooking in the hot smoke, the pieces of meat are removed from the bone by hand, cut into pieces, or gently pulled and served with bread and sauce. The crispy crust is also cut into small pieces and sprinkled over the juicy meat as additional cracklings.
The meat is best eaten with sweet-sour pickled vegetables and coleslaw, together with a variety of home made BBQ sauces.
BBQ specialties from the smoker combine juicy, tender flesh with a crisp and spicy crust, blending spice and meat flavors with the fine smoky notes of the fire. In principle, well seasoned and carefully barbequed meat does not require any sauce and is a taste statement in itself.

Raw, Burger, Rissole, and Meatball

In many parts of the world, raw and finely chopped or ground meat that is not turned into sausages is used to make pan fried and grilled specialties.

The most popular is the burger patty made from ground beef, which is best served medium, i.e., fried until still pink in the middle. In contrast to sausage meat, which is mixed with other ingredients and binding agents, the goal of a burger patty is not to produce a compact mass, but to bind the meat just enough so that it does not fall apart on the grill. Only when bitten into should the meat of the finished burger reveal its crumbly texture that, when combined with the other ingredients and the bun, produces a hearty delicacy.

Meatballs made from ground meat and other ingredients are popular around the world under many names: Boulette, meatballs, Fleischküchle, Frikadelle, Köttbullar or simply as Klops. In a slightly longer form, they are popular in the Balkans as Ćevapčići a or in Turkey as Köfte. Every cook has their own personal recipe. The ground pork, beef, or lamb is first seasoned in a variety of ways and mixed with other ingredients such as breadcrumbs and eggs to bind the mass and give it additional volume. The basis of this meat is always ground meat, which today is generally chopped mechanically and not by hand—a laborious process using large chopping knives which was common practice before the invention of useful devices such as the meat grinder.

Ground pork seasoned with salt and pepper, and sometimes garlic or caraway seeds, is a delicacy known in Germany as Mett. Fresh and raw, the mass is eaten on bread rolls garnished with onion. Another similar raw meat specialty is the tartar made from lean beef. Many butchers swear by hand-chopped tartar as opposed to ground meat. The raw, chopped beef is traditionally mixed with raw egg yolk, capers, fresh onions, salt, pepper, and, depending on the region, a variety of additional ingredients. Freshly made tartar, eaten raw, tastes best with white bread toasted a golden-brown and rubbed with a fresh clove of garlic.

Know your meat

Storing and tasting

How do I store sausage and ham?
In the ripening rooms of master butchers, sausages and hams are stored in a precisely controlled climate. Temperature and humidity are regulated so that the sausages can ripen in peace, losing weight under controlled conditions. But what happens when we take these specialties home, removing them from this perfect climate?

Whole lasts longer

A ripened sausage doesn't generally go off, it only gets harder. However, in the dry air of a modern, centrally heated house, air-dried sausage and ham specialties quickly lose moisture, easily drying out and becoming hard. When it is too hot, the fat often begins to run down the side. The sausage sweats, threatening to lose its juiciness, and become rancid. On the other hand, if it is too humid, unwanted molds may form that are anything but desirable, and are generally black or green in color.

Whole raw sausage and ham specialties, which have been ripened or smoked, are best stored in an unheated, airy pantry, hung at a temperature of 10–15°C/50–59°F. The specialties can become somewhat harder as a result, however, when left whole and uncut they can keep for several weeks.

Alternatively, the fridge's vegetable drawer can be used. However, ripened meat products should not be kept too cold as this can alter their flavor. Furthermore, fridges have a very dry climate, so the sausages should be loosely wrapped in paper or a towel.

Just enough rather than too much

Freshly cut sausage and ham keeps no longer than a couple of days, and quickly loses flavor. Artisanal specialties, made without chemical additives, are especially susceptible and have a short lifetime. Sliced, they quickly acquire oxidation flavors due to the large surface area exposed to the air. For this reason, one should only buy sufficient sliced ham and sausage from one's butcher or supplier of choice for the next few days. For longer storage periods, the sliced sausage and ham should be vacuum packed or frozen.

In the case of fresh—in other words raw or blanched specialties—the shelf life is only a few days. Lightly smoked, the meats keep somewhat longer. Wiener sausages for example, which are blanched and lightly smoked, keep for almost a week.

Fresh frying sausages should not be kept in the fridge for more than a day, and preferably fried and eaten as soon as possible. However, heating extends their lifetime. Freshly stuffed in the intestines and blanched for around 30 minutes at 74°C/165°F, the sausages keep for three to four days.

In contrast, cooked or pasteurized specialties that are filled into jars, such as pâtés or liverwurst, keep for a long time. However, as soon as the jar is opened they should be kept in the fridge and quickly eaten.

How do I conduct a sausage and ham tasting?

Today, many sausage and ham specialties have become an everyday, unquestioned culinary pleasure. However, it is sometimes worthwhile to take a closer look at what exactly it is we have on our plate or piece of bread. The act of consciously tasting can help reveal the fine differences and special qualities of the individual products and their regions. Ideally, a tasting begins with a promising exterior and ends with a long-lasting, aromatic finish.

A feast for the eyes

What does the specialty look like? What form and color does it have? Before tasting sausage and ham specialties, one should begin by examining their appearance. The exterior often reveals much about the origins of the specialty. When the product has been cut, the cross section gives the first clues as to what the sausage will feel like in the mouth. Is the sausage mass uniformly fine? Does it contain coarser pieces or little surprises such as pistachio nuts for added texture?

First smell then taste!

Whether it is a freshly cut sausage, a slice of ham, or the whole product itself, just like a fine wine it is recommended to begin by giving the specialty a thorough sniff. Our noses are considerably more sensitive than our tongues. Before the first morsel enters the mouth, it is possible to savor a wide variety of aromas that often seem to disappear after the first bite, or at least change dramatically. These first olfactory impressions reveal much about the ripeness of the meat, its manufacture, and the herbs and spices used.

Once in the mouth, it is possible to test the entire palette of aromas. Is the mouthfeel creamy, or does it have a firmer bite? What flavor does the meat have? Do certain herbs or aromas dominate, or is the combination harmonious? What about the salt content, sweetness, and acidity? Does the specialty taste as expected, or are there disappointments?

Just like a fine wine, good quality products have a long-lasting finish that reverberates on the palate.

It's the mixture that counts!

The most exciting aspect of a tasting is assembling a wide selection of different sausage and ham products, with representatives from every style. A mixed tasting composed from ripened, smoked, and blanched selections is a good way to gain an overview of a butcher's range of products, or those of a particular region.

Just like a wine tasting, one should proceed in a certain order, slowly progressing from the milder to the longer ripened and more intense flavors. Mildly seasoned blanched sausages and simple air-dried specialties should be tried before the strongly smoked and long-ripened products with intense aromas.
The same applies to the different seasonings: tasting a hot chili knacker before a mild calf's liver sausage doesn't make any sense, while the other way around can result in an exciting taste journey.

Anyone wanting to delve more deeply should try the various stages in the ripening of a single specialty, or the different terroirs. How does the taste change after 24 months compared to six months? What influence does the origin or the terroir have on the aroma?

Not too cold and not too warm

Even when tasting cold sausage and ham specialties, there is a correct temperature that brings out the best variety of aromas. Here, fat—that most important flavor carrier—is decisive. Fat doesn't unfold its aromas at low temperatures, which is why sausage and ham shouldn't be tasted direct from the fridge but at room temperature. However, it shouldn't be too hot during the tasting either, otherwise the fat will start to melt.

Portraits – heroes of the movement

The new meat culture

A new movement devoted to the rediscovery of meat and its origin, preparation, and refinement is sweeping the world. We are experiencing an international revival in which long-lost traditions are rescued from obscurity and revitalized, generating completely new constellations. The players are driven by passion, dedication, and the search for an all-embracing quality, raising the enjoyment of meat to new culinary heights.

Our journey through the world of the new meat culture begins on the farms and pastures where every meat delicacy—whether fresh, fried, or ripened—has its origin. Committed breeders, dedicated to natural, humane animal husbandry and the preservation of old breeds rather than the monotony of industrial mass production, are the basis of the new culture. Without their dedicated work on farms and pastures, these developments would not be possible. They have become indispensable partners to butchers, chefs, and meat lovers. Today, new networks are forming between the various players, generating exciting projects and outstanding pleasures.

New butchers, both men and women, are breaking with old clichés, showing that they no longer need to hide themselves and their craft as they develop a new pride and confidence in their work.
In the artisan workshops of this new movement, unique sausage, ham, and ripened meat specialties are being produced that are nowhere to be found on supermarket shelves. The resulting variety of flavors and rich depth of aromas show what this movement is all about.
In glazed butcher shops and the open workshops of the new meat schools, interested customers are now regaining an insight into the honest butchers' craft and the origins of their food. Opportunities to experience the manufacture of beloved specialties firsthand, learning everything about the appreciation of meat and the use of valuable foodstuffs, are growing by the day.

In restaurants, dinner clubs, and street kitchens, meat lovers are now rediscovering the joys of simple preparation and holistic ideals. In the kitchens, nose-to-tail, slow cooking, and genuine BBQ are reconnecting with traditions that for generations have produced fascinating specialties from every part of the animal.

The stories behind every one of this movement's protagonists are fascinating, redefining our image of the butcher, livestock farmer, slaughterer, and meat lover—stories that are representative of countless more worldwide.

Even though many of the players have caused a stir with their convictions and opinions, provoking lively discussion, every one of them is committed, heart and soul, to the preservation and revitalization of a tradition stretching back thousands of years, bringing it into our own time. They are rebellious and committed fighters for the craft, values, and taste in whose future they believe.

The revitalization of this culture is a fascinating and instructive journey, a journey which wets one's appetite for exploring this new world firsthand, celebrating the meat, artisanry, and culinary pleasures on the farms, in the butcher shops, and at the long tables.

Portraits

Lennart & Bror

IN 2013 FRITJOF ANDERSSON AND RASMUS EK OPENED THEIR BUTCHER'S SHOP, LENNART & BROR, WITH ADJOINING RESTAURANT IN THE NORTH OF STOCKHOLM. SINCE THEN THE TWO BEATLES FANS HAVE ROCKED THE COUNTER AND GRILL WITH GRANDIOSE, HAND CRAFTED MEAT SPECIALTIES.

Portraits

"Our favorite cut of meat? That's like asking us for our favorite Beatles album."

Ambitious greenhorns

The traditional road to success begins with a good education, a wealth of practical experience, and meticulous work. However, sometimes it can also be an advantage to have no idea at all. When Fritjof Andersson and Rasmus Ek made the decision to open a butcher's shop with a restaurant, they had neither the right training nor experience in the field. All they knew was that it was hard to find good meat in Stockholm and that this was not about to change unless they did something move line up.

Devoid of any know-how, they started planning from the perspective of the customer, thus free from any preconceptions. They imagined their very own favorite butcher's shop, which, in addition to the best quality meat, also included a butcher with a personal touch. The type of butcher who gives tips, fulfils special wishes, and is always approachable had completely died out in Stockholm. In order to acquire the information and skills they needed to realize their ideal, they began to build a network. This generated their most important contact: businessman, author, and butcher, Håkan Fällman.

Thrilled by the idea of the ambitious greenhorns, he became their most important mentor. Andersson and Ek learned how to butcher animals in Wales and central Sweden, organizing educational camps where they taught themselves the required theory and tasted countless cuts of meat. After two years of intensive preparation, Lennart & Bror was opened and immediately became one of the hotspots for Stockholm's culinary community. From gourmet steaks for the grill to coarse cuts for stews and braised dishes, everything that the meat lover's heart could desire is on offer—and if not, is quickly ordered.

The shop now has a network of exclusive suppliers. For example, the Havdhem pig farm, which also supplies the Swedish star cook Tommy Myllymäki, and Magnus Nilsson from the internationally celebrated restaurant Fäviken, who supplies small quantities of his own charcuterie creations. Andersson and Ek are the nightmare of every pedant: they have reached their goal without recognized training.

Portraits

103

Vom Einfachen das Gute

THE SHOP WITH THE PRETTY NAME, VOM EINFACHEN DAS GUTE (THE BEST OF THE SIMPLE), OPENED IN THE MITTE DISTRICT OF BERLIN IN 2013, DELIGHTING LOVERS OF RIPENED MEAT SPECIALTIES WITH A DELICATESSEN COUNTER CURATED BY TWO ENTHUSIASTS AND CRAMMED FULL OF HIGHLY AROMATIC SPECIALTIES—EACH WITH THEIR VERY OWN STORY.

Sausage, ham, and other stories

Nothing better expresses the essence of a delicious meal than the name of Manuela Rehn and Jörg Reuter's delicatessen: Vom Einfachen das Gute (The Best of the Simple in English). However, simple doesn't stand for the arbitrary or the plain, but for the pure and unadulterated. Products such as sausage, cheese and bread are available on every street corner. However, it has never been so difficult for consumers to find the good amongst the profusion of products in our consumer society.

Rehn and Reuter have done the searching for their customers. Their most important dictate is that the products must have a story. They know the producers personally, learning first hand what lies behind the products: where the cow was reared, what the pig ate, how long the cheese should ripen, and what makes the winegrower tick. One could make one's life easier as a small delicatessen owner. However, the idea behind all the effort is simple: when food has a story that can be told with pride, it quickly becomes apparent to customers that they are not dealing with interchangeable, everyday products.

At any rate, everything becomes clear with the first bite. When a pig has been reared on the open pastures of Andalusia feeding on acorns, the ham tastes sensationally aromatic—especially when it has ripened for 30 months. The same applies to the Txogitxu ham from 10–18 year old cows, or Salami Cacciatore from close to Parma. Naturally Rehn and Reuter don't need to travel so far for all their products. The Ahle Wurscht dealer, Carsten Neumeier, [see article below] is located in North Hesse, the Leberkäse comes from the Bavarian Rhön, and the boiled ham from Landwerthof on the Baltic coast.

The products don't necessarily have to be regional to make a good story, but regionally typical. Rehn and Reuter's approach to the theme of organic food is equally undogmatic. In times of laxer regulations for the EU organic seal, Vom Einfachen das Gute prefers to place its faith in suppliers and their own commitment to producing cleanly—A policy that functions perfectly as long as one knows whom one is dealing with.

Portraits

Labels such as "organic" or "regional" quickly become superfluous when one maintains a relationship of trust with suppliers.

Portraits
Bæst

BÆST, THE RESTAURANT FOUNDED BY CHRISTIAN PUGLISI AND KIM ROSSEN, IS LOCATED IN GULDBERGSGADE IN COPENHAGEN, DENMARK, WHERE IT HAS SERVED DELICACIES FROM REGIONAL ORGANIC PRODUCTS PREPARED IN THE BUTCHER'S SHOP AND PIZZA OVEN SINCE 2014.

New Nordic cuisine meets traditional Italian artisanry.

Never mind the pølser, here's the charcuterie

Anyone visiting Copenhagen with an interest in food generally has a colorful mental checklist that includes artistically garnished smørrebrøds, excellent craft beer, and junk food favorites such as signal red pølser and packaged chocolate milk. Pizza did not usually appear on the list, at least, not until Bæst appeared on the scene. In the heart of the Nørrebro district, which has advanced to become one of Europe's most vibrant trend hotbeds, two guys who clearly know what they are doing have opened a pizzeria. Christian Puglisi and Kim Rossen earned their spurs a few kilometers away in the world famous Noma, at a time when the restaurant was beginning to turn the conventions of international high-end gastronomy on their head. After their departure, they opened the restaurant Relæ in Nørrebro, which quickly became one of the city's culinary landmarks. Because they know people can't live off stars alone, they have now devoted themselves to the manufacture of top class dough, mozzarella, and salumi.

The Danish influence on the traditional Italian dish forms an integral part of the concept. The pizzas are sourdough, with the grain originating from local farms. In order to meet their high demands with respect to mozzarella, they produce it themselves from fresh, regional, organic milk. They have also taken things into their own hands when it comes to the charcuterie—from bresaola to ham and fennel salami, and from lardo to jerky and pork scratchings, they produce the best that the respective breed of pig or cow has to offer. And if one isn't already full from the charcuterie, then there are the delicious, atypical pizza creations from the 500-degree brick oven. Sure, even in Bæst purists can enjoy a classic Margherita with tomato and mozzarella, however, anyone who really wants to taste the Danish experience should try a variation with scratchings, new potatoes, or cornflowers. In Bæst, Puglisi and Rossen bring together the seemingly incompatible—and it works perfectly.

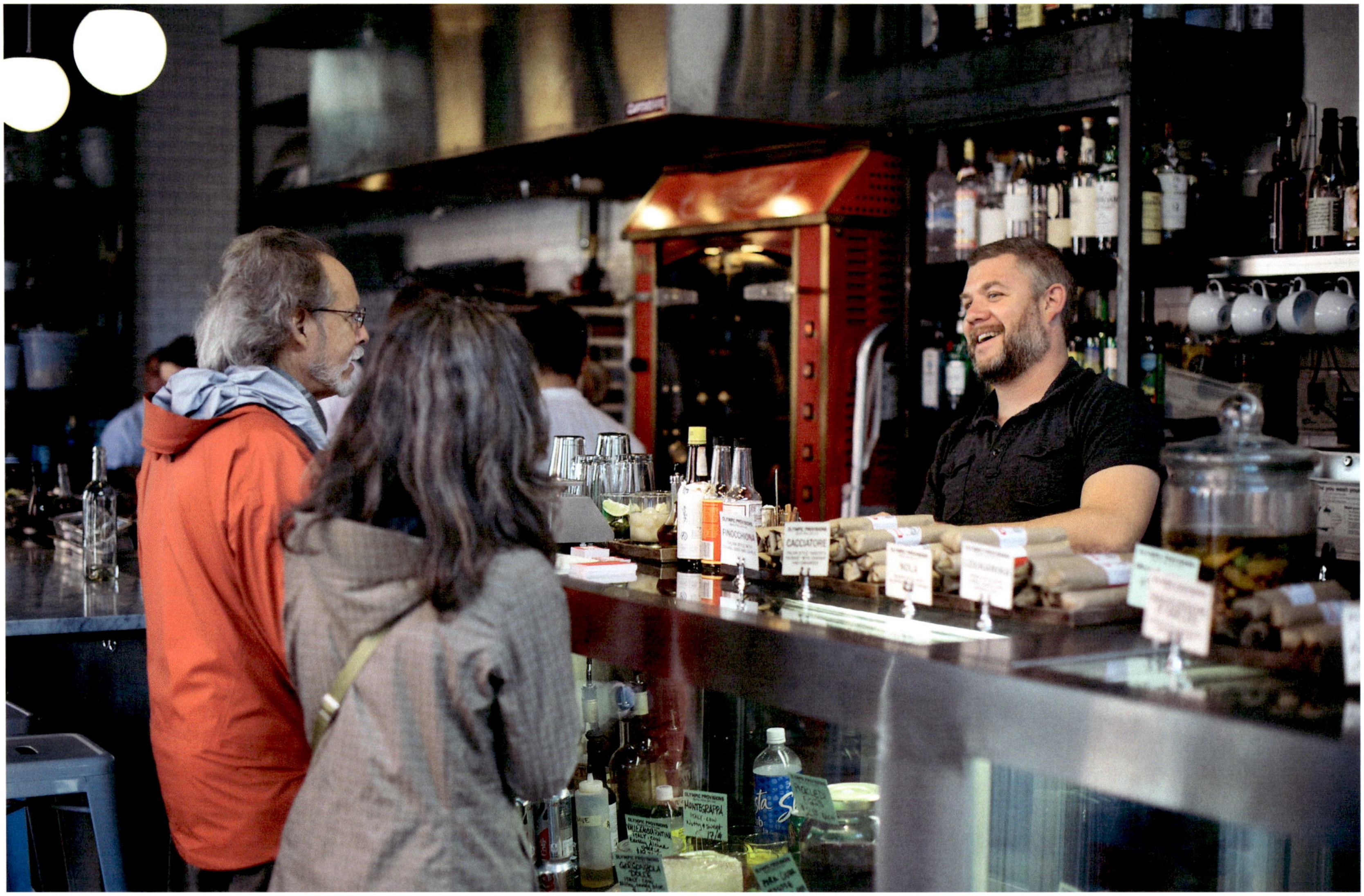
FINOCCHIONA
CACCIATORE
NOLA
MONTEGRAPPA

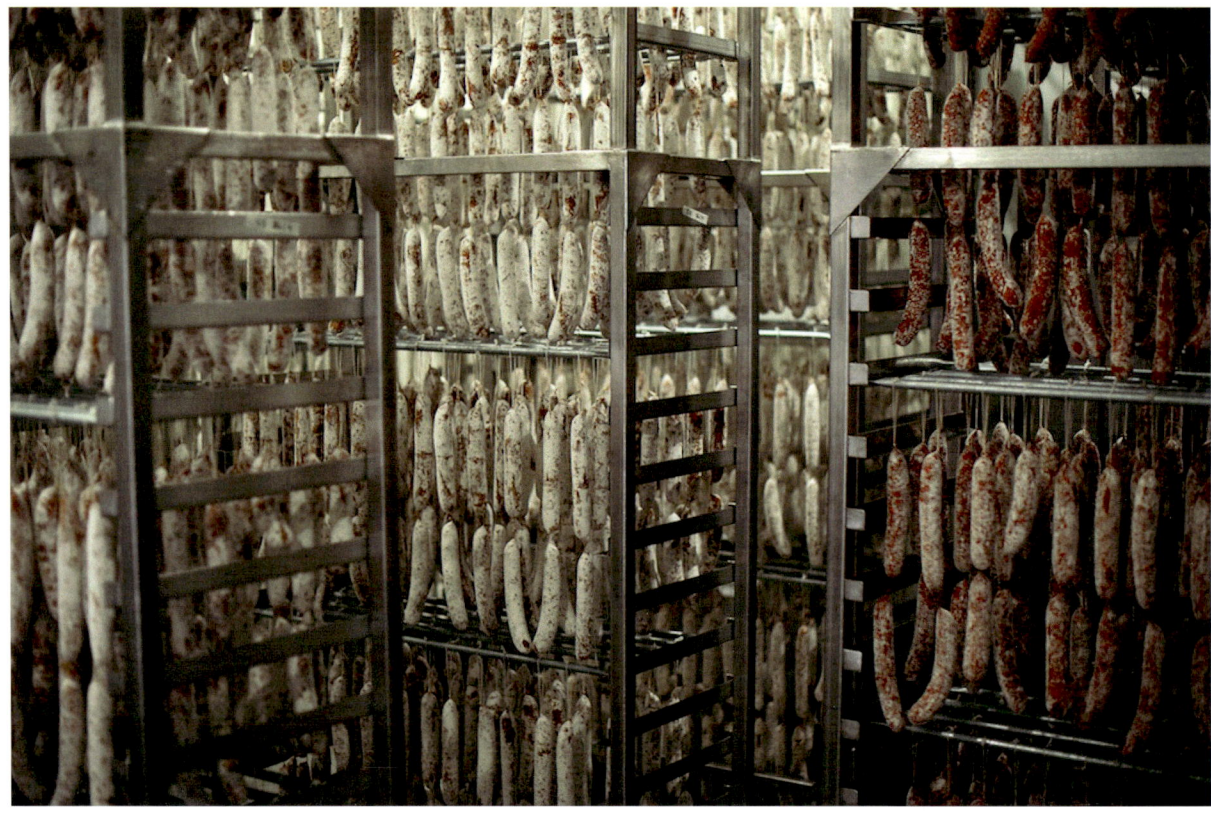

Olympia Provisions

"Charcuterie is both an art and a science. We approach it with inspired precision."

THE OLYMPIA PROVISIONS SHOP, LOCATED IN THE HEART OF PORTLAND, OPENED IN 2009. SINCE THEN THE SHOP'S RICH ASSORTMENT OF CHARCUTERIE AND THE MENU FROM THE ADJOINING RESTAURANT HAVE BEEN WOWING FOODIES ACROSS THE COUNTRY.

Medal-worthy

The Olympic Committee turned a blind eye for some time, and then they struck. Since the start of 2015, Elias Cairo's grandiose sausages can no longer be sold under the name, Olympic Provisions. Whether Olympia Provisions is a suitable replacement name is up to the individual. However, one thing is certain: if sausage making was an Olympic discipline, the charming business from Portland would be assured a place on the winners rostrum.

In the unanimous opinion of local insiders, Cairo's sausages are amongst the city's finest specialties—great praise in a food metropolis such as Portland. However, before perfecting his artisanry, Cairo undertook a long journey through Europe. He completed his chef training in Switzerland, where he discovered his passion for the art of charcuterie. His gaze then turned to Italy, falling on coppa and mortadella; in Spain he was enticed by the fire-red chorizo; and France entranced him with coarse rillette and fine pâté.

Whether he simply couldn't live without these beloved specialties upon returning to the USA, or whether he set out to delight the inhabitants of his home town with European sausage culture is unknown. However, it wasn't long before he set up his own sausage production facility. As a child he inherited a penchant for handicraft, and since he didn't want to leave anything to chance, the manufacturing process was conducted with mathematical precision from the very start. Anyone who relies solely on the magic of the natural ripening process also needs to keep a watchful eye on the environmental conditions and the quality of the raw materials.

That the interplay of the flavors in Olympia Provisions' specialties—the flavors of best quality pork, coarse backfat, sea salt, garlic, and freshly pestled herbs—achieve perfection is due to the importance given to the time factor. The ripening process simply takes time; it cannot be rushed. And suddenly it is clear why sausage making can never be an Olympic discipline—the gold medal would be awarded to the slowest competitor.

Landfleischerei Neumeier

THE LANDFLEISCHEREI NEUMEIER IN WALBURG, A SMALL VILLAGE IN THE CENTRAL GERMAN STATE OF HESSE SURROUNDED BY NATURE RESERVES, BEGAN PRODUCING SAUSAGES AND HAM IN 1968. IN 1991 CARSTEN NEUMEIER TOOK OVER THE SHOP FROM HIS PARENTS, WHICH NOW COUNTS THE FEDERAL PRESIDENT AMONGST ITS CUSTOMERS.

Portraits

Portraits

With "sch" please

That sausage is not just sausage should be clear by now. In the case of the Ahle Wurscht, this also applies to the phonetics. Anyone referring to sausage in its natural habitat of North Hessia without pronouncing the characteristic "sch" risks being laughed at. Additionally, traditional producers like Landfleischerei Neumeier are also ridiculed—at least by the large producers. Their production methods are antiquated, too inefficient, too laborious, and too expensive. Arguments that are not completely without justification, but are irrelevant in the face of the final, killer argument—the flavor.

On this issue, master butcher Carsten Neumeier is not prepared to compromise, although he is the first to admit that slaughtering single-handedly is costly in terms of both time and material. However, ultimately it is this approach that guarantees complete transparency, from the source of the animals and the quality of the meat to the slaughtering process. The fact that the immediate processing of the slaughter-warm meat has to be conducted in accordance with strict hygiene regulations is not a problem either. After all, this traditional method not only contributes to the products' characteristic flavor, but also allows Neumeier to dispense with artificial binding agents such as phosphates and citrates.

He is also intransigent when it comes to the long, dry-ripening, during which the sausages lose up to 50% of their weight. With every day in the ripening shed, the aroma becomes more and more intense. Carsten Neumeier dedicates every single step of the sausage production to the taste of his product. For anyone who has tasted his Ahle Wurscht, it is clear that it is precisely this ethos that is responsible for the difference in taste from the mass-produced sausage. The love that he heaps on his Ahle Wurscht can also be found in his liverwurst, blood sausage, and aspic, as nothing is thrown away.

By the by, this classic form of artisanry is much more fun than operating the controls of high-end machines in large-scale operations. And as quality always wins out in the end, Cartsen Neumeier can be assured of his future.

For the best tasting Ahle Wurscht, every traditional means is permissible.

Čestr

OPPOSITE THE CZECH NATIONAL MUSEUM, IN THE CENTER OF PRAGUE, YOU WILL FIND THE RESTAURANT ČESTR. SINCE 2011 IT HAS CELEBRATED EVERY PART OF THE COW—IN ITS ARCHITECTURE, THE GLAZED RIPENING ROOM, AND, NOT LEAST, THE FOOD ON ITS PLATES.

The finest from the spotted cow

Prague is a paradise for lovers of sausage and meat specialties. The market stalls abound with long-ripened and smoked specialties, private butchers foster the rich eastern European sausage culture, and the restaurants delight guests with traditional hearty fare. However, the Česká restaurant, situated between the National Museum and the State Opera, takes things one step further. Here, the animal is also celebrated in name. Česká is an abbreviation of Česká strakata kráva, the name of a Czech breed of cattle, recognizable from afar thanks to its dapper brown spots.

Employing traditional artisanry and a focus on meat from local animals, the team from Česká has gained an excellent reputation. The secret is to be found in the simplicity. Thanks to an open kitchen, the chefs not only allow customers to see them at work, but also delight in occasionally bringing the food to the table.

Meat cuisine of the highest standard doesn't have to be accompanied by pretentious behavior. Every imaginable cut of dry-aged beef—and this is meant literally—is served on rustic wooden platters. A menu consisting solely of filet would be much too boring. A steak from thick skirt—a cut of meat close to the diaphragm—provides a sensational taste experience. A grilled top blade steak or a strong bone broth is not available on every street corner, so why not?

A map, locating and explaining the various cuts of the animal, helps in compiling one's own personal menu. And when a dish is sold out, the restaurant simply offers what the farmers happen to have available, serving it with "hairy" dumplings from raw potatoes, homemade sauces, and salads with fresh vegetables from the market. And as the Česká team is happy to share their secrets, raw meat is also sold for home consumption accompanied by free, professional cooking tips.

The filet steak is obligatory. However, aficionados prefer top blade and thick skirt.

L'Antica Macelleria Cecchini

L'ANTICA MACELLERIA CECCHINI, DARIO CECCHINI BUTCHER'S SHOP WITH ADJOINING RESTAURANT IS LOCATED IN CHIANTI, OR MORE PRECISELY, IN THE SMALL ITALIAN VILLAGE OF PANZANO, AN HOUR'S DRIVE FROM FLORENCE. NOW IN ITS EIGHTH GENERATION, THE MASTER BUTCHER CONTINUES TO SERVE TOP QUALITY MEAT AT THE TABLE AND COUNTER.

"Abandon hope all ye who enter, for you are now in the hands of a butcher!"

Dante Alighieri

Between nose-to-tail and rock and roll

Anyone visiting Panzano in Chianti in search of Antica Macelleria Cecchini should close their eyes and use their ears. As soon as the raucous guitars of AC/DC can be heard then it cannot be far. Dario Cecchini, Italy's most famous butcher, is a fan of rock music, and anyone visiting his establishment is going to get an ear full of it, which does not stop culinary adventurers from around the world from making the pilgrimage to savor Cecchini's famous butcher's menu.

The aperitif is served immediately on arrival in the salesroom—a glass of light red wine with acidity that cuts perfectly through the thickly sliced fennel salami and crostinis, generously topped with lardo. Cecchini greets his guests with a handshake that could crack a coconut, and as his English, despite international acclaim, has not improved.

He directs the way to the building on the other side of the street using hands and feet. This is where the restaurant, decorated with meat cleavers, is located, and where the nose-to-tail menu from beef will be served—the perfect expression of Cecchini's philosophy. The guests are seated together at large tables and share the food, which is served dish by dish on steaming plates. The juicy roast is a dream, however, the real highlights from Cecchini's kitchen are prepared from cuts less favored by the mainstream. These include large sausages from parts of the head, simply served with a broth and a squeeze of lemon juice, strongly seasoned ragout from meat and innards on bread, and pieces of boiled meat deep fried in a beer batter. For purists, side dishes such as white beans, raw vegetables, bread and olive oil will not disappoint. No Michelin stars here, just an incomparable culinary experience.

Technology and tastes may have changed over the decades and centuries, but the esteem in which the Cecchini family hold animals remains unchanged after eight generations. Paired with their high quality standards, this has given rise to one of Europe's major hotspots for meat lovers. It is an ethos which can also be found back in the shop, where anyone interested in Cecchini's greatest specialty, the Bistecca Fiorentina, can only buy it together with other parts of the animal purely for reasons of respect.

Die Steakschaft

BUTCHER DIRK LUDWIG'S NEWLY OPENED MEAT EXPERIENCE CENTER, DIE STEAKSCHAFT, IS LOCATED IN SCHLÜCHTERN IN THE CENTRAL GERMAN STATE OF HESSE, WHERE AFICIONADOS CAN EXPLORE THE NEW MEAT CULTURE VIA BUTCHERING COURSES, MEAT SEMINARS, AND STEAK TASTING EVENTS.

The good, modern times

The Carnothek is the fulfillment of the wildest dreams of meat lovers from around the globe: a majestically illuminated, glass-enclosed ripening chamber for dry aged beef with a real salt wall. This is where the meat ripens for up to 12 weeks that Dirk Ludwig, aka "Der Ludwig," uses to make his coveted steaks—or "Schteeks" as he pronounces it. The heart of his Steakschaft in the north Hessian town of Schlüchtern is the Carnothek, simultaneously an eye-catcher, an integral part of the production process, and a symbol of Ludwig's working method.

In his business, care and quality take first place—nostalgia and references to the supposed good old days are nowhere to be found. The Steakschaft is a place where the traditional butcher's craft, combined with entrepreneurial spirit, passion, and brains, is transported into the modern age. Alongside classic methods such as wet and dry-aging, Dirk has developed his own method for ripening meat. With so-called "aqua-aging," the cuts ripen in an airtight mineral water bath. The carbon dioxide in the water produces spectacularly tender meat. Some steaks are also ripened in buttermilk or fine beech wood ashes, which lend them their own unique flavor. Whatever produces a good flavor is allowed, and conventions are there to be broken.

Ludwig's passion for experimentation does not stop at production methods—his starting products are not found on every corner. In response to those who find pork boring, there is Ludwig's T-bone steak from fat Mangalitsa pigs, which he is sure will make them reconsider. Equally impressive is the meat from old cows in Spanish Txogitxu style, a feast for lovers of intense meat flavors. And as pleasure is known to increase when shared, Dirk Ludwig has also embarked on his own educational mission. In a range of courses he demonstrates how to fry a steak correctly, make sausages, and even how to butcher an animal. Welcome to the good, modern times.

Portraits

Gebroeders de Wolf

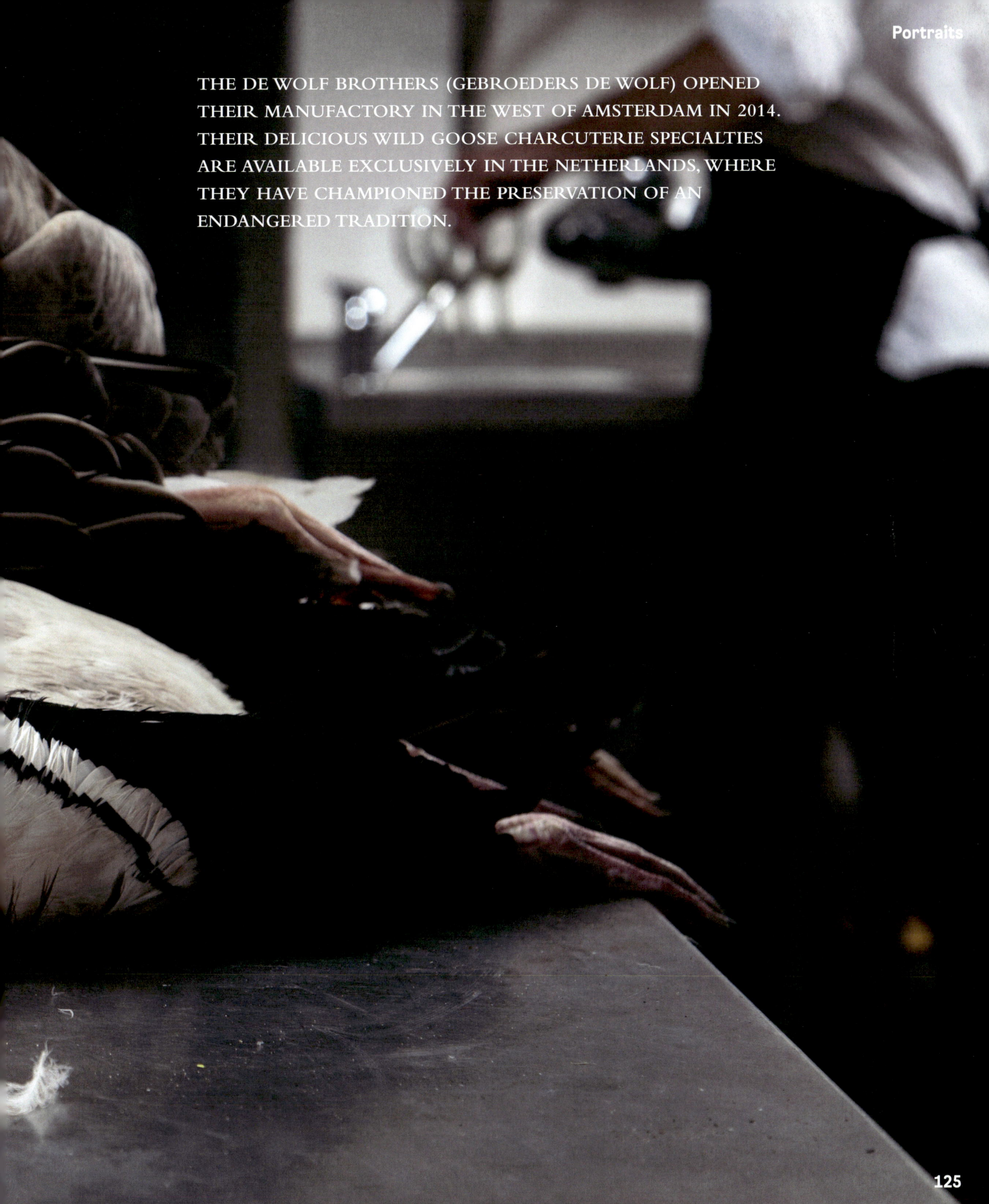

THE DE WOLF BROTHERS (GEBROEDERS DE WOLF) OPENED THEIR MANUFACTORY IN THE WEST OF AMSTERDAM IN 2014. THEIR DELICIOUS WILD GOOSE CHARCUTERIE SPECIALTIES ARE AVAILABLE EXCLUSIVELY IN THE NETHERLANDS, WHERE THEY HAVE CHAMPIONED THE PRESERVATION OF AN ENDANGERED TRADITION.

Portraits

A Question of respect

Martijn van de Reep and Tom Zinger, better known as Gebroeders de Wolf, are not your usual hunters—they can rightly claim to be the guardians of an almost forgotten tradition. As masters of wild goose charcuterie, they not only produce unique delicacies from goose meat, but also fight to redress a grave state of affairs concerning the animals.

Hunting wild geese and the consumption of their products was not unusual in Netherlands—until a decades-long ban on hunting was imposed. Over the years, the population of the animals has risen enormously, creating considerable problems for many farmers, especially in the summer months. The repeal of the hunting ban came late, perhaps too late. A large number of the birds are now shot, without subsequently being used for food production—not least because much of the knowledge of the craft techniques has now been lost. This is an intolerable situation for van de Reep and Zinger, whose love for their products can be heard in every syllable they utter. Naturally, they hunt and slaughter the animals themselves as maintaining control over the complete process is an integral part of their culinary vision.

Employing classic French methods, they produce an impressive range of products from a typical Dutch bird. The lean, dark meat can be found in intensely flavored sausages, made into wonderfully savory terrines, or smoked and cut into slices. Fattier parts, such as the legs, are used to make delicate rillettes and hearty confit. All the products have an intense flavor, which, regardless of what part of the animal they are made from, make the hearts of game connoisseurs beat faster.

It is a question of honor for the Gebroeders de Wolf that nothing is thrown away out of respect for the animals. Their success has also proven them correct. More and more delicatessens across the country are clamoring for the wild goose charcuterie from the brothers..

Portraits

Everything has to be made oneself—the single-handed execution of the complete production process is obligatory for Zinger and van de Reep.

Le Bourdonnec

YVES-MARIE LE BOURDONNEC, FRANCE'S MOST WELL-KNOWN BUTCHER, IS A LIVING EXPONENT OF GOOD MEAT WHO VOCIFEROUSLY DEFENDS HIS CONVICTIONS. HIS UNIQUE MEAT SPECIALTIES, WHICH SO MANY OF HIS COUNTRYMEN SWEAR BY, HAVE BEEN AVAILABLE IN HIS BUTCHER'S SHOP ON THE AVENUE VICTOR HUGO SINCE 2012.

The rebel

At the tender age of 10 it was already apparent that Yves-Marie Le Bourdonnec was different from other children, insisting on being present when his uncle, the village butcher, came to slaughter the family's hand reared pig. Captivated by the beauty of the scene, it was clear to him that he wanted to be a butcher—and as quickly as possible.

In 1992 Le Bourdonnec opened his first business, Le Couteau d'Argent, in Asnières near Paris at the age of 19. With every passing year his reputation as a meticulous quality fanatic rose, and in 2012 he opened his first shop in the center of the capital, followed by two more.

Le Bourdonnec loves raw meat. Tender and rich in flavor, with little collagen, and a balanced fat structure are properties achieved by dry-ripening the meat for between 40 and 60 days, with gut instinct and experience deciding on the precise timing. However, it is the rearing of the animals that he sees as decisive for the best quality. Nothing is possible without stress-free husbandry, natural grass fodder, and the right terroir. One minute—terroir? The right habitat is just as important for Le Bourdonnec as it is for a winegrower cultivating regionally typical vines. Amongst others, Galician Red cattle and Longhorns from North Yorkshire are sold as terroir meat.

He is less disposed to French breeds, which given their high collagen content, are more suited to stewed dishes rather than grilling—a sentiment that doesn't make one many friends in France. After expressing this opinion on a TV show, he was expelled from the national butcher's association. That he is not frightened of controversy is also shown by the fact that he refuses to serve certain star chefs for personal reasons.

Le Bourdonnec is concerned about more than just producing the finest quality meats. He also wants to repair the system, seeing himself as a pioneer of a new movement of butchers who share his values. He promotes the younger generation, assisting with training events, and works closely with breeders to produce ever better results. His critics accuse him of a penchant for self-promotion. Ultimately, however, the results have proven him right.

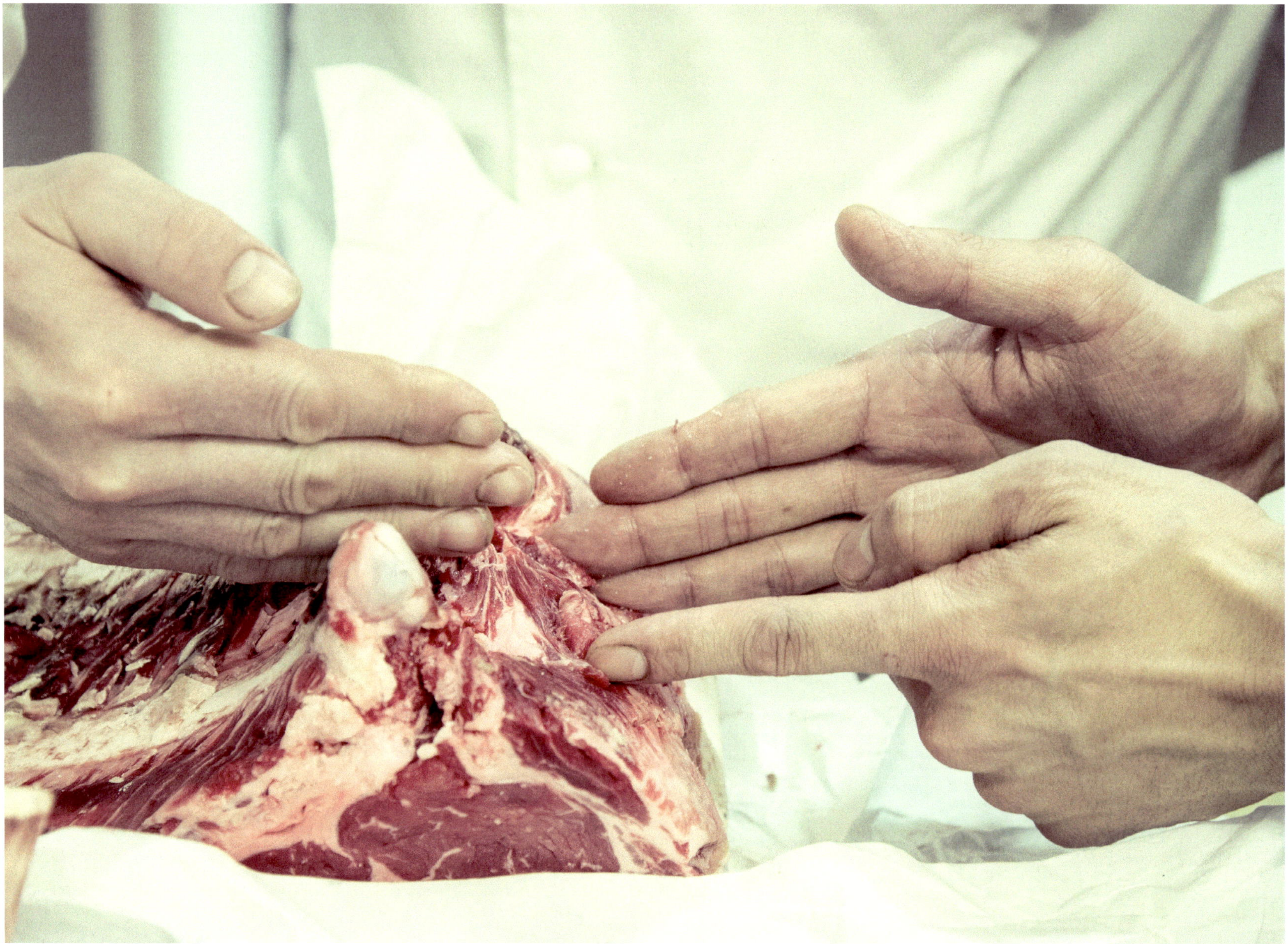

Portraits

Portraits

Yves-Marie Le Bourdonnec wants to do more than produce the best meat. He wants to repair the system.

Portraits

Salt & Time Butcher Shop

The Salt & Time Butcher's Shop and Salumeria with integrated restaurant can be found in Austin, Texas in the south of the U.S. Since 2010 it has produced exquisite specialties from meat supplied by regional ranches: home-made frying sausages, salami, and smoked meats as well as pickles, stocks, and matching sauces.

At the right time and the right place

It began at a farmer's market where Ben Runkle, an acknowledged devotee of European charcuterie, first sold his cured ham and sausage products. He named his stand Salt & Time, after the two essential ingredients in the refinement of raw meat for production of palate-teasing delicacies.

Runkle's products quickly advanced to become an insider tip amongst local culinary enthusiasts, and he soon got to know the master butcher, Bryan Butler, over a sausage. In order to expand their range of products, the two joined forces, opening their own shop in 2013. A short while later, word of mouth reached the local and national media, and reporting went through the roof. The niche business specializing in small takeaway snacks soon mushroomed into a full-scale restaurant, with cook Josh Jones's burgers being listed amongst the "21 Essential Hamburgers in America" by the national foodie portal, Eater—the ultimate accolade.

Everyone wants meat from Salt & Time. However, they don't always make it easy for their customers with their rigorous nose-to-tail ethos. Pork breast, matambre meat rolls from beef flank steak, and lamb belly are generally not the most popular parts of the animal. However, Salt & Time have made it their mission to exploit the potential of these cuts to the fullest.

In the restaurant and butcher's shop, traditional methods are employed, but not always according to old recipes, with exciting new creations sold alongside classics such as fennel salami, chorizo, and mortadella. Whether it is salami with Chilean Pequin chilies, coppa with citrus and cumin notes, or hot N'Duja Tejano spread—international influences, especially Central and South American, characterize the work of Salt & Time. In contrast, the meat is supplied from Texan sustainable farms, generally in the form of whole animals. For the purchase of Akaushi cattle, Dorper sheep, and Red Wattle pigs, long-term partnerships have been concluded with farmers, relieving them of a little of the market pressure. By such measures, Runkle, Butler, and Jones have endeared themselves to suppliers, not to mention their expansive fan base.

Portraits

Schlachtfest

SINCE 2014 A GROUP OF ENTHUSIASTS IN THE KREUZBERG DISTRICT OF BERLIN HAVE BEEN STEELING THEMSELVES IN THE CULINARY ART OF USING THE WHOLE ANIMAL. THAT THIS IS ANYTHING BUT A SOBER AFFAIR IS DEMONSTRATED BY THE SCHLACHTFESTE, A SHOWCASING OF NUMEROUS DISHES IN CELEBRATION OF THE SLAUGHTERED COW, PIG, OR SHEEP.

A lively celebration in honor of tradition

Large crowds in Berlin's Markthalle Neun in the heart of Kreuzberg are not unusual, especially since advancing to become the city's food melting pot over recent years. However, on this day the people are not queuing for gourmet burgers, kimchi, or mezze, but for pickled trotters, deep-fried ears, and blood sausage.

We are at the second Schlachtfest, and this time it is the "Pig Edition"—a culinary meeting convened by food artisans. The chefs Susan Choi and Stefan Endres from Mr. Susan; Lode van Zuylen and Stijn Remi from Lode + Stijn; master butcher Simon Ellery from The Sausage Man Never Sleeps; and creative director Kavita Goodstar drew their inspiration from the tradition of the village festival known in Germany as Schlachtfest. Although the founders have their roots in different parts of the world, they were all inspired by the same idea of a lively village celebration where everyone comes together to share a meal from a slaughtered animal.

They decided to transport this experience to the reality of today's Berlin. At the end of 2014 they began organizing quarterly celebrations in cooperation with selected farmers from the Brandenburg region, at which an animal is prepared and eaten, nose-to-tail. Shortly before the event, it is communally slaughtered and butchered. The start was made with a Charlois cow from Bernau. Lode + Stijn lovingly prepared the organs, Mr. Susan enticed with a Korean BBQ, and Kantine 9 served chips fried in smoked beef fat.

At the following Pig Edition, two free-range Saddleback pigs from the Gut Hirschaue farm supplied a fantastic broth made from the heads, and gnocco fritto was deep-fried in the fat, while butcher Simon Ellery excelled himself with his sausages. Grilled heart and dumplings from head and tongue were among the highlights at the lamb-themed Schlachtfest. Every part of the animal is equally important, the processing a question of respect for the life of the animal and the environment.

For ticket holders, there are a limited number of places for those wishing to participate in the slaughtering and butchering of the animals. For a stronger connection to the food on the plate; in honor of the rich tradition of the Schlachtfest; and because it tastes damn good.

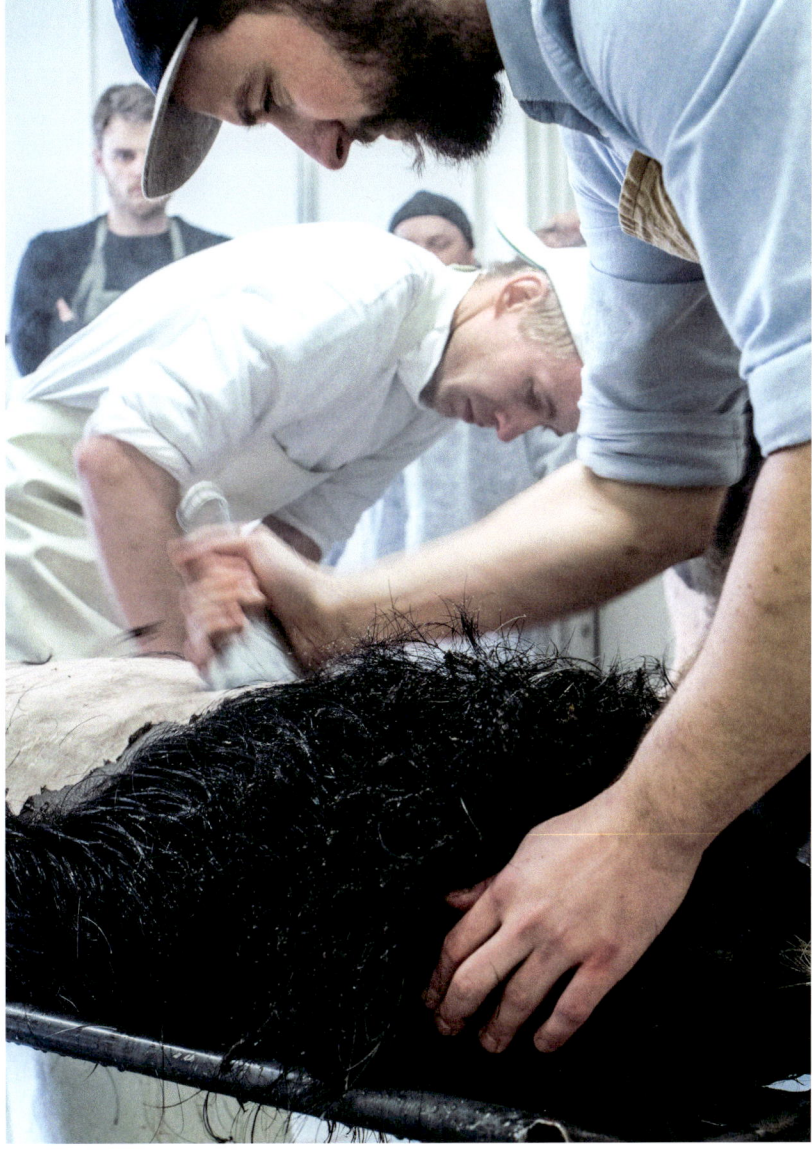

Portraits

The main goal is to transport the tradition of the Schlachtfest, where the whole village comes together, to the metropolitan context.

Portraits

B.E.S.H.

THE PICTURESQUE HOHENLOHE REGION OF BADEN-WÜRTTEMBERG IS THE STOMPING GROUND OF THE FARMER'S COOPERATIVE BÄUERLICHE ERZEUGERGEMEINSCHAFT SCHWÄBISCH-HALL E.V., KNOWN AS B.E.S.H. FOR SHORT. SINCE 1988 IT HAS FOUGHT FOR THE PRESERVATION OF OLD ANIMAL BREEDS USED FOR THE PRODUCTION OF DELICIOUS SPECIALTIES.

Savior of the black spotted pig

It may appear paradoxical to eat animals in order to save them. However, the pig breed known as the Swabian-Hall swine would no longer exist if it wasn't for a group of regional farmers, led by Rudolf Bühler, who decided to start breeding and slaughtering them again. In 1982 the old breed from the Hohenlohe region in the northeast of Baden Württemberg was faced with extinction, displaced by other, high performance breeds that could be more effectively employed in mass production. This was an intolerable situation for Rudolf Bühler.

Together with other farmers, he kept the remaining animals and meticulously set about increasing their numbers. First a breeding association was founded, followed by an agricultural producers cooperative, the Schwäbisch-Hall e.V., for the joint marketing of the products—a gift for Swabia's culinary enthusiasts. The meat of the slowly growing Swabian-Hall swine excels in every respect. With its fine marbling and greater tenderness, it easily beats the supermarket competition. Its pleasantly hearty character is shown to perfect advantage in well-ripened salami, or freshly ground and spread raw on a roll to make German mettbrötchen.

In the beer gardens, pork shoulder and ham hock entices guests, and anyone who has ever tried the air-dried ham will never return to the mass produced varieties. The stubbornness of Bühler and his compatriots has paid off. Step by step they have established their own production chain for the beloved cloven-hoofed animals with black heads. Since 2001 the cooperative has even had its own abattoir, thus gaining complete control of the production process including the slaughter of the animals. Under strict, self-imposed guidelines, the farmers rigorously maintain their course, and their numbers are increasing. BESH now has around 1,400 farmers in is ranks.
Bühler and his compatriots have seen with their own eyes how quickly a breed of pig can be brought to the edge of extinction, and don't intend to let this happen again. That their endeavors have also provided undreamed of taste experiences is a welcome side effect.

Without the efforts of a number of passionate farmers, the Swabian-Hall swine would have long been extinct.

Portraits

Naše maso

IN 2014, THE SMALL BUTCHER'S SHOP NAŠE MASO OPENED IN PRAGUE'S OLD TOWN. SINCE THEN THERE HAVE BEEN LONG LINES OF CUSTOMERS QUEUING FOR TARTAR FROM CZECH BEEF, AND SAUSAGES FROM PŘEŠTICE PIGS. AND FOR THE REALLY HUNGRY THERE IS THE SHOP'S INTEGRATED BISTRO.

Portraits

Burger joint with star quality

At no other location in Prague is there such a high concentration of specialist shops than in the Dlouhá Gourmet Passage. However, anyone searching for Naše maso only has to look for the longest queue. Shortly after opening, the rumor made the rounds of local foodies that this was where the city's best burgers were fried—first by word of mouth, then via the international rating portals.

Expectations were naturally very high. Dalibor Křivánek had left Michelin rated Degustation Bohême Bourgeoise to work as head chef and sales manger at the small butchery with tiny bistro. František Kšána Jr. is the son of a legendary master butcher from Prague, who continues his father's life work with bravura. On top of this, Naše maso has a committed owner behind it, Tomáš Karpíšek's Ambiente group, which has caused a stir in the Czech food scene with its high-end restaurant and shop concepts.

However, the team itself passes on the compliments to their farm suppliers. Heifers from Zbiroh, which, thanks to sophisticated fodder, produce meat with the best possible fat structure, resulting in an incomparably tender mouthfeel; Přeštice pigs from the west of the Czech republic, an old breed that grows slowly, also accumulate lots of tasty fat. Over recent decades the population reached dangerously low levels after the animals were removed from mass production due to their inefficiency. Resourceful butchers such as Kšána brought about a renaissance of the breed as free-range pigs, and today customers tear the wonderfully intense sausages out of his hands.

Then there is the obligatory beef from Czech Fleckvieh, a hallmark of the Ambiente chain. It is especially aromatic, and, at Naše maso, is used to make steak tartare to die for. No product is without its name. The producers are proud of their goods and delight in highlighting their special qualities—a concept that is so well received that a second shop had to be opened in the Dlouhá Passage, which exclusively sells freshly packed meat.

But what about the burger? It consists of a bun, meat, gherkin, and homemade mustard. Nothing more, nothing less—and it is perfect.

Tourists and locals are crazy about Naše maso's burgers and steak tartare. Unfortunately, the number of tables can be counted on one hand.

Portraits

Underground Food Collective

THE UNDERGROUND FOOD COLLECTIVE IN MADISON, THE CAPITAL OF THE U.S. STATE OF WISCONSIN, WAS FOUNDED IN 2009. HERE OLD BREEDS OF PIG AND GOAT REARED ON FARMS FROM THE SURROUNDING REGION FORM THE BASIS FOR CHARCUTERIE SPECIALTIES INSPIRED BY ITALIAN, SPANISH, AND FRENCH DELICACIES.

You can take the butcher out of the underground, but you can never take the underground out of the butcher.

The sausage guerrillas

Anyone operating underground is hard to find. However, this characteristic provided the Underground Food Collective from Madison with a decisive advantage over other companies—extravagance. As a catering service, they were never bound to a set cuisine in the early days anyway, which didn't stop news of the passion and finesse of this loose group of culinary enthusiasts from getting around.

When there was no alternative to opening their own restaurant, they launched the Forequarter, which was an immediate success. Over time, however, Jonny Hunter, Ben Hunter, and Mel Trudeau developed a special relationship to meat and charcuterie, which up until then the collective had only bought as ingredients for its ingenious menus. Though they had long since left the underground, their DIY mentality remained, so they taught themselves how to slaughter and butcher whole animals, freeing themselves from their dependence on suppliers of sausages and other products.

Underground Meats was born. Ripened goods from whole muscles such as pancetta or coppa form part of their product range, however, the specialty of these self-made butchers is their salami. They produce Tuscan fennel salami and soppressata with red wine and thyme according to traditional recipes, tickle the taste buds with smoky chorizo and hot ghost chili salami, and always have seasonal surprises in store.

Underground Meats works closely with small farmers—bloated trading structures are anathema to them—obtaining their pork from old breeds such as Tamworth, Black Mulefoot, and Red Wattle, which have all been reared with respect for the environment and the quality of life of the animals. A unique specialty is their goat salami from the male animal, which on dairy farms are often killed senselessly, being of no use for milk production. And, as befitting true guerrillas, they share the knowledge they have acquired in order to broaden the movement. Hunter and company not only hold butchering courses for potential competitors, they have also posted their meticulously developed quality management plan as an open source document on the Internet to help up-and-coming colleagues over the hurdle of USDA certification—an alternative to the mainstream.

Portraits

Smoking Goose

AT THE COUNTER OF THE SMOKING GOOSE BUTCHERS IN NORTH DORMAN STREET IN INDIANAPOLIS, ONE IS IMPRESSED BY THE THE NUMEROUS HANDMADE AND SLOW-RIPENED SPECIALTIES. SINCE 2007 THE SHOP HAS SPECIALIZED EXCLUSIVELY IN MEAT FROM HEALTHY ANIMALS SUPPLIED BY SMALL FARMERS FROM THE SURROUNDING STATE OF INDIANA.

Portraits

Inspired by the passion of the farmers supplying his shop, Chris Eley set out to produce his own sausages.

From Indiana with love

Chris Eley loves three things: his wife Mollie, good food, and his hometown of Indianapolis. This is where he cut his teeth in the world of gastronomy, which ultimately led to culinary school in Chicago. With sound training in his back pocket, he returned in 2007 to unite his three great passions, opening Goose the Market—a delicatessen with a generously proportioned meat and sausage counter—together with Mollie.

As they both focused on suppliers from Indianapolis, they soon established close trading links with local food artisans and farmers. They got to know a cheese producer with his own dairy herd—who also keeps Berkshire pigs on the side that are fed on the resulting whey—and the farmers from the neighboring Conner Prairie living museum that rear the endangered Ossabaw Island hogs by employing methods of the nineteenth century.

Inspired by the passionate work of the farmers, they soon aspired to their own manufactory for sausage and ham specialties. In 2011 they opened Smoking Goose, which is now considered one of the city's major culinary highlights. Today they have around 40 products permanently on offer, including numerous specialties where Chris Eley has indulged his passion for experimentation. For example, the Stagberry Salame made from elk and dried blueberries, a harmonic combination of game and fruit in sausage form; and the Ciauscolo with fennel seeds, orange peel, and wort from a neighboring brewery, which is inspired by a central Italian specialty.

Despite all the enthusiasm for new flavors, the classics also have their place—from soppressata and merguez to andouille, the evergreens of the international sausage culture are all meticulously produced by hand. Both the filling of the sausages in natural gut and the tying of the nets for the air-drying of the salami are carried out manually. For Chris and Mollie Eley, real meat has its own story, which they gladly tell—it is all part of the Smoking Goose philosophy.

Portraits

Ark of Taste

THE ARK OF TASTE ARCHIVES THOUSANDS OF ENDANGERED DOMESTIC ANIMAL BREEDS, PLANTS, AND FOOD SPECIALTIES FROM AROUND THE WORLD. THE FIRST PASSENGERS FROM THE INTERNATIONAL PROJECT SET UP BY THE SLOW FOOD ORGANIZATION CAME ON BOARD IN 1996. SINCE THEN THEIR RANKS HAVE GROWN CONTINUALLY.

Portraits

The archive of the almost forgotten

The Ark of Taste can be described as a number of things: a protective measure for animals threatened with extinction, an international archive of regional kitchen cultures, and a potpourri of rare products for ambitious culinary enthusiasts. Maybe the most beautiful description sees the ark as an invitation to get to know, rediscover, and actively preserve a treasure trove of regional food cultures scattered throughout the world.

In 1996 it was founded by the Slow Food Foundation for Biodiversity in order to compile a list describing virtually forgotten foods, thus making a contribution to their preservation. This list includes both threatened breeds of farm animals and crops, as well as traditional, artisanal food products. In order to be added to the foundation's list, the item must meet criteria that go beyond its status as an endangered product. These include an extraordinary flavor and a character that lends its identity to the respective region. The products are compiled and described in cooperation with agricultural scientists, botanists, and veterinarians.

In 2015 the Ark of Taste included over 2,500 food items from around 125 countries. The list is publicly available on the website of the Slow Food Foundation for Biodiversity, and classified according to country and food category. From the Mutura sausage from Kenya and the Canadian Bay of Fundy algae, to the Taiwanese Maqaw mountain pepper and the pasture-reared Limpurger bullocks from southern Germany—the Ark of Taste provides a unique insight into the variety of the world's food cultures while highlighting the breeds and varieties that are in need of greater attention. It is only by getting to know the endangered products that consumers can make an active contribution to their preservation, whether by eating less of them or starting to consume them in order to support the producers.

In accordance with the motto "Saving by eating," passengers in the Ark have outstanding qualities and contribute to the identity of their native region.

Hood Food

SINCE THE BEGINNING OF 2015, THE CREATIVE DINNER CLUB, HOOD FOOD, HAS TOURED THE SWISS CAPITAL OF ZURICH WITH ITS DELICIOUS EVENTS. IN THE PROCESS THE THREE YOUNG CULINARY ENTHUSIASTS VALENTIN DIEM, LAURA SCHÄLCHLI, AND FANNY EISL TRANSFORM UNUSUAL AND SIMPLE PRODUCTS FROM THE LOCAL AREA INTO TASTY MORSELS.

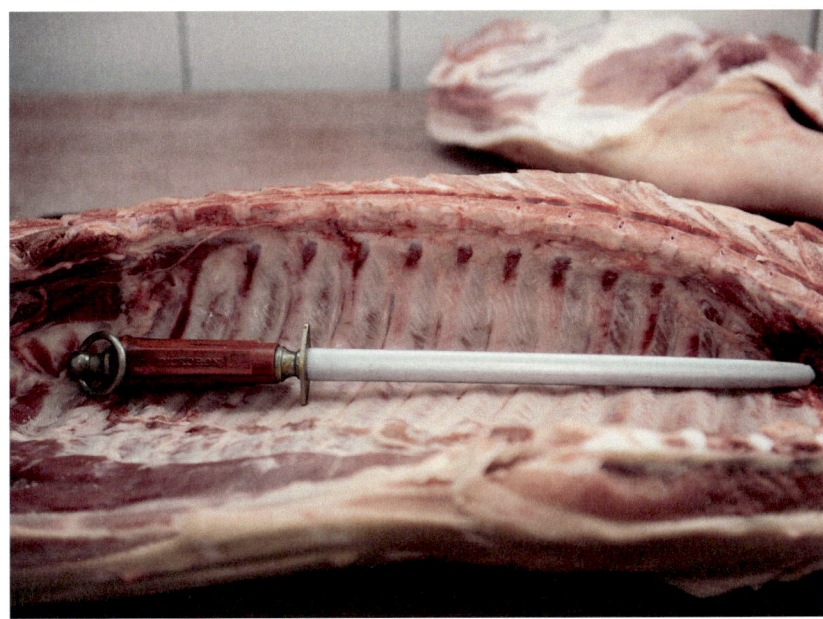

Avant-garde on the road

Valentin Diem is both a cook and a phantom. His avant-garde creations pop up continually at different sites throughout Zurich, outside the mechanisms of a normal restaurant business. While operating Vale Fritz, he rented the kitchen of a small bed and breakfast, running a catering service, and occasionally serving a classic menu in the dining room. Enter Fanny Eisl and Laura Schälchli.

While Eisl worked frequently with Diem within the context of her design studies, Schälchli contributed her widespread gastronomic knowledge from the Pollenzo Cookery School, which was developed by the University of Gastronomic Sciences in collaboration with Slow Food. As a trio they set out to bring a splash of color to Zurich's culinary scene in the form of theme-based pop-up restaurants.

With Wood Food they made a roaring start. Based on the theme of wood, guests were seated at long wooden tables, while Valentin Diem cooked at the open fire. The menu included smoked breasts of duck and carp, grilled lamb hearts, and a fantastic sausage seasoned with a dash of white wine infused with wood. For the latest event they drew inspiration from their immediate environment. Hood Food takes the regional-based approach one step further. In search of the best products from their immediate neighborhood, they met the farmer couple, Sennhauser, who breed pigs by leaving the majority of the work to nature.

The menu, served for a month in the Tiefenbrunnen mill, was built around the pigs of the Demeter-certified farmers from Rossrüti, which were prepared nose-to-tail, or vom Schnörrli zum Schwänzli as the Swiss say. Diem served little works of art such as stuffed pig's stomach with lemon verbena, dried filet, braised cheeks, and stinging nettle blood sausage—always with a special eye for flavor, texture, and appearance. Side dishes included dandelion flowers, watercress velouté, birch tar, and cheese curd spätzle noodles, all with a clear reference to the neighborhood. Regardless of the next theme they choose, anyone in Zurich who values good food should keep their eyes open for Diem, Schälchli, and Eisl.

Diem, Schälchli, and Eisl's theme-based pop-up restaurants add a new facet to Zurich's culinary scene.

Arche de Wiskentale

CHRISTOPH AND ISABELL WIESNER'S FARM, ARCHE DE WISKENTALE, IS LOCATED IN THE HEART OF NATURE IN WISCHATHAL IN LOWER AUSTRIA, WHERE THE FAMILY HAS BRED THE OLD MANGALITSA BREED OF PIGS IN A BIOLOGICALLY CIRCULAR ECONOMY SINCE 1999.

Fluffy bandits

When the trees around the Arche de Wiskentale farm in the Lower Austrian wine district have been nibbled and plants uprooted, when the nights are filled with a low grunting, then the "Banditos" are out and about again. However, there is no cause for alarm. This is not evidence of a marauding biker gang, but Christoph and Isabell Wiesner's woolly pigs. After spending the first weeks of their lives with their mothers, they are free to explore their surroundings—their nickname comes from their habit of letting it rip once in a while. For the Wiesner family this is quite normal.

The Arche de Wiskentale farm operates according to natural cycles. Although specialized in Mangalitsa pigs, they also cultivate a variety of crops, which alongside fruit and vegetables includes sunflowers for producing oil. Throughout the farm one encounters freely roaming domestic geese, wild turkeys, and ducks, which the children tend to. Specially kept bees pollinate the plants, and the animal fodder is largely self-grown. Going against every efficiency and profit maximization trend, farms such as the Arche de Wiskentale are fascinating examples of the successful cooperation of man, animals, and plants. And, not least, they produce food of the highest quality, such as the air-dried ham modeled on Serrano, which ripening for up to three years.

The Mangalitsa pigs' generous proportions of fat finds its way into the ham where it is a carrier of wonderful aromas. The Wiesner's are devotees of international meat culture. Within the context of a farmyard party, they served a pig wrapped in stinging nettles and vine leaves, cooked in a hole in the ground according to the Hawaiian Luau tradition—a smoky and juicy delicacy. Anyone keen to sample the classic, though no less delicious products such as bacon, Käsekrainer sausages, or fresh meat need to keep an eye on the calendar. The animals are only slaughtered in the fall, and the woolly pig specialties are in great demand.

Portraits

For the Wiesner family it is not about growth and efficiency, but successful cooperation between man, animals, and plants.

Portraits

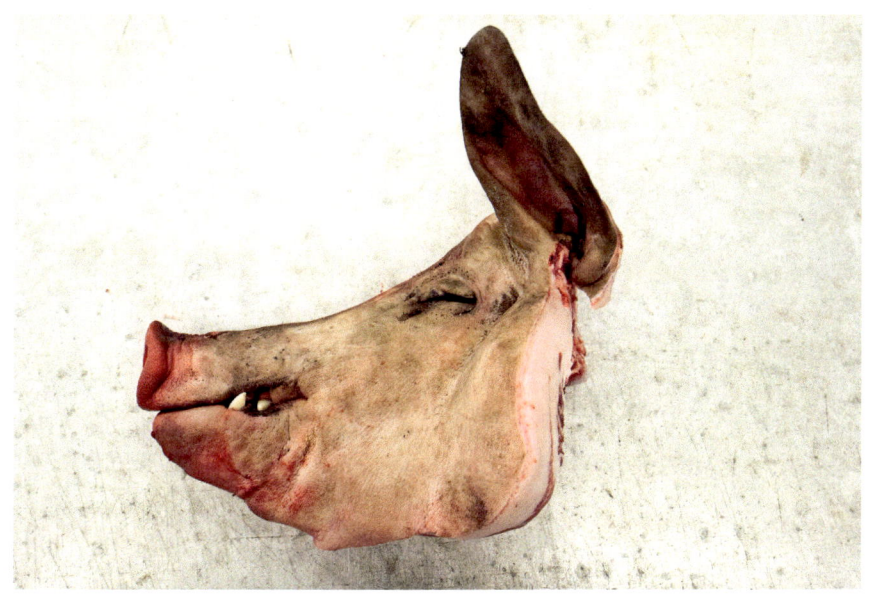
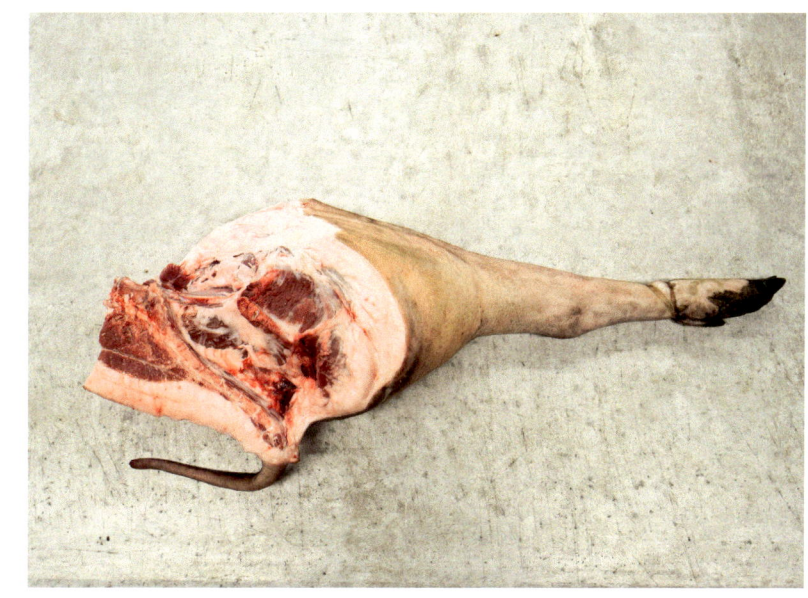

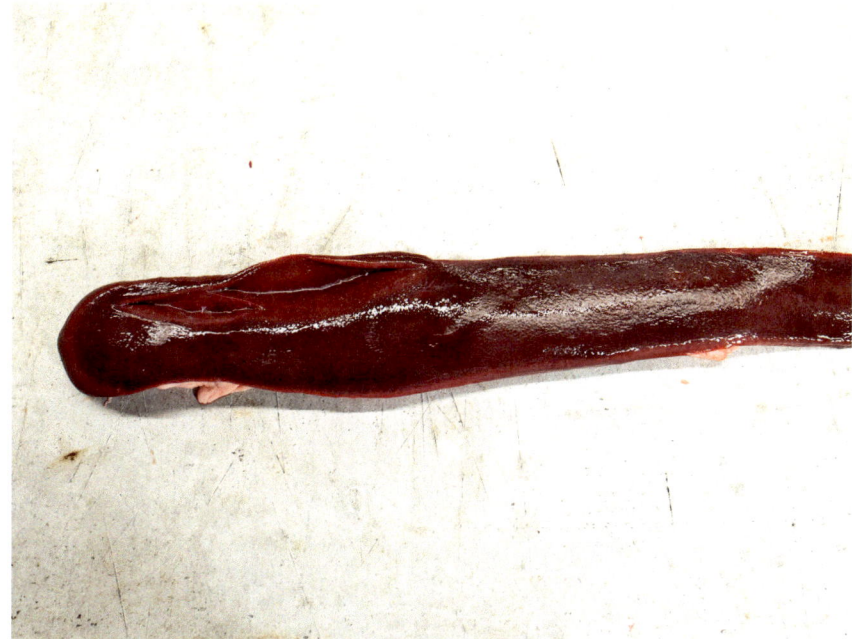
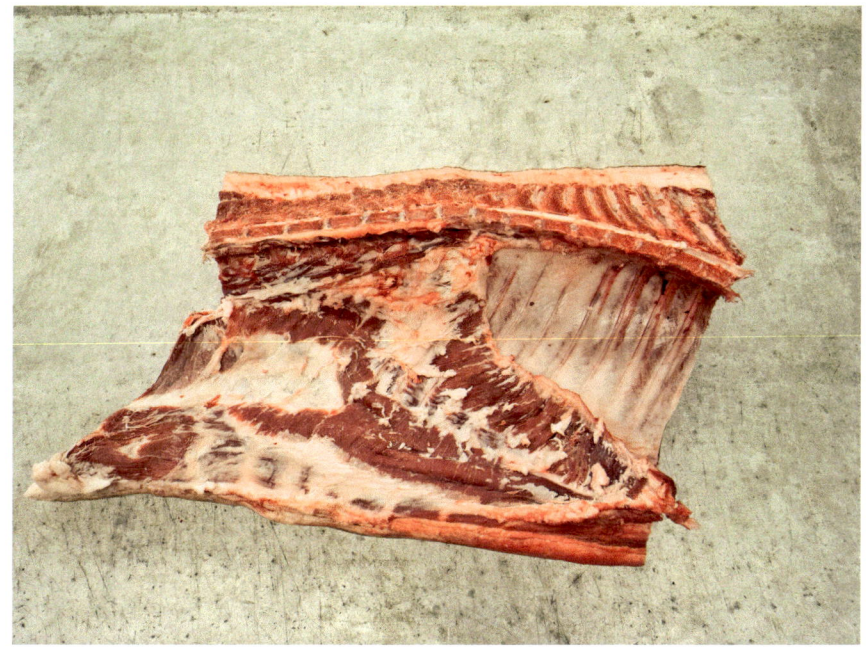

Portraits

Brandt & Levie

Between sausage manufacturing and a rock festival

With the two larger than life crossed meat cleavers over the entrance, you cannot miss the butcher's shop Brandt & Levie. The logo adorns aprons, advertising brochures, and, not least, the shop's products. The young founders Jiri Brandt, Samuel Levie, and Geert van Wersch know that in this day and age good products also need visual recognition value. Their clean, cool design has even earned them a Red Dot design award. However, they also know that good design can never compensate for poor quality, especially when it comes to sausage and meat.

All three already had experience as cooks, however, they lacked the know-how to launch their bold dream of establishing their own high-end sausage production company. So they went to Italy to learn first hand from the best producers, where even the figurehead of the Slow Food movement, Carlo Petrini, had a few tips for them.

Back in Amsterdam they started immediately, visiting farmers from the region and establishing direct trading links with those who shared their philosophy of respect for animals. From the purchased pigs they made air-dried and fresh sausage as well as ripened specialties from whole muscle such as pancetta, coppa, and a variety of hams. However, Brandt, Levie, and van Wersch really excel when it comes to salami. New creations with lavender and rose petals or chipotle chili and cacao regularly delight their adventurous clientele.

The young butchers also celebrate their nose-to-tail approach in other, unusual ways. Excess lard is used to make soap, and the blood flows into the hotdogs, which, amongst other places, are sold from the shop's own food truck—a mobile gourmet sausage diner that now appears regularly at food and music festivals.

At Brandt & Levie, the sausage has been successfully elevated to part of a young, everyday culture. More and more delicatessens in and around Amsterdam now stock the butcher's specialties, and after only four years they have been forced to move to larger premises.

THE BRANDT & LEVIE MANUFACTORY BEGAN GRINDING MEAT AND STUFFING SAUSAGES IN AMSTERDAM IN 2011. SINCE THEN THE YOUNG BUTCHERS' COLORFUL PRODUCT PALETTE HAS GROWN STEADILY AND THE SPECIALTIES CAN NOW BE BOUGHT AND SAVORED THROUGHOUT THE DUTCH CAPITAL.

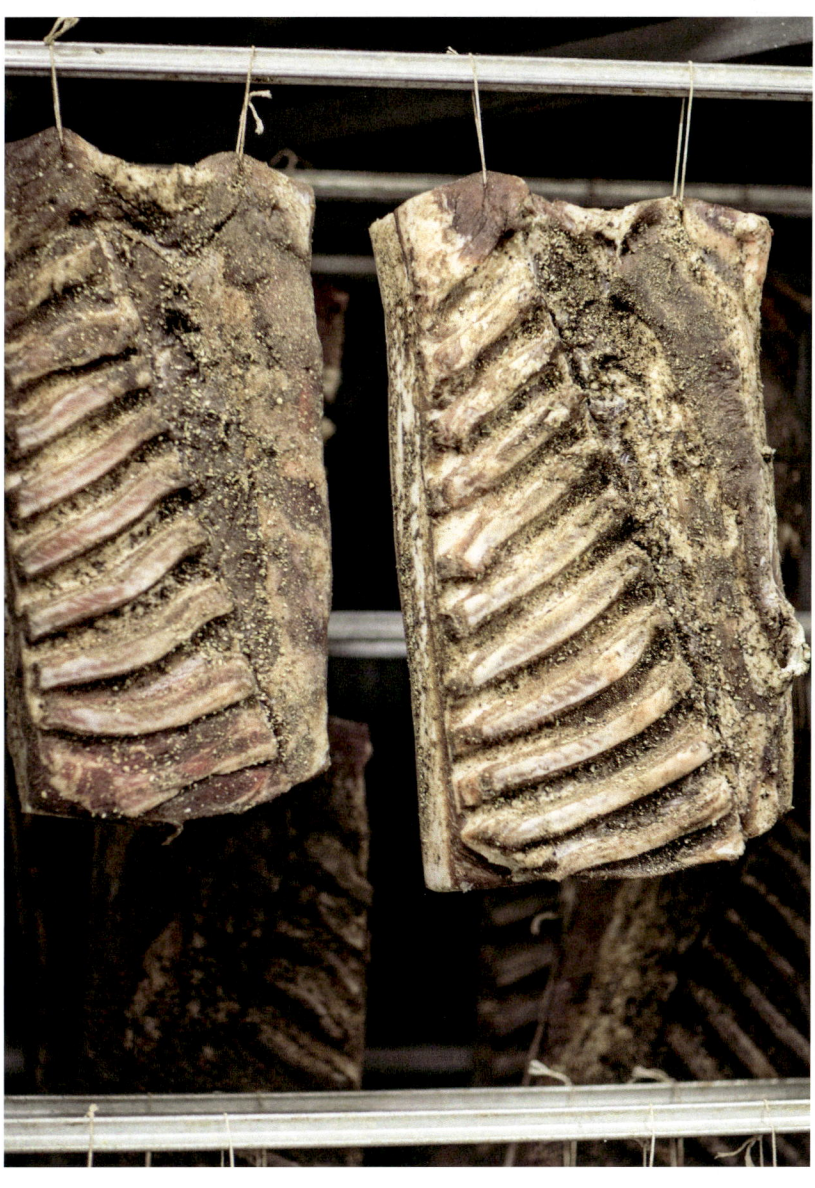

With rigorous artisanry and matching design, Brandt & Levie have elevated the sausage to an integral part of a young, everyday culture.

Portraits

Fleischerei Scheller

MASTER BUTCHER AND COOK, CARSTEN SCHELLER'S MANUFACTORY IS LOCATED IN RONNEBERG NEAR THE LOWER SAXONIAN CAPITAL OF HANOVER. "THE ONLY THING YOU REALLY NEED TO MAKE SAUSAGES IS GOOD MEAT," STATES THE FOURTH GENERATION BUTCHER, "AFTER ALL, YOU ONLY GET OUT WHAT YOU PUT IN."

Portraits

According to the best family tradition

"Between 'as always' and 'as never before'" is how master butcher Carsten Scheller from Ronnenberg near Hanover describes his product range. In this case, as always extends back over seven decades to the founding of the business by the husband and wife team, Hermann and Helene Scheller in 1938. Back then, purchasing whole animals directly from farmers was commonplace. Today, it is only practiced by the better representatives of the butcher's craft, a philosophy that enables one to select meat of the best possible quality.

In the case of the Schellers, they chose the Rotes Höhenvieh, a breed of cattle reared in the Weser Uplands, which 20 years ago had been reduced to a population of just 40 animals. Committed breeders readopted the breed, which, thanks to free-range husbandry on pastures rich in herbs, produces especially fine-fibred meat. The calves originate from the Adrianenhof farm in East Friesland where they graze on lush salt meadows close to the coast. The pigs come from Eichenhof, a regional producer cooperative made up of family farms that ensures complete transparency down to the individual farmer.

A number of the products are also reminiscent of the grandfather's creations, in particular the great family specialty—the juicy-piquant Klinkerschinken, a brick-shaped ham from the haunches of the Hildesheimer Bördeschwein pig. According to a recipe passed down from generation to generation, it is seasoned with a finely composed herb mixture, and during ripening is washed weekly with a strong beer.

So much for the as always—but what about the as never before? In the first instance, this is to be found in the relationship between butcher and clientele. Carsten Scheller has broken down the barrier of the sales counter, inviting customers to take a look behind the scenes. In the "Gaumenwerk" he holds sausage-making courses, organizes nose-to-tail tastings, and explains every aspect of the origin, slaughter, and quality of the meat. In short, he educates his customers to become empowered consumers, promoting the butcher's craft in the process, which aspires to far more than just producing the best quality meat.

Direct trade with the farmers, honest artisanry, and transparency—what was a matter of course for Carsten Scheller's grandfather is now more important than ever.

Portraits

Offal Wonderful

AT THE RANCHO LLANO SECO'S DINNER CLUB THE FOCUS IS ON THE ENJOYMENT OF THE WHOLE ANIMAL. THE OFFAL WONDERFUL EVENT, INITIATED IN 2013, REINTERPRETS TIME-HONORED COOKING TRADITIONS, INVITING PARTICIPANTS TO OAKLAND, CALIFORNIA TO EXPAND THEIR CULINARY HORIZONS.

Hurrah for the fifth quarter

When the crew from the Llano Seco farm extended an invitation to their event at the 2014 Eat Real Festival in Oakland, people came in droves—and they all wanted to see was blood. It was the second event organized by the Offal Wonderful campaign, an initiative to promote the consumption of innards, which are erroneously considered animal waste products.

On this day blood was declared the main theme, with a program including a presentation on the international importance of blood as food, and a blood sausage tasting. However, the organizers of Offal Wonderful are not generally concerned with feeding festival visitors, who already take a keen interest in their diet, but with the reinvigoration of the culinary culture associated with the "fifth quarter," as the Italians call the less popular parts of the animal. With the rise of cost-efficient, mass-produced meat in the industrial nations, the consumption of innards sank continuously, and with it the knowledge of their tasty preparation.

Olivia Tincani and Charlie Thieriot from Llano Seco could no longer sit back and let this development take its course. As employees of a traditional livestock business, everything to do with slaughtering was a theme close to their hearts, so together with the Eat Real Festival and the Butchers' Guild, they initiated the Offal Wonderful campaign. This was greeted enthusiastically by local gastronomes. From BBQ food trucks and fine dining restaurants to pizzerias and gourmet sandwich shops, chefs that were keen to integrate dishes made with innards into their menus immediately came forward. And their creations go well beyond the familiar dishes with liver and kidney.

At the Offal Wonderful events they place animal parts such as heart, stomach, ears, skin, and the meat of the head at the center of their dishes. Through such initiatives they not only awaken the spirit of discovery in their guests, but also promote a food culture whose horizon extends far beyond filet and schnitzel.

As a result of cost-efficient mass goods, consumers in the industrial nations have become accustomed to a uniform taste. Offal Wonderful aims to re-expand their culinary horizon.

Portraits

Hatecke

BUTCHER, LUDWIG HATECKE'S MAIN SHOP HAS BEEN LOCATED IN SCOUL IN THE SWISS CANTON OF GRAUBÜNDEN SINCE 1955, WITH FURTHER OUTLETS NOW RECENTLY OPENED IN ZERNEZ AND ST. MORITZ. TODAY, THE BUTCHER'S PURIST MASTERPIECES DELIGHT MEAT LOVERS WORLDWIDE.

Meat purism from the Swiss mountains

Even his grandfather slaughtered and butchered the family's animals in the old farmhouse in the Swiss Canton of Graubünden—now home to the Hatecke meat manufactory.
The methods used to make the specialties haven't changed much over the last 200 years either. To this day traditional handicraft is still employed from slaughter to sale.

Nevertheless, the butcher's shop has little to do with the dusty kitsch of a bygone era of traditional costumes. This is because of Ludwig Hatecke, who struck out on a new path in the mid-1980s, refurbishing the shop.

Instead of ornate, rustic oak, he opted for minimalist architecture that placed the focus on the meat specialties. The range of products was also reduced, now largely consisting of the core product, not thousands of side products and varieties of sausage—just good, refined meat. Nothing should distract one's attention and "meat should taste like meat," states the purist, Hatecke, echoing with the popular design principle of less is more. This motto also applies to the new product forms and packaging, as the Swiss butcher is convinced that "what is good must also look good."

Ludwig Hatecke also has high standards when it comes to the origin and quality of the meat. As one of the few butchers in the Canton who still slaughters himself, the raw goods for his specialties are drawn exclusively from regional farmers and hunters operating in the mountains and fields of the Engadin. Only the Madagascan pepper comes from further afield.

Hatecke is now renowned for his dried meat specialties, such as Bündnerfleisch and Salsiz, far beyond the borders of the small alpine country. The Salsiz, an air-dried raw sausage from beef, venison, or chamois, is pressed into a triangular shape unique to Hatecke. This makes it easier to cut.

Ludwig Hatecke loves the interplay of old and new, the traditional and the modern. It is the right mixture that makes the butcher's profession exciting and ensures that the handicraft has a future. In his opinion, the best reward for his work is that his son will continue the butcher's dynasty.

Portraits

"What is good must also look good."

Portraits

Portraits

Herrmannsdorfer Landwerkstätten

IN 1986 KARL LUDWIG SCHWEISFURTH REALIZED HIS DREAM AT THE GATES OF MUNICH. TODAY HIS SON KARL RUNS THE HERRMANNSDORFER COUNTRY WORKSHOPS IN THE SOUTHERN BAVARIAN TOWN OF GLONN, WHICH, IN ADDITION TO THE FARM AND BUTCHER'S SHOP, ATTRACTS VISITORS WITH ITS BAKERY, BREWERY, CHEESE DAIRY, PUB, AND THE ARTISAN WORKSHOP—AN ACADEMY FOR GOOD FOOD.

From factory production line to porcine paradise

The young Karl Ludwig Schweisfurth was deeply impressed by the huge slaughterhouses he saw in New York and Chicago in 1950. Inspired by this model, he transformed his parents' business back in Germany into Europe's most modern meat goods company, whose production lines would soon process three hundred pigs per hour.

The break came in the 1980s when his sons refused to follow in his footsteps and he took a look in the sheds where the animals for his industrially produced sausages were reared. What he saw gave him cause for thought, and he began to question his business model.

In 1986 it was clear: "I am going to give up the business and start again, with ecological farming and food production." The sausage factory was sold and in its stead, together with his sons, he established an ecological flagship project close to Munich. The goal was to realize, as closely as possible, the ideal of a "sustainable, respectful approach to animals, plants, people, and land."

For over 20 years, ecological food of the finest quality has been produced in Herrmannsdorf, and today, in addition to the farm and butcher's shop, the country workshops now include a bakery, cheese dairy, and brewery. The products are sold in shops in the nearby metropolis of Munich, or on site in the farm shop and pub.

Anyone interested in finding out more about the work in Herrmannsdorf can learn directly from the masters of their craft in the "Artisan Workshop" belonging to the farm's own "Academy for Good Food," where courses are offered on baking, making sausages and preparing meat.

The butcher's shop is supplied by a network of over 100 ecological farmers who employ stress-free slaughtering methods, processing meat while still warm. The butchers now produce over 100 different varieties of sausage and ham, including some of Germany's best, which have been aged in stonework ripening cellars. One such meat is the legendary air-ripened ham from the farm's own free range pigs that graze on open pasture, foraging for worms—a happy pig's life forms the basis for the numerous Herrmannsdorfer specialties.

Portraits

"Everything we do is characterized by a responsible attitude towards life and all its necessities: to land, water, and air, as well as plants, animals, and people."

Karl Ludwig Schweisfurth

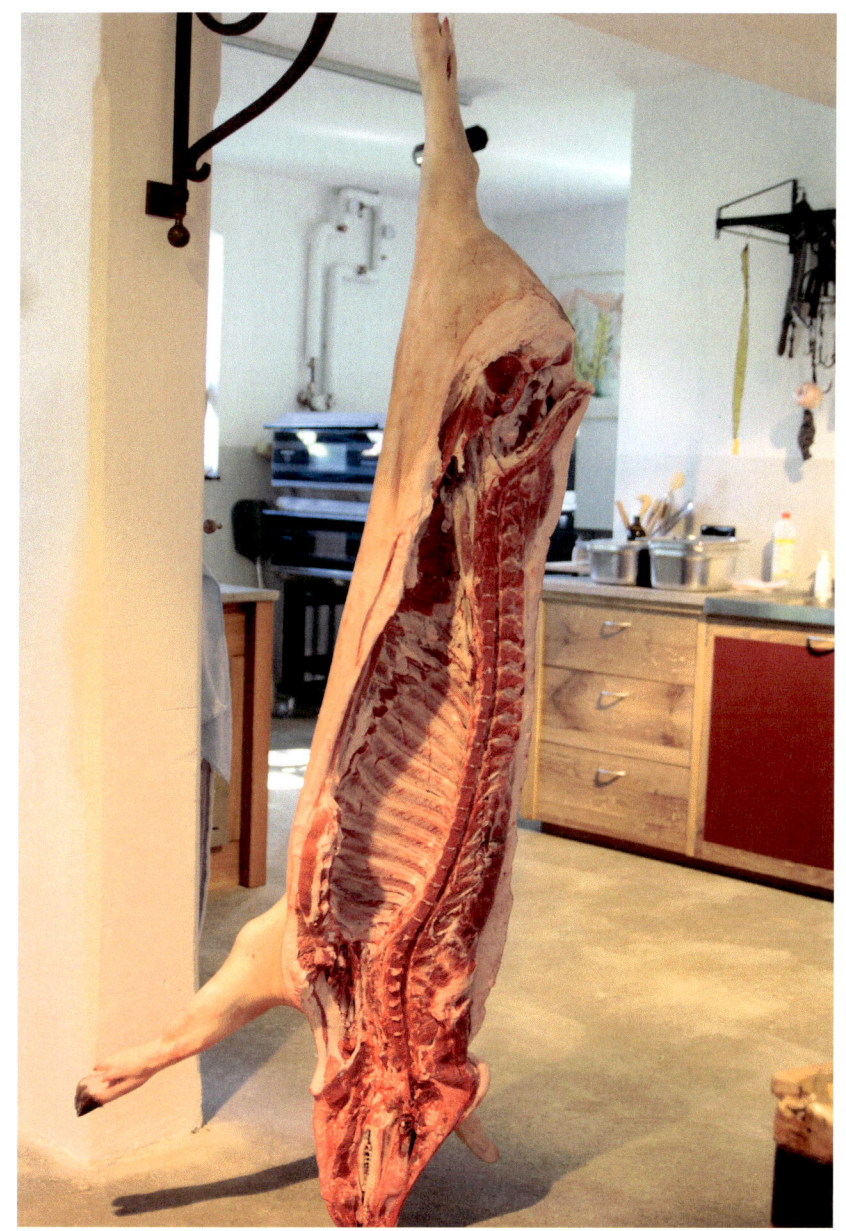

The Meat Hook

THE BUTCHER'S SHOP, THE MEAT HOOK, WAS FOUNDED IN THE DISTRICT OF BROOKLYN IN NEW YORK IN 2009, AND IN 2014 WAS FOLLOWED BY THE MEAT HOOK SANDWICH SHOP. TODAY THE SPECIALTIES PREPARED ACCORDING TO THE CREDO "REGIONAL, SUSTAINABLE, AND TASTY" HAVE GAINED A REPUTATION FAR BEYOND THE BORDERS OF THE WILLIAMSBURG NEIGHBORHOOD.

The metropolis's neighborhood butcher

Brent Young, Ben Turley, and Harry Rosenblum do not just see their butcher shop in the Williamsburg district of Brooklyn, New York as a place where you can buy good food. It is also an important part of a lively neighborhood. It should be a place where people can discuss, meet, and learn from one another.

It is these encounters that the founders of Meat Hook value—not just those over the shop counter, but also those outside the metropolis. They are proud of the fact that they know everyone by name that has handled the meat before it lands in their refrigerated display case in New York. The three founders see close and fair business relations in the region as the basis of their butcher shop, and they also attempt to inform their customers on this principle. Everyone should consider who they give their food dollars to.

The Meat Hooks are pioneers when it comes to sustainable meat in the American metropolis. The only meat on offer is that from animals who have been reared with access to open pasture and natural fodder on small farms in the adjoining states of New York and Pennsylvania.

Once they have been brought to New York, the animals are butchered before the eyes of the customers. It goes without saying—from tail-to-nose.

In addition to numerous fresh meat specialties and a whole armada of fresh frying sausages, the butcher's shop also sells all the cold cuts required for the perfect sandwich: mortadella, pâté, ham, porchetta, and delicate roast beef.

In the shop's own seminar room, customers are taught that a pig is not just composed of pork chops and pork belly, but that exciting dishes can also be made from the neck, ears, or meat of the head.

"We believe that everyone should have access to good food, in all of its forms, wherever they are." The founders have remained loyal to this ideal to this day. This was not an easy path to take. However, without this ethical backbone, the Meat Hooks are convinced that their efforts would have been pointless.

Portraits

"We believe that everyone should have access to good food, in all of its forms, wherever they are."

Portraits

The Rough Kitchen

THE ROUGH KITCHEN'S STREET FOOD STAND IS LOCATED IN AMSTERDAM'S NEWLY OPENED FOOD HALLS WHERE SINCE 2014 THE TWO FOUNDERS, MARCUS POLMAN AND JORD ALTHUIZEN, HAVE BEEN SMOKING THE BEST QUALITY MEAT IN THEIR PRIZED AMERICAN SMOKER, IMPORTED DIRECTLY FROM THE HOME OF BBQ.

An homage to the pig

The food halls in the Oud West district of Amsterdam have rapidly metamorphosed into a hotspot for the Dutch capital's foodies. Stands offer all kinds of delicacies, from Asian wraps to pulled pork slowly cooked for 16 hours in the Rough Kitchen's smoker—the brainchild of Marcus Polman and Jord Althuizen, two meat enthusiasts who have had a long love affair with good products.

Jord Althuizen originates from the wild, rustic street kitchen scene, having toured festivals for years with his mobile street kitchen, Smokey Goodness. He was one of the first to bring the American BBQ tradition to the Netherlands. Marcus Polman is primarily a journalist and author of numerous standard works on the perfect steak and the best pork delicacies. While Polman's books have been read worldwide, Althuizen can also look back on international success—in 2014, a jury in Estonia voted him World Barbeque Champion for his whole hog (a whole pig cooked over an open fire).

With Rough Kitchen the two crusaders joined forces to share the "whole beauty of genuine meat culture" with their guests. The founders see their project as a tribute to the pig, which the two committed carnivores prefer smoked or grilled over an open fire.

The basis of their cuisine is pure-breed Duroc, Berkshire, and Bentheim Black Pied pigs supplied by small regional farmers—the starting point for juicy sandwiches with pork belly and chimichurri sauce or pulled pork. Each week there are new dare-to-dine dishes, such as the delicious pig's head in aspic, characteristic of the nose-to-tail philosophy.

In cooperation with regional artisan butchers, the Rough Kitchen also serves old Dutch specialties such as the blood sausage known locally as balkenbrij, and dark Dutch bacon smoked and dry-ripened for over a year. The goal of the founders is to reacquaint today's foodies with older specialties, and help preserve their country's culinary heritage. The successful start in the food halls is soon to be followed by further outlets.

Portraits

"A concept from two carnivores in heart and soul."

Portraits

Wurstgalerie

SINCE 2014 THE SAUSAGE GALLERISTS FROM KITCHEN GUERRILLA, PETER INHOVEN AND HENDRIK HAASE, HAVE BEEN ORGANIZING CULINARY EXHIBITIONS IN BERLIN AND DÜSSELDORF. THE WORKS—PRODUCED, GRILLED AND EXHIBITED ON LOCATION—ARE ENJOYED BY ART LOVERS TOGETHER WITH A COOL GLASS OF PILSNER URQUELL STRAIGHT FROM THE BARREL.

Keep calm and eat a Wurst!

The Amuse Bouche hangs from the ceiling and consists of a curtain of sausages that every guest has to bite their way through before taking a seat. Throughout the room, arranged next to a long table, are numerous installations from which hang a multitude of rustic sausages. Some with a fine mold, others with a rough peppercorn crust, and more still with a delicious golden-brown smoked color. Welcome to the Wurstgalerie (sausage gallery)!

The Kitchen Guerilla team from Hamburg is experienced in occupying restaurants, sailing boats, and other unusual places, turning them into creative dinner clubs with their surprising ideas. For the founders Koral Elci, Olaf Deharde, and Onur Elci, food and communal eating help promote cultural exchange. For the Wurstgalerie they collaborated with the sausage impresario Hendrik Haase, and the artisan butcher Peter Inhoven to host an evening at Berlin's old Malzfabrik (malt factory), dedicated to the sausage theme. As sausages and beer have formed a perfect pair since time immemorial, it is fitting that the event is supported by a Czech brewery.

Germany is known as the land of sausages, but the country's culinary heritage is currently in a sorry state. Many sausage eaters are no longer familiar with the butcher's craft. Honest artisans are becoming a rarity, many recipes have disappeared, and the majority of consumers know very little about the variety and origin of good craftsmanship. On this evening, this is all about to change in an entertaining, and above all, tasty fashion.

While the cooks start the grill, master butcher Peter Inhoven wields his sausage stuffer, filling a variety of creations that will later land on the plates of the guests treated to this live demonstration. A projector installation shows the manufacture of the specialties in films and photos, from the pig to the sausage. And between the various courses, sausage impresario Haas holds a dinner speech on sausage culture. Throughout the evening, guests are invited to leave the table and help themselves to the installation exhibits. Many of them taste their way through the variety of the sausage culture for the first time, taking the tip of their favorite sausage home with them at the end of the evening.

Grrls Meat Camp

SINCE 2012 THE "SISTERHOOD" OF THE GRRLS MEAT CAMP HAVE REGULARLY PITCHED THEIR TENTS AT DIFFERENT LOCATIONS IN THE U.S. AND FRANCE, PROVIDING A FORUM WHERE FEMALE FARMERS, CHEFS, AND BUTCHERS CAN PRACTICE THE BUTCHER'S CRAFT AND LEARN FROM EACH OTHER. THE CAMP'S SPIRIT CONTINUES TO INSPIRE A STEADILY GROWING COMMUNITY OF FOLLOWERS.

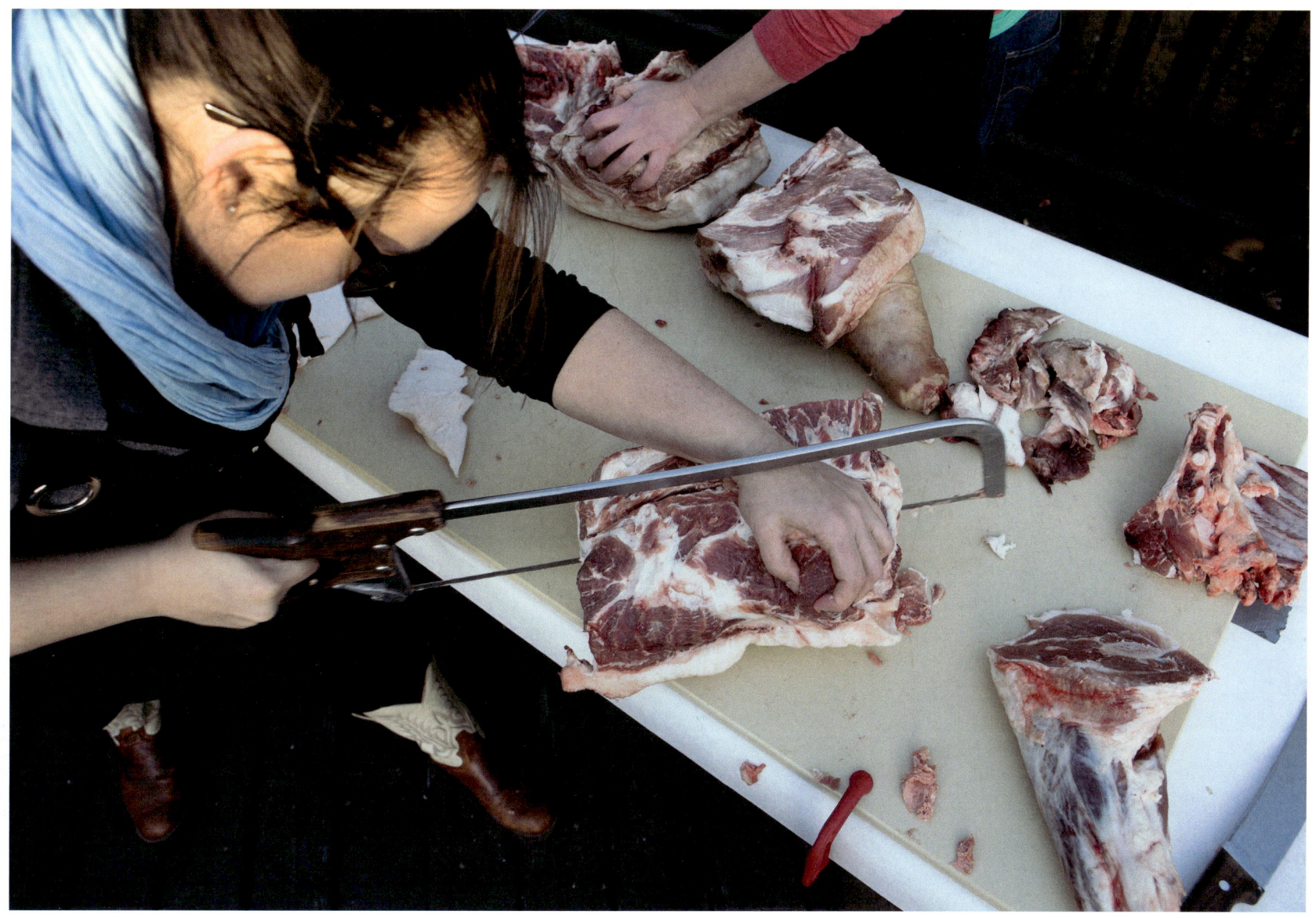

Meat is women's business!

Twenty years ago, Californian chef, Kate Hill, set out to learn everything about the French butcher's craft from the locals in her new home of Gascony, a region of southern France where the fine art of charcuterie begins with the slaughter and ends with a rich variety of specialties made from every part of the animal.

At the cooking school she founded locally, Hill soon began to pass on her newfound knowledge of French country cuisine and slaughtering to other enthusiasts. One of her first students was Camas Davis from Portland, who was renowned in the USA as the founder of the so-called Portland Meat Collective, a public butcher's school that offers courses in good meat practices.

Davis was quickly followed by a further dozen women at the French culinary retreat, resulting in the first Grrls Meat Camp. At today's annual three to four day event, everyone is invited to attend, from beginners to professional butchers.

For Hill, the aim of the camp is to build a strong sisterhood where women can inspire each other and share their knowledge of the old craft. The ultimate goal is to create an association that lends a voice to female farmers, butchers, chefs, and teachers—all those women whose daily work is shaped by animal farming and meat.

Grrls Meat Camp is designed as a place where a real exchange of ideas can be nurtured, an approach that has already received a large echo in the digital world. On the movement's Facebook page, hundreds of activists discuss ideas and provide mutual assistance on a daily basis. However, what was missing was a real place to meet.

The world of women working with meat is still young, nevertheless it is growing steadily and increasing numbers of women have come to appreciate the atmosphere of the new feminine meat movement. However, Kate Hill sees Grrls Meat Camp as just the beginning. "When women share knowledge and experiences with each other, supporting each other and working together, then this produces something magical," says Hill. Not to mention the incredibly tasty pâté, ham, and fantastic sausage the women produce, which can be admired online.

Portraits

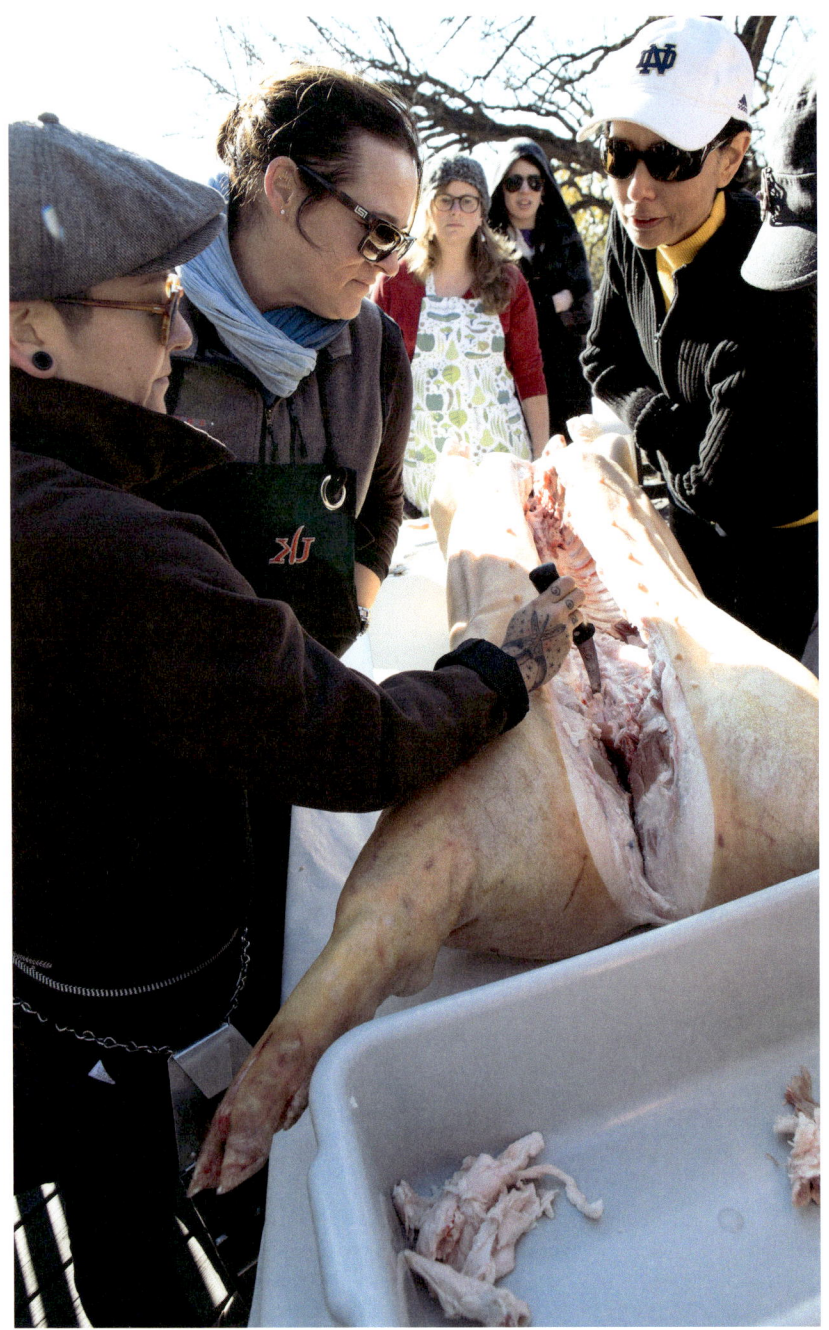 

"To inspire, instruct, and initiate a sisterhood of farmers, butchers, cooks, and teachers, giving voice to women working with food animals and meat." Kate Hill

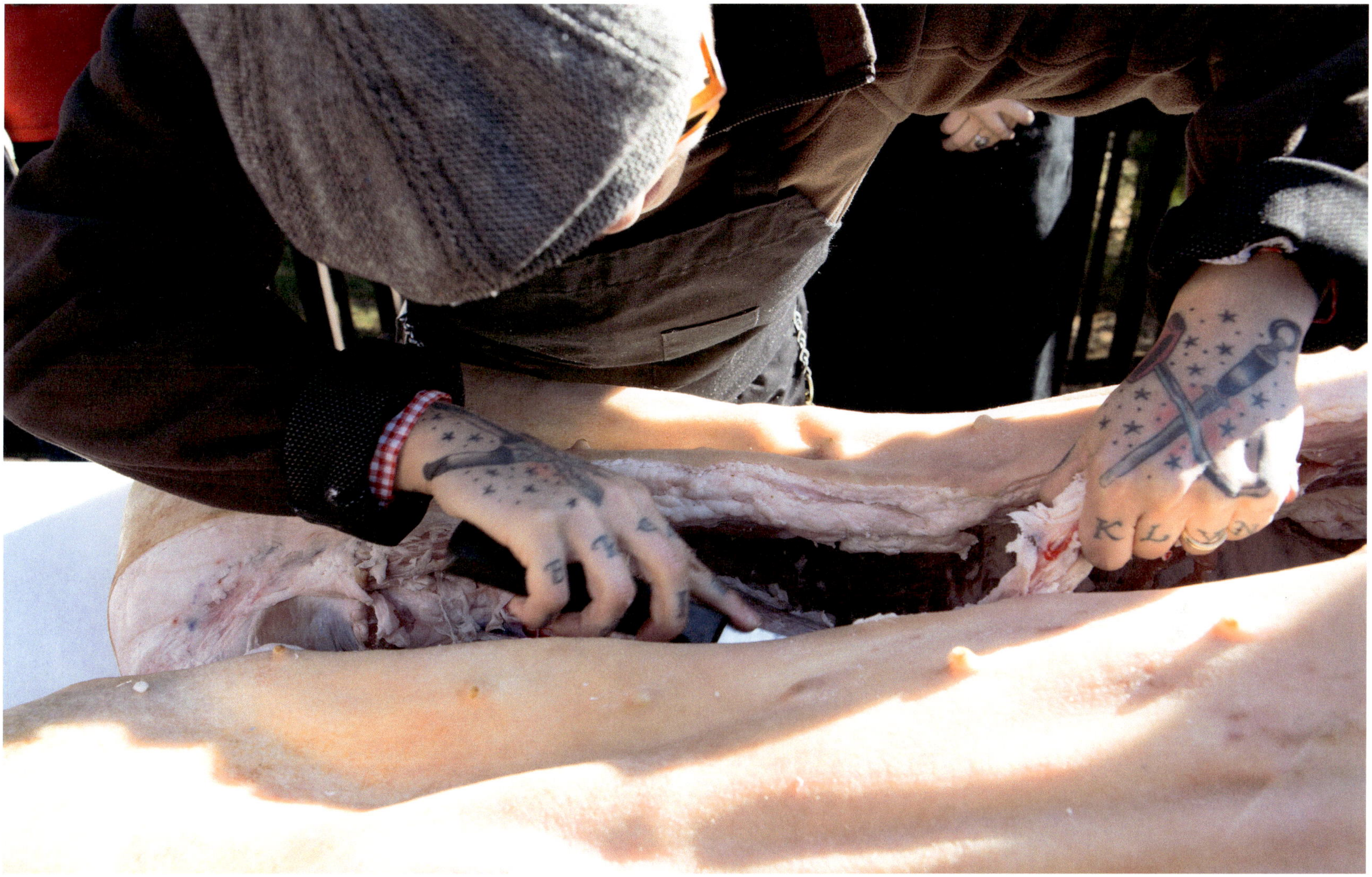

Portraits

Adam Danforth

ADAM DANFORTH IS AN ITINERANT BUTCHER WHO TRAVELS THE LENGTH AND BREADTH OF THE UNITED STATES SLAUGHTERING ANIMALS AND PASSING ON HIS KNOWLEDGE IN WORKSHOPS. IN THE PAST HE WIELDED THE KNIFE AT MARLOW AND DAUGHTERS IN NEW YORK CITY, AND ON DAN BARBER'S BLUE HILL FARM.

Saving the art of respectful slaughter

"Eat less meat, eat better meat" is the credo of the young butcher Adam Danforth from Ashland, Oregon. Armed with this conviction, he travels the length and breadth of America, slaughtering animals for farmers on their homesteads and passing on his experience to interested meat eaters in numerous courses.

With the aid of his workshops and books in which he has set down his knowledge, he attempts to preserve the lost art of respectful slaughter. His goal is to reawaken the memory amongst course participants that the enjoyment of meat is shaped by a connection between man and animal. One life is given for another.

"During every slaughter I feel this reverence for the animal," stated Danforth. "As an animal's blood flows over my hands, I form what is, to me, a sacred pact in which I commit to honoring the animal's sacrifice." He is conscious that not every meat eater can enter into this extremely intimate relationship with the animal. Nevertheless, he is convinced that "anyone who eats the meat is connected to the animal through every cell they consume."

Meat is the most valuable and the most expensive food that we eat. On top of that, it consumes the most natural resources in a world that we have already brought to its limit.
For Danforth, eating less meat also means knowing precisely where the meat on our plates comes from. A life reared on pastureland in a natural environment is just as important as species-appropriate fodder. This meat may be somewhat more expensive than the products from industrial livestock farming, but good quality has its price.

Danforth the butcher now eats half the amount of meat he used to, and delights in the better quality, even when it sometimes costs twice as much. However, anyone who thinks Adam Danforth is concerned with meat as the new status symbol is mistaken. "It is about my wellbeing and the wellbeing of the animals."

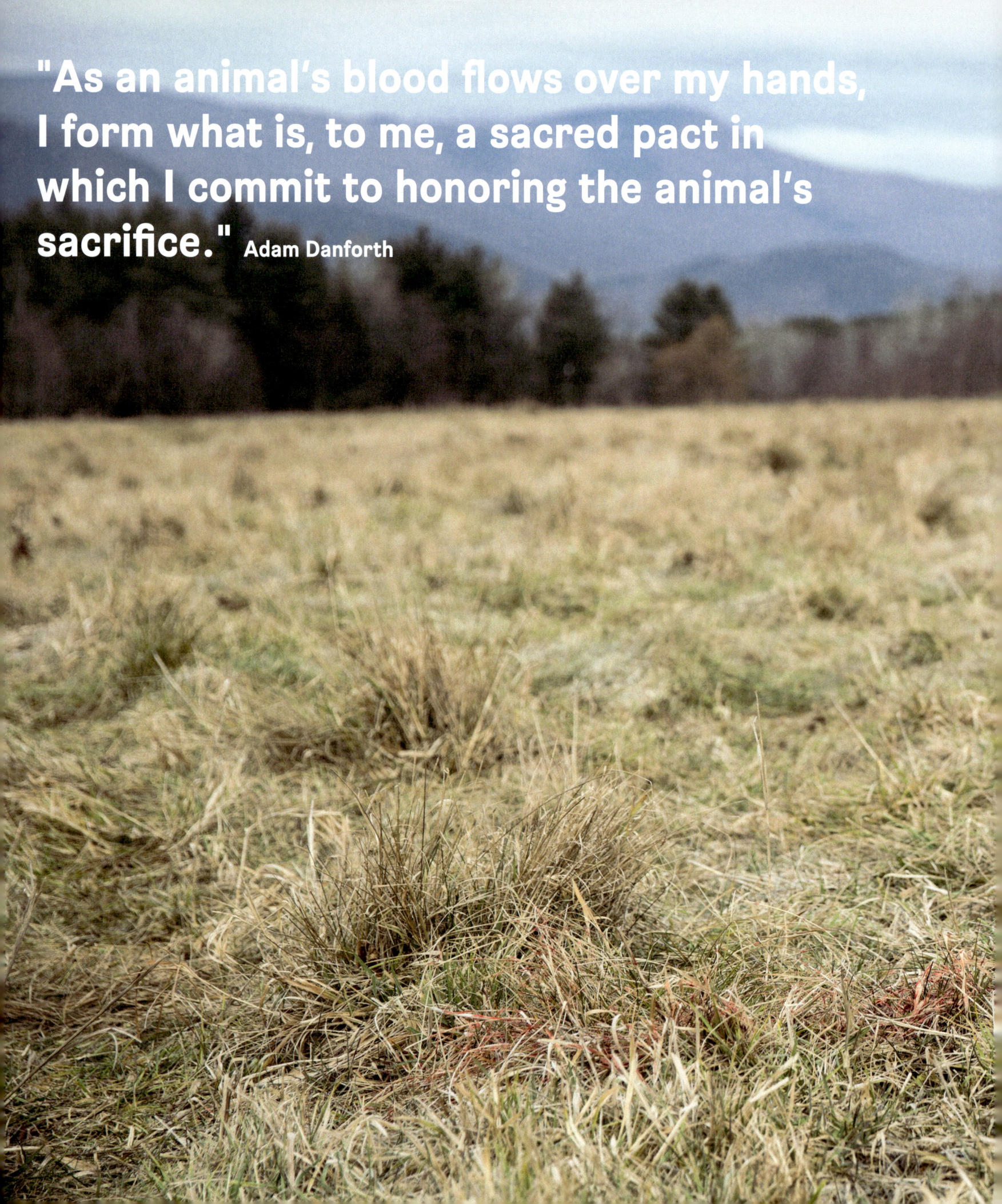

"As an animal's blood flows over my hands, I form what is, to me, a sacred pact in which I commit to honoring the animal's sacrifice." Adam Danforth

Gut Hirschaue

SINCE 1992, THE HIRSCHAUE FARM IN BIRKHOLZ NEAR BEESKOW, AROUND 100 KM FROM BERLIN, HAS BEEN HOME TO DEER, MOUFLON SHEEP, AND MÄRKISCHE SADDLEBACK PIGS REARED ON THE OPEN EXPANSES OF LOWER LUSATIA. TODAY, BOTH VISITORS TO THE GAME RESTAURANT AND GOURMETS FROM THE NEARBY CAPITAL RAVE ABOUT THE MEAT WITH ITS UNIQUE FLAVOR.

Half wild but twice as good

Wild goings-on at the gates of Berlin. In 1992 Hartmut Starr began building an enclosure on his land in the Mark Brandenburg, planting trees and bushes in the fields. After all, the wild animals from his breeding program should feel comfortable in their new home. Today, more than 1,000 fallow deer, red deer, and mouflon (European wild sheep) live on the organic farm that is now run by his son Henrik.

In addition to the wild deer, Märkische Saddleback pigs can now be seen foraging in the fields and wallowing in the dirt to their heart's content. This special cross between wild boar and an older Saddleback breed is much more robust than modern, overbred pigs, and is happy living free-range throughout the year. Due to their wild boar traits, the animals grow considerably slower than their industrially farmed colleagues, and only reach slaughter weight after one and a half years. However, the slower growth results in a unique quality of meat with excellent marbling, now proving popular amongst increasing numbers of meat eaters in the nearby metropolis—as well as enrapturing Berlin's high-end gastronomy.

The pigs, deer, and mouflon forage independently for their own food. Using a sophisticated crop rotation system with a multi-year cycle, the committed breeders provide the animals with regular supplies of lush, healthy green fodder, letting the animals wander from field to field. In winter they are fed additional hay and take special delight in the specially gathered acorns. The pigs are also fed a type of organic muesli produced on the farm from corn and grain.

Instead of subjecting the animals to the unnecessary distress of capture, loading, and a long journey by lorry, they are killed outside in the field, stress-free, with a well-aimed bullet. From there they are transported to the farm's own butchery, where they are cut and made into fine sausage and ham specialties. In the farm shop and restaurant, customers can taste their way through the wild selection, experiencing the meats' unique flavor. And anyone who wants to know more can join Henrik Staar on a hike through the enclosure's colorful animal world—one-of-a-kind in Europe.

"If you know where and how your roast was produced, then you are promoting a responsible approach to the animals and the land. The conscious enjoyment of meat not only conserves the environment, it also has much more to offer in terms of flavor."

Portraits

Portraits

IN THE TOWN OF PARCHTITZ IN THE CENTER OF RÜGEN, GERMANY'S LARGEST ISLAND, YOU WILL FIND MARCUS BAUERMANN'S RÜGENER LANDSCHLACHTEREI WHERE HE HAS BEEN SLAUGHTERING, STUFFING SAUSAGES, AND RIPENING MEAT SINCE 1998. TODAY THE UNIQUE FLAVORS OF THE BALTIC SEA SPECIALTIES ARE KNOWN THROUGHOUT GERMANY.

Rügener Landschlachterei

The sausage philosopher from the Baltic coast

"For me, food is happiness," says Marcus Bauermann. "A piece of liverwurst prepared in the morning from fresh meat and eaten at lunchtime. Fresh as a clear mountain stream winding its way through forests and meadows, bubbling with the whole vitality of nature," is how the sausage should taste from his country butcher shop on the Baltic coast.

Here, liverwurst is always slaughter-warm, meaning it is made immediately after the slaughter, stirred by hand and then filled into jars. Bauermann is convinced that "anything else would deprive the sausage of its erotic." All of his sausages and cold cuts are made from the meat of animals he has slaughtered, animals reared by regional farmers that the butcher knows personally. For Bauermann, eating happy sausage also means actively promoting animal welfare. In addition to the sausage pigs—sometimes weighing several hundred kilos—endangered Pomeranian sheep are also used for the production of his specialties, which today are amongst the finest Germany has to offer.

His salamis, naturally ripened in the Baltic air, are free from artificial, laboratory-made additives, containing just fresh herbs and spices, good wine, and the mold that gives the ham and sausages their final appearance—as white as the chalk cliffs for which the north of the island is famous.

However, Bauermann is convinced that good sausages must consist of more than just meat, pork belly, and seasoning. "Love and the conviction that honest food is the basis of happiness" are equally important. The master butcher with a distinctive walrus moustache has won many friends with this philosophy and the resulting specialties.

Producing salami and ham in this manner is hard work, "just as friendship or love can sometimes be hard work too," states Bauermann. However, the resulting pleasure makes all the effort worthwhile. When the master butcher speaks of the revitalization of traditional sausage culture, he is referring to nothing less than the pursuit of happiness.

Nevertheless, making good sausages is not an occult science for Bauermann, but honest artisanry that he is happy to share with anyone interested. Anyone experiencing a Lust auf Wurst (a craving for sausage) will find all the recipes he uses on a daily basis in his book of the same title.

Morgan Ranch

JAPANESE CATTLE ARE NOT EXCLUSIVE TO THE PASTURES OF THE FAR EAST. FOR OVER 20 YEARS THEY HAVE ALSO BEEN GRAZING IN THE SANDHILLS OF NEBRASKA IN THE MIDWEST OF THE U.S. THE MORGAN RANCH, FOUNDED IN 1934, IS NOW RENOWNED WORLDWIDE FOR ITS TENDER AMERICAN WAGYŪ BEEF.

Portraits

Japanese delicacy from the pastures of North America

Twenty-five years ago, American farmer Dan Morgan had to listen to Japanese business associates telling him that the meat from his cattle was good, but not good enough. Although hard hit by the criticism, the American breeder did not become demoralized. Instead, he rose to the challenge and decided to rear Japanese Wagyū cattle—the gold standard for top quality beef—in America. Although the whole world raved about the ultimate pleasure of Kobe beef, the black Wagyu cattle were rarely found on pastureland outside of Japan. This was largely because of Emperor Meiji who, at around the turn of the century, decreed that it was no longer permitted for cattle to leave or enter his country. The goal back then was to maintain the purity of the native breeds, and it is only in recent years that these strict export regulations have been somewhat relaxed.

At the beginning of the 1990s, there was only one option for the ambitious breeder from Nebraska, and that was to borrow an original Japanese Wagyu bull, which he had to return to the island immediately after obtaining the sperm cells. Over the years that followed these adventurous beginnings, Morgan has succeeded in establishing an almost pure-breed herd of American Wagyu cattle.
The animals are reared on the open pastures of Nebraska, completely free range, and without the use of growth hormones or preventative antibiotics. In addition to the natural fodder of the Nebraska Sandhills, 210 days before slaughter the cattle receive extra feed in the form of corn, alfalfa, mash, and minerals.

The Morgans personally control every step in the production of their meat: breeding, calving, selection and classification, fattening, transport, monitoring of the slaughtering and meat production, packaging, and dispatch. Morgan is convinced that this is the only way to produce meat of such high quality. With its fine veins of fat, the beef has a special buttery and nutty taste, and after years of hard and passionate work on the Morgan ranch, comes incredibly close to the Japanese original.

Wurst Gang

SINCE 2012, WURST GANG HAS TOURED THE SAUSAGE KITCHENS AND PIG SHEDS OF POLAND AND GERMANY. THE TWO TRAVELING COMPANIONS, GRZEGORZ ŁAPANOWSKI, ONE OF WARSAW'S MOST WELL-KNOWN COOKS, AND FOOD ACTIVIST, HENDRIK HAASE FROM BERLIN, ARE UNITED IN THEIR LOVE OF THE TRADITIONAL BUTCHER'S CRAFT.

Portraits

Two-man German-Polish sausage appreciation society

Everything began with a warm-smoked wild boar from a Polish artisan butcher, and a long-ripened raw sausage from a German country butcher. As chance would have it, Grzegorz Lapanowski and Hendrik Haase, two culinary enthusiasts with a passion for good meat and sausage, met one day in Amsterdam. It quickly became clear to the two activists from the Slow Food Youth Network that they shared more in common than just their passion for good sausage—an important part of both Polish and German cuisine. They were also united in a common struggle to preserve the artisan culture threatened on both sides of the border.

In Poland, as in Germany, the loss of large numbers of butchers who pursue an honest trade is painfully felt. Old polish and German pig breeds are threatened with extinction, and on both sides of the border small artisan businesses are struggling with EU regulations that make life almost impossible.

Smoking over an open fire, a method employed for centuries to produce Poland's typical hot-smoked specialties, has almost disappeared along with the natural aging and ripening of German raw sausage in old barns. What was okay for centuries, a part of the tradition, is now considered unhygienic and must yield to the clinically-clean stainless steel of mass production methods.

Instead of succumbing to lethargy, however, the two friends embarked on regular road trips under the name Wurst Gang, visiting butchers, farmers, restaurants, and street food stalls still committed to the sausage culture. Together they now stuff, cook, and taste their way through Poland and Germany's sausage cuisines, creating self-made Schlackwurst, Kaszanka, Mettwurst, and Kabanosy en route. From the treasures they bring back from their travels, they set to work in the kitchens of Berlin and Warsaw, creating dishes such as fresh frying sausages with Jerusalem artichoke and baked apples, smoked venison sausages with herb pasta, and pho with fresh duck sausage.

At cross-border tastings, such as the Sausage & Beer Market at Markthalle Neun in Berlin, they have set about sharing their mutual love of sausages with an international public. As Wurst Gang, they have also documented their travels, recipes, and experiences in pursuit of the origin of their native sausage cultures in image, sound, and text. A book on this unique friendship is currently in progress.

Two culinary enthusiasts with a passion for sausages—a project devoted to Polish-German culinary culture.

Recipes

LODE & STIJN

Sausage matters

For Jörg Förstera from the artisan butchers Kumpel & Keule in Berlin, a good sausage is the sum of all its components. In addition to natural ingredients such as high quality meat from humanely reared animals and aromatic herbs, factors such as time, passion, dedication, and a sense of responsibility play an important role in the making of a good sausage.

Recipes

The young master butcher has selected three recipes from his repertoire for this book that can be successfully made at home using simple equipment and a modicum of skill. The recipes have been inspired by visits to meat artisans in northern France, Italy, England, and Spain.

In principle, not much is required to make homemade sausages: good meat, salt, spices, a few fresh herbs, and a casing into which to stuff the final mixture.

A simple hand operated meat grinder is sufficient for the production of small quantities, although slightly more powerful electronic tabletop devices are now affordably priced and suitable for the home. Furthermore, some food processors also have attachments that can be used to grind meat.

Simple funnels with a large enough opening, available from DIY shops, can be used for filling the casings. More practical are metal sausage fillers, which are also available for smaller quantities and are perfect for sausage amateurs.

It is better to order the right meat and appropriate casings in advance, as not every butcher caters for customers who wish to buy the individual components for their home-stuffed frying sausages.

In the kitchen

The two cooks, Lode van Zuylen and Stijn Remi, have gathered a wealth of meat experience in Europe's star restaurants. As core members of the Schlachtfest Berlin team (pages 134–137), they are responsible for preparing the delicacies from every part of the slaughtered animals in the dinner club's kitchen—from nose-to-tail. They delight guests with delicious and creative dishes, which are often made from unfamiliar cuts of meat and innards. The two cooks see the challenge as creating surprising dishes from good ingredients without being pretentious. At the heart of Lode & Stijn's kitchen are the products themselves.

Ox tail croquettes, chicken liver pâté on crackers with hazelnuts, and blood sausage with smoked trout—with the recipes on the following pages, specially created for this book by the two chefs, the new meat movement's nose-to-tail philosophy can find its place in the domestic kitchen, producing new, delicious culinary surprises for the home table.

The following pages also include useful tips and instructions on combining a steak or a selection of sausage and ham specialties with freshly made dips and sauces to produce new taste sensations.

JÖRG FÖRSTERA

Blood sausage
with smoked trout and raw potato salad

Preparation

- Make sure to take the trout out of the fridge about an hour before eating to ensure it is at room temperature.

- Thinly slice the cauliflower on a mandolin and place the slices in cold water with some ice cubes to make them crisp.

- For the potato salad, heat up a good dash of butter in a small pan until light brown in color and remove from heat.

- In the meantime, cut four slices of the blood sausage and fry them until they are nice and crisp on both sides.

- Slice the potatoes wafer thin on a mandolin and toss them in the warm browned butter, keeping them slightly raw.

- Take the cress or arugula and mix with the cauliflower, season with pepper, salt, olive oil, and a splash of fresh lemon juice.

- Assemble the trout on the plate, then the potatoes, blood sausage, and salad. Finish with some extra browned butter.

Ingredients
(Serves 4)

4 slices blood sausage

2 filets smoked trout

2 potatoes

½ cauliflower

1 lemon

4 oz cress or arugula

¾ cup butter

Chicken liver pâté
with crackers, hazelnuts, and brown beer syrup

Preparation

- Trim the chicken livers, removing any tubes and bloody bits.
- Melt a bit of butter in a wide frying pan until it just begins to bubble.
- Add the livers and fry quickly until they acquire a gentle color on all sides but are still lightly pink in the center.
- Transfer to a plate and set aside.
- Add the diced bacon to the pan and fry until cooked.
- Add the shallots and gently cook over a low heat until soft and translucent.
- Stir in the garlic, thyme, and some freshly grated nutmeg. Now add the Marsala, cook for 1 minute and add the butter.
- Leave it to melt and remove the pan from the stove. Mix everything in a food processor until quite smooth..
- Spoon into a bowl and season generously.
- For the brown beer syrup, cook the beer in a small pan over a medium heat until reduced to a thick syrup.
- At this stage it is still very bitter, so add some agave syrup to achieve the right balance between sweetness and bitterness.
- Serve the pâté generously spread on whole-wheat crackers, dusted with chopped hazelnuts, and a sprinkle of beer syrup.

Ingredients
(Serves 6)

1 lb. chicken livers

¼ cup butter, softened

½ lb. bacon, diced

2 large shallots, finely diced

4 garlic gloves, finely diced

2 cups dark brown Ale

handful hazelnuts

thyme

nutmeg

Marsala wine

sea salt

fresh ground pepper

agave syrup

Aspic
with fresh parsley

Preparation

- Boil the water, add the sugar and salt until dissolved, and add the spices. Remove from heat and allow to cool. When cooled, add the pig head and keep in the fridge for six days (if you have too much brine, just use as much as you need and keep the rest for other usages).

- After six days, discard the liquid and keep the head in the fridge in plain water for one more day.

- Cut the vegetables, put them in a pot with the head, and fill with water. Boil gently until the meat is tender (in order to test, poke the cheek with a knife, it should feel like soft butter. If you are not sure, it is always better to cook the head a little bit longer than not long enough).

- Take the meat out of the liquid and let it cool down. Drain the liquid through a sieve and reduce to about one liter. Place the gelatin in cold water. When the gelatin is softened, add it to the liquid and keep warm.

- Pick the meat from the bone, add to the liquid, and add some freshly chopped parsley. Mix in some pepper and salt and pour into jars. Close the jars so they vacuum-seal.

- If you prefer, you can spread some softened lard on the top just before closing the lid.

Ingredients
(Makes 4 jars)

½ pig head

2 fennel bulbs

2 onions

1 leek

5 garlic bulbs

2 stalks celery

2 leaves gelatin

parsley

lard

for the brine:

1 gal. water

2 cups sugar

2 cups salt

12 juniper berries

12 black peppercorns

2 bay leaves

Lamb heart
with lamb tongue knödel (dumplings) and green peas

Preparation

- Dice the onions and fry until golden brown. Put the tongues in a pot with water, garlic, bay leaf, and off-cuts from the onion. Cook on a low heat until the meat is tender (you can test this by pinching the tip of the tongue with your fingers).

- Transfer to a plate and let cool until the meat is cold enough to peel the skin from the tongue. Cut into small cubes.

- Cut the bread into chunks of about ½ x ½ in. Mix the milk with the egg yolks, salt, and pepper and add to the bread crumbs together with the diced tongue and onions.

- Whisk up the egg whites until they are white and fold into the bread mixture. Chop some parsley and mix in. If you feel the mixture is a bit dry, just add a little more milk.

- Fill a pot with water and bring to boil. Transfer the mixture to a towel (or two if you want smaller rolls) and roll the mixture tight, making sure to press out as much air as possible, then secure the edges with kitchen twine.

- Gently cook in the water for 20 minutes, remove, and place in iced water. When cold, cut into slices.

- It is best to make the knödel the day before so it is cold and firm, making it easier to slice.

- Slice the lamb hearts in half. Remove most of the fat from the outside and any hard parts or pieces of blood. Keep them cold in the fridge.

- Peel the green peas and cook them briefly in hot water. Cool them in iced water. When they are cold, transfer to a bowl.

- Fry the slices of knödel in butter until golden brown on both sides.

- Stew up the peas in some chicken stock (page 223) or water with a bit of butter, pepper, and salt.

- Season the heart with salt and pepper and fry vigorously in a casserole pan with some sunflower oil. Cut into thin slices straight from the pan so they are still raw on the inside.

Ingredients
(Serves 4)

2 lamb hearts

2 lamb tongues

2 lbs. green peas

1 ½ cups milk

2 egg yolks

2 egg whites

3 slices day old white sourdough bread

2 onions

2 garlic cloves

parsley

bay leaf

Chicken stock

Preparation

- Take the chicken and press down on the ribcage to crack the bones—this releases flavor from the bones.

- Place the chicken in a pan and add about 1.3 gal. of water.

- Chop all vegetables into rough pieces leaving the skin and peel on.

- Bring to a boil and add the other ingredients, boiling slowly for four hours. Skim off any foam with a ladle or slotted spoon.

- Strain the broth and leave the chicken to cool. When cooled down, pick all the meat from the chicken and save it to serve in your broth or to make a terrine or salad.

Ingredients
(Makes about 3 liters)

1 chicken

2 onions

1 fennel bulb

1 kohlrabi

3 celery stalks

1 tsp black pepper

2 bay leaves

4 garlic cloves

thyme

Salsiccia
with gnocco fritto and fennel salad

Preparation

- Mix the fresh yeast with lukewarm water and add the flour, salt, and softened lard. Mix until well combined. Transfer to a container and let cool for eight hours or overnight.

- Place a pot with about 0.3 gal. of oil on the stove and keep it at 354.2°F.

- Divide the dough into balls of around 2 oz. each. Dust the table with flour and flatten the balls until they are about ⅛ in. thick. Dust off the flour and fry them one by one, gently spooning the oil over the dough so they pop into nice round balls. Flip them over and take them out when they are golden brown.

- Slice the fennel thinly on the mandolin and put the slices in iced water for around one minute. Drain well and mix with olive oil, salt, pepper, chopped dill, and some lemon juice.

Tip

- Fry up some salsiccias (pages 248–251) and serve them with gnocco fritto and fennel salad.

Ingredients
(Makes 20)

4 cups strong white flour, such as Manitoba

1½ cups water

½ tsp fresh yeast

½ tsp salt

1½ oz. lard, softened

2 fennel bulbs

dill

sunflower oil

Goulash
with sourdough bread fried in lard

Preparation

- Heat up a solid pan, preferably cast iron. Cut the meat into cubes about 1 × 1 in. and sprinkle with salt and pepper. Add a healthy amount of lard to the pan and fry the meat until it acquires a nice brown color.

- In the meantime, cut the onions into rough squares. When the meat has reached the right color, add the onions.

- After a minute or two, add the garlic, about half a tablespoon of black cumin, paprika powder, fennel seeds, and dried marjoram.

- You can add the tomato paste after about two minutes. You will need to stir regularly to prevent it from burning.

- After about two or three minutes, add the tomatoes, paprika, and potatoes, all chopped into rough cubes.

- Add about 0,4 cups of water and a bay leaf, cover the pan with a lid, and let it cook on low heat for about one and a half hours, stirring occasionally.

- The goulash is ready when the potatoes are cooked and the meat is tender.

- Add salt and pepper to taste.

- For the sourdough toast, heat up a frying pan, spread lard on both sides of the slices, and fry until they acquire a nice color.

Tip

- Serve the goulash with some thinly chopped raw bell pepper and onion, chopped parsley and dill, and some finely grated lemon zest.

Ingredients
(Serves 4)

1 lb. beef brisket or neck

2 cloves of garlic

3 onions

3 bell peppers

3 tomatoes

4 potatoes

1 tbsp tomato paste

1 bay leaf

4 slices white sourdough bread

lard

paprika powder

black cumin

fennel seeds

dried marjoram

1 sprig dill

1 sprig parsley

1 lemon

Saucisse de Toulouse
with lentil salad and baked apple

Preparation

- Finely dice the onion and fry gently in a pot with a good amount of olive oil. Finely chop the garlic and add to the onions.

- After a minute, add the lentils, a few sprigs of thyme, and cover with chicken stock (page 223). Stew gently until the lentils are cooked. Drain any leftover liquid and spread out on an oven tray to cool.

- Heat the oven to 390°F and bake the apples for about 15–20 minutes.

- Chop the spring onions, parsley, dill, and coriander and mix. Add to the cooled lentils and mix to taste with olive oil, lemon zest, lemon juice, pepper, and salt.

- Fry the Saucisse de Toulouse (see recipe Salsiccia pages 248–251) and serve with the lentil salad and half of a baked apple.

Ingredients
(Serves 4)

1 lb. green lentils

1 red onion

2 garlic cloves

2 spring onions

1 tbsp oliveoil

2 apples

1 sprig thyme

1 sprig coriander

1 sprig parsley

1 sprig dill

1 lemon

Osso buco

Preparation

- Add flour to a soup plate and season it with pinches of salt and pepper.
- Dust the pieces of veal shank in the seasoned flour, shaking off any excess.
- Heat a tablespoon of butter and a splash of olive oil in a shallow casserole dish that is large enough to hold the veal pieces in a single layer. Add the veal and cook until browned on both sides, then remove from the pan and set aside.
- Chop the onions, carrot, and celery in cubes about ½ × ½ in. Finely chop the garlic.
- Add the garlic, onion, carrot, and celery and cook until softened. Return the veal pieces back to the pan and add tomatoes, cut into eight pieces, and cook for another two minutes.
- Add white wine and cook until it has reduced by half.
- Add the stock, herb bunch, a little salt and pepper, and bring to a gentle simmer. Cook for about two hours until the meat is very tender and comes off the bone. Turn the veal once or twice to ensure it is not cooking dry. If needed, add some more stock or water.

Tip

- Serve the osso buco with a classic risotto or a creamy potato puree.

Ingredients
(Serves 4)

4 slices veal shank

1 ⅔ cup flour

2 garlic cloves

2 onions

2 celery sticks

1 carrot

1 large glass of white wine

3 tomatoes

¾ cup chicken stock (page 223)

bay leaf, thyme, sage, and rosemary herb bunch

1 pinch salt and pepper

Oxtail croquettes
with mustard

Preparation

- Sprinkle the oxtail pieces with salt and pepper and fry on all sides in a pan with some sunflower oil. Place them in a large pot and cover with water.

- Cook the oxtail pieces until tender and transfer to a plate. Let them cool until you are able to pick the meat from the bone.

- Finely dice the onions and fry until they acquire a light brown color. Transfer to the meat.

- Soak the gelatin leaves in cold water to soften them. Melt the butter in a pot, add the flour, and stir for about two minutes.

- Add the milk in five parts, taking care that the milk is incorporated every time you add it to the mixture. Make sure the mixture does not burn. Add the gelatin and mix well.

- Add the meat and onions, some freshly grated nutmeg, and salt and pepper to taste. Transfer the paste to a container and let it cool down overnight in the fridge, covered with baking paper.

- The next day, divide the paste into 12 pieces and roll into rough cylinders. Put them in the freezer. When they are frozen, take them out and dust with flour.

- Whisk the egg whites so they loosen up. Fill up a bowl with breadcrumbs, enough to coat all croquettes twice. Roll the croquettes one by one through the egg whites and then in the breadcrumbs.

- When you have breaded them all, dip them again one by one in the egg whites and breadcrumbs.

- After about one hour you can deep-fry them in sunflower oil. Make sure the oil is around 356°F.

- Fry until golden brown and crispy and serve with mustard (page 242).

Ingredients
(Makes 12 croquettes)

4 lbs. oxtail, sawed into pieces

2 oz. butter

½ cup white flour

5 cups milk

2 onions

2 leaves gelatin

2 egg whites

breadcrumbs

nutmeg

mustard

Beef & marrow pie

Preparation

- Season the beef shank with salt and freshly ground pepper. Heat some sunflower oil in a large pot over a high heat and sear until brown on all sides.

- Glaze with the wine and reduce up to half of the liquid.

- Add the carrot, onion, celery, garlic, and bay leaves and cover with chicken stock (page 223). Cover and gently cook for about three hours until the meat is tender. Remove from the heat and let cool. Refrigerate overnight.

- Remove from the refrigerator and skim the fat off the surface. Warm the mixture until it becomes liquid, take out the meat, pull from the bone, and chop into small pieces.

- Strain the liquid from the vegetables and keep separate. Mix the meat with the vegetables.

- Roll out the puff pastry dough to about ¼ in. thick. Cut out circles that fit the size of your pie forms. Put one piece of bone marrow in the middle of each pie form and add the beef mixture around it until it covers the sides.

- Place the pastry on top of each pie and seal the sides. Use the tip of a small knife to make a hole above the bone marrow.

- Leave in the fridge for at least 30 minutes. Preheat the oven to 390° F. Break an egg into a bowl and add a little water, brush the egg mixture onto each pie, and place in the oven.

- Cook until the pastry is golden brown and the bone marrow a nice roasted brown.

Ingredients
(Serves 6)

2 ⅔ lbs. beef shank

1 ⅔ cups red wine

1 carrot, roughly chopped

1 onion, quartered

2 celery sticks, roughly chopped

6 garlic cloves

3 bay leaves

1 pint chicken stock (page 223)

6 pieces bone marrow (select the smaller, longer ones)

6 sheets puff pastry

freshly ground black pepper

Steak
with sauce choron and watercress salad

Preparation

- Ask your butcher for a well-aged, fat-marbled piece of steak, preferably from an older cow. These usually have more flavor. Slowly brown the butter in a small pan until it is light brown and acquires a nutty smell. Put the pan aside but make sure it stays warm. The particles at the bottom, even when they are slightly darker brown, are exactly what you want for your sauce choron.

- Heat up a frying pan—preferably a heavy bottomed one. Sprinkle the steaks with salt and pepper and add them to the pan when the sunflower oil starts to smoke.

- Fry on both sides until they are a nice brown, caramelized color. Add a dash of butter and turn them for about half a minute. Transfer to a plate and cover with aluminum foil.

- Mix the egg yolks with approximately 0.2 cups of vinegar (you can add more when the sauce is ready) and some salt in a small pot.

- Put the pot on a low heat and start to whisk. Make sure to keep whisking so that the mixture does not burn or scramble. If you have the feeling it is proceeding too fast, just take the pot off the heat and keep whisking. When it has reached a nice volume, take the pot off the heat and gently add the butter.

- Don't do it too fast, otherwise the sauce may split. When all the butter is incorporated, add about two or three tablespoons of tomato paste according to taste. Keep warm.

- Mix the watercress with some finely chopped shallots, good olive oil, and some freshly squeezed lemon juice.

- Slice the steak, sprinkle with some fresh ground pepper and sea salt. Serve with the warm sauce and salad.

Ingredients
(Serves 4)

2 steaks, about 11 oz. each

$2/3$ cups butter

6 egg yolks

$1/2$ lb. watercress

2 shallots

vinegar

tomato paste

lemon

Tartar
with fried capers and juniper berries

Preparation

- Finely dice the shallots. Dry the capers on paper. Fry them in sunflower oil at 356°F. Season with salt and pepper.

- Grate a tablespoon of juniper berries on a fine hand grater or in a mortar. Finely chop the chives.

- Cut the meat into small cubes or pass it through a meat grinder.

- Mix all the ingredients except for the fried capers. Add pepper, salt, and about a tablespoon of water.

- Squeeze the mixture through your fingers to make the tartar smooth and somewhat sticky.

- Serve with the fried capers, some slices of white sourdough bread, and a light salad.

Ingredients
(Serves 4)

1 lb. beef filet, lean and well aged

3 shallots

1 oz. capers

1 bunch chives

juniper berries

Guinea fowl terrine
with prunes

Preparation

- Soak the plums according to the type you are using. If they are very dry, put them in water for an hour or two before starting the recipe.

- Cut the legs and wings from the carcass and cook together in the chicken stock.

- Take out the carcass with the filets when the meat is cooked. The legs and wings will need a little bit longer. When all the meat is ready, remove it from the bones.

- Reduce the stock until you have 0,3 gal. left.

- Put the gelatin in cold water to soften.

- Add about two tablespoons of apple butter to the reduced stock and remove from heat. Season with salt and pepper and add the gelatin.

- Mix the meat with salt and pepper and add to the stock.

- Chop the plums if you prefer them smaller.

- Line a cake tin with baking paper and fill it up with the mass. It is important to put the terrine under pressure, so cover it with plastic or baking paper and place another cake tin filled with water on top. Place in the fridge overnight. Cut into slices immediately before serving.

Ingredients
(Makes 1 terrine)

1 guinea fowl

1 gal. chicken stock (page 223)

4 leaves gelatin

½ lb. dried plums

2 tbsp apple butter

Recipes

Sides

Pickled radishes

Preparation

- Mix the sugar, salt, and vinegar until dissolved and pour over the radishes. Leave overnight for the sweet and sour flavors to mix and mingle or, if this is not possible, leave at least three hours before serving.

- Pack into a large airtight container or wide necked jam jars.

- Store in the fridge and use within two weeks.

Ingredients
(Makes 2 jars)

2 lbs. radishes

1 ½ cups sugar

1 tbsp salt

¾ cups cider vinegar

Mustard

Preparation

- Grind the whole mustard seeds for a few seconds in a spice or coffee grinder, or by hand with a mortar and pestle. They should remain largely whole as you will also be using mustard powder.

- Pour the semi-ground seeds into a bowl and add the salt and mustard powder. Pour in the water or beer, salt, turmeric, and honey. Stir well.

- When everything is incorporated, let it sit for up to 10 minutes. The longer you let it sit, the mellower the mustard will be.

- When you are ready, add the vinegar.

- Pour it into a glass jar and store in the fridge. It will be runny at first, but will thicken overnight.

Tip

- Wait at least 12 hours before using.

Ingredients
(Makes about 1 glass)

2 oz. mustard seeds

2 oz. mustard powder

1 oz. water or beer

3 tbsp cider vinegar

2 tsp salt

1 tsp ground turmeric

2 tbsp honey

Piccalilli

Preparation

- Cut the vegetables into small, even, bite-sized pieces. Place in a large bowl and sprinkle with salt. Mix well, cover the bowl with a tea towel, and leave in a cool place for 24 hours, then rinse the vegetables with ice-cold water and drain thoroughly.

- Blend the corn flour, turmeric, mustard powder, mustard seeds, cumin, and coriander to a smooth paste with a little vinegar.

- Put the rest of the vinegar into a saucepan with the sugar and honey and bring to a boil. Pour a little of the hot vinegar over the blended spice paste, stir well, and return to the pan. Bring gently to boil for 3–4 minutes to allow the spices to release their flavors into the thickening sauce.

- Remove the sauce from heat and carefully fold the well-drained vegetables into the sauce. Pack the pickle into warm, sterilized jars and seal immediately.

- Leave for 4–6 weeks before opening.

Tip

- Use within a year.

Ingredients
(Makes 3 jars)

6 ½ cups washed, peeled vegetables – select 5 or 6 from the following:

cauliflower or romanesco

green beans

cucumbers

courgettes

green or yellow tomatoes

carrots

small silver skinned onions

peppers

2 tbsp fine salt

2 tbsp corn flour

2 tbsp turmeric

2 tbsp mustard powder

2 tbsp mustard seeds

1 tsp crushed cumin seeds

1 tsp crushed coriander seeds

2 ½ cups cider vinegar

1 ½ cups granulated sugar

2 oz. honey

Recipes

How to make: Liverwurst

244

Preparation

1. For the broth, place the half pig head in a saucepan together with the diced vegetables, parsley, crushed garlic cloves, and spices, cover with water and simmer for two hours. While the broth is cooking, weigh the herbs, salt, and spices and grind them in a pestle and mortar.

2. During the last hour of cooking, add the fat and remaining coarsely cut meat (with the exception of the liver) to the broth and reduce the heat to a low simmer.

3. Soak the gut for the sausage in warm water, cut into lengths of about 8 inches and tie one end with twine.

4. Remove all of the meat from the broth and allow it to cool somewhat. Remove the meat from the bone. Separate the bone and the gristle. While the meat is cooling, remove the bile ducts from the raw liver and coarsely grind.

Recipes

5 Coarsely grind the cooked meat and onion and add to the liver.

6 Add the spices, herbs, and salt and mix well by hand.

7 Fill the seasoned and well-mixed sausage mass into the natural gut, if possible while still warm, avoiding air cavities.

8 After filling, tie the other end of the gut with a piece of twine.

9 Blanch the filled and tied liverwurst at 158–165°F in the remaining broth (topping up with warm water if required). The broth must not boil, so it is advisable to check the temperature with a thermometer and adjust the heat accordingly. The blanching time is dependent on the thickness of the sausages. As a rule of thumb, blanch for three minutes for every ⅛ th in diameter.

10 After blanching, briefly rinse the sausages in warm water and allow them to cool in a cold place (hung up or on a grill). After cooling, the sausages should be stored in the fridge and will keep for between three to six days at a temperature below 45° F.

9

Tip

- Don't throw away the broth used to blanch the liverwurst. It is delicious and makes a tasty soup, either pure or with a handful of pearl barley. The sausage broth can also be reused as a stock for other dishes!

Ingredients
(4½ lbs of sausage)

Broth

1 bunch soup vegetables: carrots, celery, leek, parsnip, parsley

1 large onion

bay leaves, pimento seeds and cloves of garlic

Meat

½ pig head

28 oz pork belly without bone

14 oz pork dewlap

14 oz pig liver

Spices

1½ oz sea salt

2½ tbsp freshly ground pepper (black)

¼ oz raw sugar

1 tsp marjoram

1 pinch thyme and lovage, dried

1 pinch pimento, caraway seeds, ginger, mace, grounded

1 large onion

½ sprig fresh oregano

Casing

Pork chitterlings (inquire at your butcher)

For tying the sausages

Twine

Recipes

How to make: Salsiccia

Recipes

Preparation

1. Remove the fat and any bones, sinews, and skin from the meat with a sharp knife. This step is known as trimming and can also be carried out by your butcher to save time.

2. Coarsely cut the meat into walnut-sized pieces and refrigerate well prior to grinding. Pass the cold meat through the meat grinder using a coarse disc. In the case of the salsiccia, the very coarse disc can be used.

3. Precisely weigh the spices, other ingredients, and salt, then mill or grind in a pestle and mortar. Wash the fresh herbs and then chop finely with a knife. In the case of the salsiccia, peel the garlic and ginger, and grate the lemon peel. Place the ground sausage mass in a large bowl, add the weighed spices, chopped herbs, and other ingredients, and then mix and knead by hand.

Recipes

Important

4   The sausage mass must be kneaded until it binds nicely. To test whether it has bound sufficiently, take a piece of the kneaded mixture in your outstretched palm and turn your hand over. If the sausage mass remains stuck to the palm it has the right consistency and can be filled.

5   Now press the sausage meat into the sausage filler while excluding as much air as possible.

6   Soak the intestine in warm water and then slide it over the filling tube until only a small section protrudes.

250

Recipes

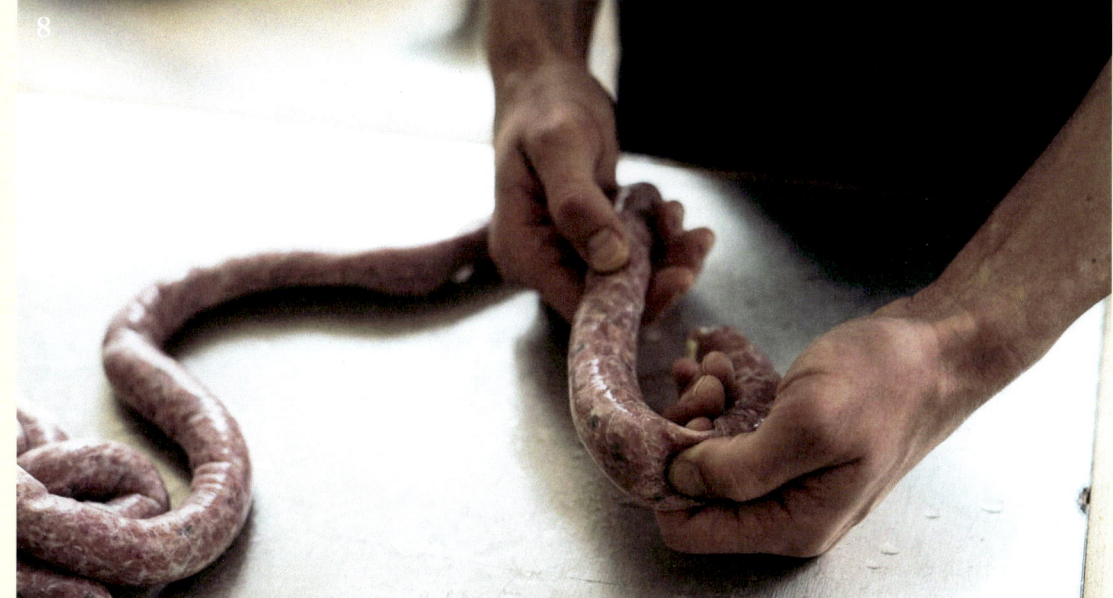

Ingredients
(4½ lbs of sausage)

Meat

35 oz pork belly without bone

17½ oz leg of veal

17½ oz pork loin without bone

Spices

1¼ oz sea salt

¼ oz raw sugar

2 tsp fresh ground white pepper

½ sprig oregano

½ sprig thyme

4 garlic cloves

1 piece of fresh ginger (about the size of a thumb)

1 red chili pepper

sage leaves

lemon peel

Casing

Sheep's small intestine (inquire at your butcher)

7 Now carefully press the sausage mass until it reaches the opening of the filling tube to expel any excess air, tie the end of the intestine, and fill loosely to make a very long sausage.

8 Now twist the long sausage by hand to make individual pieces of desired length. Press the sausage together at the desired intervals, using the thumb and finger, and twist with the other hand. Take care that the sausages are not filled too tight as there is a danger they may burst.

Tip

- Fresh frying sausages should be fried or grilled on the same day. Always keep freshly ground meat and filled sausages refrigerated prior to stuffing or cooking!

Index

Special Thanks by Hendrik Haase

I would like to thank all those who have made this book possible with their contributions: Vanessa, Beatrix, Benedikt, Robert, Sven, Silvio, Jörg, Lode, and Stijn. A special thanks goes to all those who found time, between the barn door and the shop counter, to inspire us with wonderful impressions of their work.

The Authors

Hendrik Haase
Food activist, bon viveur, and enthusiastic educator. As a graduate communication designer and culinary curator, Haase has helped build a new movement in which farmers, butchers, cooks, and connoisseurs explore new paths in meat matters. In addition to saving the world's culinary heritage, his main passion is the preparation and exploration of food as an everyday, lived, aesthetic practice.

Benedikt Ernst
After completing his studies as a nutritional scientist, Benedikt Ernst first turned to the writers craft in Hamburg. As a freelance author, he works regularly for the online edition of essen&trinken, the magazine, Szene Hamburg, and the blog Mit Vergnügen, which explores the city's culinary life. Ernst is co-founder of the online food magazine *Smak*.

Beatrix Eichbaum
As a passionate connoisseur, copywriter, and PR specialist for food and beverage, Beatrix Eichbaum has demonstrated a fine nose for aromas and quality. For the dynamic networker, self-confessed meat lover, and press officer for the renowned premium meat supplier OTTO GOURMET, everything revolves around good meat from humanely reared animals—both professionally and privately.

A
Adam Danforth
Pages: 196–190
Country: USA
Photo credit: Joe Keller (pp. 196, 198), Ken Goodman (p. 197)

L'Antica Macelleria Cecchini
Pages: 120–123
Country: Italy
Photo credit: L'Antica Macelleria Cecchini

Arche De Wiskentale
Pages: 158–161
Country: Austria
Photo credit: Jürgen Schmücking

The Arc of Taste
Pages: 150–153
Country: Italy
Photo credit: Presìdia of Slow Food

B
Bæst
Pages: 93, 108–111
Country: Denmark
Photo credit: Per Anders Jörgensen

B.E.S.H.
Pages: 99, 138–XX
Country: Germany
Photo credit: Hartmut Seehuber (pp. 99, 140, 141), Ricarda Grothey (pp. 138, 139)

Brandt & Levie
Pages: 162–165
Country: Netherlands
Photo credit: Brandt & Levie

C
Čestr
Pages: 118–119
Country: Czech Republic
Photo credit: Honza Zima, (p. 119 top), David Háva (p. 119 bottom), Filip Šlapal (p. 118)

D
Die Steakschaft
Pages: 122–123
Country: Germany
Photo credit: Der Ludwig

F
Fleischerei Scheller
Pages: 164–169
Country: Germany
Photo credit: www.meikebergmann.de

G
Gebroeders de Wolf
Pages: 124–127
Country: Netherlands
Photo credit: Rogier Chang
www.chang.nl

Grrls Meat Camp
Pages: 192–195
Country: France
Photo credit: Jennifer Marx

Gut Hirschaue
Pages: 38, 200–203
Country: Germany
Photo credit: Hendrik Haase

H
Hatecke
Pages: 174–177
Country: Switzerland
Photo credit: Benjamin Hasenclever & Sascha Mieke, (pp. 175–177), Filip Zuan (p. 174)

Herrmannsdorfer Landwerkstätten
Pages: 10, 31, 34, 35, 178–181
Country: Germany
Photo credit: Herrmannsdorfer Landwerkstätten (pp. 10, 31, 34, 35, 178–180), Viviana D'Angelo (p. 181)

Hood Food
Pages: 154–157
Country: Switzerland
Photo credit: Lukas Lienhard (p. 155 bottom left), Nick Lobeck (pp. 154, 155, 157)

Index

L

Landfleischerei Neumeier
Pages: 58, 64, 65, 114–117
Country: Germany
Photo credit: Jörg Teuber (pp. 114, 115, 116, 117 top),
Hendrik Haase (pp. 58, 64, 65, 117 bottom)

Le Bourdonnec
Pages: 128–131
Country: France
Photo credit: Fred Marigaux

Lennart & Bror
Pages: 100–103
Country: Sweden
Photo credit: Erik Lindvall, (pp. 101, 102, 103), Tobias Regell (pp. 100, 103 bottom)

M

Morgan Ranch
Pages: 206–207
Country: USA
Photo credit: Thomas Ruhl, www.port-culinaire.de

N

Naše maso
Pages: 142–145
Country: Czech Republic
Photo credit: Honza Zima (pp. 142, 143, 144, 145 top and bottom right), Martin Faltus (p. 145 bottom left)

O

Offal Wonderful
Pages: 2, 170–173
Country: USA
Photo credit: Fare Resources

Olympia Provisions
Pages: 112–113
Country: USA
Photo credit: Robyn Von Swank (p. 112, 113), David Reamer (p. 112 top)

R

Rügener Landschlachterei
Pages: 204–207
Country: Germany
Photo credit: Hendrik Haase

S

Salt & Time Butcher Shop
Pages: 90, 132–133
Land: USA
Fotos: Kate LeSueur

Schlachtfest
Seiten: 40, 45, 46, 50, 94, 134–135
Country: Germany
Photo credit: Hendrik Haase

Smoking Goose
Pages: 148–149
Country: USA
Photo credit: Kelley Jordan Photography (p. 149 top), Corrie Quinn (p. 149 bottom), Brittany Sanders (p. 148)

T

The Meat Hook
Pages: 182–185
Country: USA
Photo credit: Liz Barclay

The Rough Kitchen
Pages: 3, 186–189
Country: Netherlands
Photo credit: Kyonne Leyser (p. 189 top), Remko Kraaijeveld (pp. 3 left, 186), Saskia van Osnabrugger (p. 189 bottom)
The Rough Kitchen (p. 187)
Additional credit: Sander de Ponti (Foodstyling), Jan Willem van Riel (Styling)

U

Underground Food Collective
Pages: 146–147
Country: USA
Photo credit: Emily Julka

V

Vom Einfachen das Gute
Pages: 89, 104–107
Country: Germany
Photo credit: Caro Hoene (p. 105), Autumn Sonnichsen (p. 89, 104), Axel Mosch (p. 106)
Ashley Ludaescher (p. 107)

W

Wurstgalerie
Pages: 96, 190–191
Country: Germany
Photo credit: Daniel Banner

Wurst Gang
Pages: 2, 13, 208–209
Country: Germany
Photo credits: Paulina Małyska (pp. 2 top left, 13, 209 bottom), Julián Redondo Bueno (p. 208), Krzysztof Kozanowski (p. 209 top)

Imprint

Crafted Meat

The new meat culture: craft and recipes

This book was conceived, edited, and designed by Gestalten.

Edited by Hendrik Haase, Robert Klanten, and Sven Ehmann

Preface by Hendrik Haase
Texts "The animal" by Hendrik Haase (pp. 8–39)
Texts "The cuts" by Beatrix Eichbaum / Otto Gourmet (pp. 40–57)
Texts "Charcuterie" by Hendrik Haase (pp. 58–89)
Texts "Know your meat" by Hendrik Haase (pp. 90–95)
Texts "Portraits" by Hendrik Haase (pp. 98–99, 174–203, 206–209) and Benedikt Ernst (pp. 100–173, 204–205)
Texts "Recipes" by Hendrik Haase (pp. 212–213), Lode van Zuylen and Stijn Remi (pp. 214–243), and Jörg Förstera (pp. 244–251)

Editorial management by Vanessa Obrecht
Translation from German by Colin Shepherd
Proofreading by Transparent Language Solutions

Photography by Silvio Knezevic (pp. 2 bottom, 3 right, 30, 42, 44, 60, 63, 66–86, 92, 98, 210–253)
Additional images by Hendrik Haase (pp. 4, 8, 20, 21, 33)
Illustrations by Oriana Fenwick (pp. 2 top right, 14–19, 24–29, 32, 36, 37, 39, 48, 52, 54, 58)

Graphic design by Sandra Schwaiger, Jeannine Moser, and George Popov
Typefaces: Bembo by Stanley Morison and Brezel Grotesk by Stefanie Preis

Printed by Offsetdruckerei Grammlich, Pliezhausen
Made in Germany

Published by Gestalten, Berlin 2015
ISBN 978-3-89955-637-7

German edition
ISBN 978-3-89955-595-0

British edition
ISBN 978-3-89955-596-7

© Die Gestalten Verlag GmbH & Co. KG, Berlin 2015

All rights reserved. No part of this publication may be reproduced or transmitted in any form or by any means, electronic or mechanical, including photocopy or any storage and retrieval system, without permission in writing from the publisher.

Respect copyrights, encourage creativity!

For more information, please visit www.gestalten.com.

Bibliographic information published by the Deutsche Nationalbibliothek:
The Deutsche Nationalbibliothek lists this publication in the Deutsche Nationalbibliografie; detailed bibliographic data are available online at http://dnb.d-nb.de.

None of the content in this book was published in exchange for payment by commercial parties or designers; Gestalten selected all included work based solely on its artistic merit.

This book was printed on paper certified according to the standards of the FSC®.